PALM

THERAPY

Dr. M.E.Johnson
1823 Rue Pinot Blanc
San Jacinto, CA 92583
909-487-1259

PALM THERAPY

Program Your Mind Through Your Palms—A Major Breakthrough in Palmistry

by

MOSHE ZWANG

with

DIANA ZWANG & YARON SWERY

Ultimate Mind Publisher, Los Angeles, California

Printed in the Untied States of America

First Edition, July, 1995

Publisher's Cataloging in Publication Data:

Zwang, Moshe
        Palm Therapy : program your mind through your palm—a major
        breakthrough in palmistry / Moshe Zwang, Diana Zwang, Yaron Swery

        p. cm.
        Includes bibliographical references and index
        Preassigned LIBRARY OF CONGRESS CATALOG CARD NUMBER: 95-090168
        ISBN 0-9645519-2-6

        1. Palm Therapy. 2. Self Help (Psychology) 3. Alternative Medicine.
        4. Success. 5. New Age. 6. Palmistry. 7. Acupuncture.
        8. Spritual Healing.   I. Title.

        Book design: Diana Zwang
        Illustrations: Moshe Zwang

Palm Therapy is the trademark of Moshe Zwang.

Dedication

I dedicate this book to the memory of my late father, Dr. David Zwang, a scientific researcher of pharmacology and professor of chemistry in Buenos Aires, Argentina, inventor of many chemical formulas and a master of Chess. His deep understanding of life and his profound wisdom were the inspiration and the very first trigger toward the founding and developing of Palm Therapy as well as in other areas in my life.

MOSHE ZWANG
Founder of Palm Therapy

Contents

Important Notice

WARNING - DISCLAIMER: The information written in this book is for the interest of those who wish to have general information of the subject matter.

Many of the statements contained in this book express the opinion of the authors who are neither medical doctors nor psychologists. Many of these opinions, which include the theory and practice of Palm Therapy and other alternative methods, have not been investigated or approved by any government or regulatory agency.

It is sold with the understanding that neither the publisher nor the authors are engaged in rendering medical, psychiatric, psychological, financial, legal, or other professional services.

This book is intended as an informational tool. It should not be a substitute for any treatment, counseling or diagnosis made by your physician or other licensed health professional. It should not be used for self-diagnosis or self-treatment of mental disorders or any other diseases or disturbances. If counseling or expert assistance is needed, the services of a competent professional should be considered. Pregnant women, children and those with cardiac or other special problems are especially urged to see their physicians. Ultimately, you, the reader, must take full responsibility for your health. Always consult with your doctor before taking any advice from a book.

Every effort has been made to make this manual as complete and accurate as possible. However there may be mistakes both typographical and in content.

The publisher and the authors disclaim any responsibility or liability to any person or entity for any consequences, loss or damage, which may result, or alleged to be caused, directly or indirectly, from the use of the information in this publication

If you do not wish to be bound by all of the above mentioned, you may return this book to the publisher for a refund within thirty days from date of purchase, along with a proof of purchase, including place, date, and receipt. Please write to the publisher first for return authorization.

REMEMBER NOTES: The notes of "Remember" within the text are reminders within a specific issue. It is IN ADDITION to the "Warning-Disclaimer" (above), which applies to the whole concept and the text of this book.

CASE HISTORIES: All of the names and personal data in this book have been altered in order to respect the privacy of each person. Any similarities to real persons are coincidental.

REPETITIONS: This work includes various new concepts and ideas. In order to make it easy and clear to the reader, the important ideas and aspects in this book are mentioned in more than one place in the text.

TRADEMARKS: All terms that are known to the publisher and the authors as registration marks, trademarks or service marks, were mentioned as such. The publisher and the authors cannot attest to the accuracy of this information. Use of terms in this book should not be regarded as affecting the validity of any registration, trade or service marks.

Acknowledgements

With this acknowledgment, I wish to thank my family and friends. Although they are not directly involved in the founding or development of Palm Therapy, by being supportive and unconditionally loving all the way, they gave me the support needed to develop this therapy.

I am thankful to my friend, Mr. Zeev Toren, who combines spirituality, persistence, willpower, and wisdom with the practical daily life, for his support and encouragement while developing Palm Therapy and my other creations. And to his wife, Simha Toren, for her warm, loving personality, combined with spirituality, dedication and caring for others, for her support and encouragement.

To my mother, Pnina, for dedicating her life to raising the family with love, caring, devotion, and values which have been inspiring to the whole family.

To my sister, Adriana Zwang, the genius artist, whose talents and achievements were enlightening for me; her art works were displayed in famous museums all over the world including the British Museum (1983, 1985); her masterpiece "Green Planet" (1986) for the International Year of Peace, sponsored by the United Nations won first prize both for its high artistic level and for its expression of the aspiration for peace and understanding between nations.

To my sister, Taly, who is blessed with wisdom, many talents and a pure heart, for her cheerful spirit which has been inspiring to me.

To my gifted brother, Rafi, whose mathematical and logical thinking, which made him a champion both in Math and Chess contests were inspiring as well. And to his family.

To my sister, Sylvia, who is blessed with will-power, a loving personality and dedication. And to her family.

To my sister, Shirley, for her constant support, wisdom, profound insight, and deep understanding of human nature which together with kindness and caring for others, makes her one of the best inspirations for creativity and success.

To the parents of my wife, Diana—Joseph and Hanah Aharony—for raising such a loving, spiritual and gifted daughter. Without her dedication, this book would have been delayed for years. Also, to Diana's sister, Drora and her family, and to her brother, Shlomi, and sister, Judith.

To Yaron's parents, Menashe and Rachel Swery, for raising such a spiritual, talented, dedicated son. God bless you!

To Yaron's brother, Yecheskeel (Hezy), who is blessed with wisdom and a warm, loving heart. Also a special dedication and acknowledgement to his late brother, Yegal, a unique personality, smart and sensitive to life, whose fate-Karma took him away so early.

(continues)

Acknowledgements (continues)

Special Thanks :

To Marilyn Gellis, Ph.D, in clinical psychology, the founder of the Institute for Phobic Awareness, Phobics Anonymous, World Service Headquarters, for her kindness and her advice.

To Gregory Goldman, M.D., an expert in internal medicine, one of the most knowledgeable persons in classical Homeopathy, for his inspiring wisdom.

To David Nahum, the chairmen of the Israeli Vegetarian Association, a leader in the fields of vegetarianizm and alternative medicine, for his friendship and support during my initial clinical work in Israel.

To Abraham Aven-Hen Ph.D, for his support and wise approach to life.

To Moshe Olshevsky, O.M.D., for his freindship and support while we were teaching at the Israeli College of Naturopathy.

To Shlomo Noy, M.D., Yael and Abraham Beharav, Ph.D., Esther Drogova, M.D., David Azaria, M.D., Shoshana Alon N.D.,Batia Patal M.D., and to all of my ex-colleagues who contributed to the development of alternative medicine in Israel.

To Dr. Carson Dunlop, who was the dean of the Naturopathic School, Renfrew, England, for his inspiring, deep insight into the health of human beings and deep understanding of healing at the three levels of existence, the body, mind and soul.

To my friends, Yehoshua Shwizter, Daniel Hadad and Oded Kupelnic, sea captains, for their loyalty and all the great, inspiring days in the Israeli Merchant Marine.

To Alicia Ghiragossian, Ph.D., J.D. in Law (Argentina), for her inspiring talks and ideas.

To Gill Boyne, the founder of the Hypnotism Training Institute, the president of the Hypnotist Examining Council of California and the founder of a new technique in Hypnotherapy-the transforming therapy–for his inspiring works.

A special Acknowledgment to those who helped during the process of the creation of this book:

To Elizabeth Kimberlin, for the initial proofreading and the help in the editing of this book. Her consistency and unconditional devotion are highly appreciated.

To Kevin Boren, for typing the extensive bibliography of this book.

To JoAnn Block and to Colette and Michael Petros, for their help during the initial process of typsetting this book.

And to all others, too numerous to mention, who helped and contributed to the preparation of this book.

— Thank You All —

Foreword

During my training in Jungian analysis in Israel, I was first introduced to palm reading as a form of "psychological testing." I also had the opportunity to compare the results to the more traditional tests, as several of my patients had both types of test done.

At that time I was impressed as to how accurate and constructive a tool palm reading was for diagnostic purposes and to give direction regarding career development, talents, relationships, etc.

However, when Moshe Zwang first talked to me about his method of Palm Therapy I was very skeptical. In order to convince me Moshe volunteered to come to my office and demonstrate his method, working on a few of my patients for free.

I took the challenge and chose two patients with severe and chronic problems which have lasted more than ten years. These patients were under my care for one year. One patient suffers from severe panic disorder, the other from severe impulse control disorder including compulsive gambling and other compulsive behaviors. I tried medications with these patients, as well as extensive psychotherapeutic techniques, with only temporary minor improvements. These patients also received during the years different forms of therapy from a variety of therapists. Nothing was helpful. Therefore, I felt that any improvement would be significant. Also, we have an objective way to measure success, i.e., the frequency of panic attacks or gambling sprees.

Moshe was kind enough to come to my office once a week for the last seven weeks, for 45 minute sessions with each one of these patients. To my amazement, I must admit that both patients are feeling much better subjectively. Objectively, there were no gambling sprees, and the frequency and severity of the panic attacks decreased to a great extent.

This is, of course, not a scientifically designed, double-blind study. The numbers are not statistically high enough to reach any conclusions. Yet, it is still compelling and it certainly deserves more clinical trials.

I must admit that I still don't know how it works or why. On the other hand I also still don't know the exact mechanism by which aspirin works.

It is always possible it was a placebo effect, but it is very unlikely, as I had tried different placebos with these patients before and they didn't work.

When working with the patients, Moshe bonded with them. They liked him and respected him. They opened up to him and shared with him their feelings, etc. I sat in the room as an observer, and it was difficult for me to categorize what type of "psychotherapy" he was using. Apparently, there was none, although on occasions he asked them to visualize themselves at the peak of their symptoms while he worked on their hands.

Both patients were impressed enough with the results that they asked to continue with the Palm Therapy, privately. They are now motivated enough to drive a long distance to his office and to pay his fee.

It was a real pleasure for me watching Moshe at work. I cannot deny the remarkable results occurring in such a short period of time. I will definitely continue watching my patients for long term results. However, at the present time I already have become curious enough to ask Moshe to teach me his technique.

—Daphna Slonim, M.D.
Diplomate, American Board of
Psychiatry and Neurology.
Medical Director D.S.A. Medical Clinic
Beverly Hills, California

Introduction

Palm Therapy is a breakthrough in the field of scientific palmistry. It combines ancient wisdom with theories based on advanced brain researches. It is an efficient, easy to apply method which uses the hand/mind connection in order to allow each one of us to achieve optimum potential, emotional balance, success and fulfillment in any area of life. This vital connection will be discussed in Section One of this book.

Palm Therapy, as a pathway to reach your goals, takes you through three stages: *the Balancing Stage, the Release Stage* and *the Fulfillment Stage*. While the first two stages are short as to time periods, the third one is a continuous process of development and growth at all levels of one's existence—the body, mind and soul.

1

A simple stimulation on the palmar creases/lines and other parts of your hands which are related to the aspects of your personality and well-being can help you reshape your personality and get the best from yourself. You also can use it in daily life situations when you need that extra energy, that emotional strength and the mental abilities to perform, to react and to achieve. It can be done anywhere and at any time.

The balancing effect of Palm Therapy on the mind is rapid and effective with proven results. It may not surprise you. After all, we are in the era of utilizing fast techniques for the benefit and evolution of humanity. The world of today is characterized by advanced technology with faster, more efficient tools and machines in every aspect of life.

Recently, we received information about other psychotherapies and various techniques which can also bring results faster than ever before. For example, the ability to desensitize phobias and panic disorders that have been unsuccessfully treated for years in just a few visits or sometimes in a single session with effective results.

The following are a few of the **rapid results methods**, new generation of therapies:

Psychotherapy Techniques (Eye Movement Desensitization and Reprocessing, *The Callahan Techniques ™, etc.)
Some psychotherapy techniques can achieve fast results. These include the Eye Movement Desensitization and Reprocessing (**EMDR™,) which was developed by Dr. Francine Shapiro, or the Callahan technique by Dr. Roger Callahan. These techniques work quickly on desensitization of phobias, anxiety disorders and other undesirable problems.

*The Callahan Techniques, is a trademark of Roger J. Callahan, Ph.D.
**EMDR is a trademark of Francine Shapiro, Ph.D.

Hypnotherapy (Transforming Therapy by Gill Boyne)
Among the fastest methods for healing by hypnosis is the Transforming Therapy which was developed by Gill Boyne. This efficient technique uses the state of trance in order to create a real transformation in the client's life.

Allergy Desensitization (Nambudripad's Allergy Elimination Techniques)
Allergy desensitization techniques including the Nambudripad's allergy elimination techniques which were developed by Dr. Devi S. Nambudripad. The methods for desensitization of allergies is done with rapid results by stimulating specific acupuncture points while holding the allergen, or its representative, close to the body.

Acupuncture (Koryo Hand Acupuncture)
Another aspect well-worth mentioning is the advancements in the field of acupuncture with the development of the Koryo hand acupuncture by Dr. Tae Woo Yoo. In this technique, the mind and body are treated through hand acupuncture with fast and convincing results. (Koryo hand acupuncture is another reinforcement to my hypothesis regarding the complete netlike energy pathways of the hand as discussed in this book. Various therapies, including Palm Therapy, activate part of these pathways to create a systematic technique.)

Success Techniques (Cybernetics, Neuro-Linguistic Programming)
Success techniques such as Cybernetics which was developed by Maxwell Maltz., M.D., F.I.C.S. and Neuro-Linguistic Programming (NLP), which was developed by Dr.

Richard Bandler and Dr. John Grinder proved to bring fast and efficient results to those who practice them correctly.

In concluding this partial list of rapid results therapies and techniques which now Palm Therapy enters, we can see that this is the beginning of a new era of therapies having one thing in common—rapid and efficient effects.

Comparing Palm Therapy to any other existing rapid result method does not reduce nor imply a decrease in the value and effectiveness of that technique. For the therapist it may be a good clinical approach to study as many of the rapid results therapies as possible since they may be used as complementary tools.

For some people, one of the methods applied may be more effective than the others. To other individuals, a combination of a few techniques may be better.

Is each new technique/therapy a unique phenomenon or is it a part of the human ability to heal rapidly when provided with the right tools?

Are the manifestations of these various techniques only coincidental? Does the basic mechanism behind their healing process really differ one from another?

While evaluating the rapid effect of Palm Therapy it was necessary for me to try to understand its place among other methods. Is Palm Therapy a unique finding?

After much consideration of the subject, I am convinced that all rapid result therapies work on the same healing factor within the human mind using different methods and theories of "how it works". Of course, each therapy method stands by itself with its own practitioners and advocates. The differences are in the technique, method, level of professional requirements to practice the technique, and even the level of involvement in the client's life. But as mentioned, there is one thing in common— their rapid and efficient effect. At a certain time during the course of the treatment in most of these methods, the clients are asked to focus their thoughts on the trauma or negative memory, or on the allergen or its representative. This is done in order to bring the problem into a person's awareness. Then each of the techniques uses its own tool to desensitize the problem by applying a stress reduction technique. It can be induced by rapid eye movement, stimulation of certain pressure points, acupuncture, Palm Therapy, hypnosis and other body/mind healing methods. During the process, the individual actually reexperiences the memory of the problem along with a sensation of complete relaxation. This process replaces the negative physical and emotional reaction of that individual towards the negative event that initiated his/her physical or mental problem with a relaxed state of mind, leading to the desensitization of the problem/allergy, etc. When that individual tries to reexperience the trauma, the negative events, or the physical/emotional sensation related to that event, he/she actually finds out that it is not the same anymore. An instant healing process has taken place. (In the case of the allergy desensitization technique, holding the allergen or its representative during the process just emphasizes that one's awareness participates in the rapid healing methods.)

This is actually the main mechanism behind the success of the various rapid result therapies, including Palm Therapy.

I believe that the success of these techniques work especially when they deal with the memory storage of the individual. At some point in the past, the subject had some traumatic event/s which one was unable to deal with satisfactorily to resolve the problem, fear or stressor. The solution, then, was to store it. The body and mind constantly do it. According to the Oriental medicine theory and some Western theories, this storage is accumulated with other experiences during one's lifetime. Eventually, it affects the individual in the form of mental/emotional disorders or physical ailments. Some are considered to be mild while others may be severe in their manifestation. The duration of the outbreaks can differ as well and unless one learns how to release them, one can expect, at some time in life, to experience the result of this negative, unsolved storage.

The rapid results therapies have the ability to release or to desensitize the traumas, the physical and emotional sensations which are related to these traumas or to the unsolved emotional pain.

After the therapy, the client still may remember the traumatic events or unwanted situation, but they no longer can affect him/her. As stated above, the techniques differ from each other, but they all activate the healing forces within our minds which then helps us to get rid of the symptoms caused by these events.

This hypothesis, initially, may sound complicated, but we need to remember that our mind is powerful. It is capable of self-healing and balancing. If we give our mind the ability to do so, it will release the symptoms of emotional and/or physical disorders in a very short time, thus overcoming specific problems. The therapy, then, can be directed towards fulfilling goals in one's life.

Understanding this rapid healing mechanism helps us to realize that there are potentially endless forms for releasing/desensitizing the negative effects of events from the mind's storage. This implies that, in the future, we can expect, in addition to advances in Palm Therapy, many new and innovative techniques/therapies bringing fast and efficient results which will further benefit humanity.

Applying this hypothesis to Palm Therapy means that my discoveries in this field are only the initial steps. I do believe that although rapid and effective results can be noted with the use of Palm Therapy, it will be advanced much further during the years to come as research in this method continues.

Meanwhile, I have decided to publish my findings so that you can benefit from the theory and practice of Palm Therapy now.

In **Section One** you will read about the hand/mind connections based on works of brain researches, neuroscientists and on old wisdom. It describes the various mind/brain activities; your emotions, thoughts and behavior as manifested in the body chemistry, in your handwriting or drawing and in the lines of the palms of your hands. In this section you will also read about the hand/mind connection and the quantum mechanics theory as applied to Palm Therapy.

Section Two will take you through the three stages of Palm Therapy: the Balancing, the Release, and the Fulfillment. Each stage illustrates the progress and the changes that you may go through with Palm Therapy—from stress, guilt, fears and frustration into relaxation, mental/emotional balance acceleration of your talents and fulfillment of your goals via the triggering of success and other characteristics through your hands. It probably sounds amazing or unbelievable, but it works !

Section Three deals with the various aspects of traditional and scientific palmistry. In this section you will read about the history of palmistry. Throughout this section, I will also share with you my recent findings in this field as discovered during my work to develop Palm Therapy. These include addictive attachment patterns and the prenatal life as seen in our hands. This section also incorporates some vital information regarding the application of Palm Therapy.

Section Four will provide you with the practical guidelines for the application of Palm Therapy and its three stages. The suggestions in this section are designated for healthy individuals who further wish to reinforce their emotional balance in various daily life situations, accelerate success and develop talents and energies to their fullest potential. In this section, you will also find some information on how to overcome allergy symptoms which affect many otherwise healthy individuals.

New ways to awaken ESP through Palm Therapy's stimulation is also included in this section. You need to complete the first two stages of Palm Therapy before attempting to stimulate your ESP as directed in this book.

Section Five deals with various mental disorders. The first chapter of this section indicates some of the factors in the body, mind and soul which may be responsible for the development of mental disorders.

A separate chapter is dedicated to the description of each group of disorders, the way they are seen in the hand and the suggested Palm Therapy technique for each. Among them are anxiety disorders, mood disorders, hyperactivity disorder and others. THIS SECTION IS FOR INFORMATION ONLY. It is neither intended for self-diagnosis nor for self-treatment (also see "Important Notice" at the beginning of the book). This part can be used as a reference. We designed it so it will not affect your understanding of Palm Therapy. You may wish to refer to a particular disorder that is of interest to you, then continue with the next section. This is possible, but please read the introduction for Section Five first.

Section Six is designated to acquaint the reader with some of the many possible combinations of Palm Therapy with other alternative healing methods simultaneously. This includes Palm Therapy with aromatherapy, bioenergy, hypnotherapy and others.

Appendixes. In Appendix A you will find a brief description on the anatomy of the hand. You may want to refer to it before or while you are reading the section about palmistry.

More information about some of the many scientific or alternative healing methods that can be incorporated with Palm Therapy is presented in **Appendix B**.

Bibliography The Bibliography in this book is a very extensive one. It is divided into seven main parts: palmistry, Western medicine, psychiatry, psychology, alternative medicine, metaphysics and physics. It is an important part for those of you who may wish to further investigate these topics.

***

Palm Therapy is designed to help you fulfill your goals and achieve your success through the releasing of any negative thinking or behavior patterns you may have developed, whether due to stressful prenatal life, childhood events, life stressors or even due to some body disfunctionings. It helps to dissolve fears, hate, guilt and sorrow. It helps to promote relaxation, better relationships with others, happiness, well-being and harmony of your body, mind and soul.

I believe this book can bring more love, happiness, and peace to humanity. When fears, hate, jealousy, and other negative emotions dissolve and are replaced with joy, fulfillment and success, the hearts of all humanity will naturally unite!

Read this book thoroughly. Share it with others as well. The more people all over the world who practice Palm Therapy, the better world it will be. If you find this information helpful, please recommend this book to others. Networking is the fastest and most powerful way to share it. **Together we can make the change for better, happier, loving human beings!**

SECTION ONE

THE HAND
AN EXPRESSOR
OF THE MIND/BRAIN ?

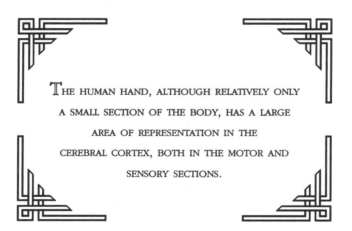

THE HUMAN HAND, ALTHOUGH RELATIVELY ONLY
A SMALL SECTION OF THE BODY, HAS A LARGE
AREA OF REPRESENTATION IN THE
CEREBRAL CORTEX, BOTH IN THE MOTOR AND
SENSORY SECTIONS.

1

The Hand/Mind Connection

Anne, a 32-year-old, was introduced to me by one of her girl-friends. Anne had suffered from grieving for the last five months. Her beloved husband, with whom she had spent seven years of her life, and to whom she had given all of her love, was gone. He had died suddenly in a car accident. Anne was in a very bad emotional state which interfered with her normal activities at home and at work. She could not concentrate. She spent hours dreaming about him and cried most of the time. Nothing could really replace Jim.

I observed both of her palms. I then asked her to concentrate on her most painful memory of Jim. It was the day she realized that he would never come back to her. Her eyes filled with tears as she did as I said. I then started stimulating certain palmar creases/lines and minor lines on her palm. "This is called Palm Therapy," I explained to her and started to talk about anything but her husband. After about four minutes I asked her: "Now tell me, Anne, how do you feel?" She was silent for a moment and then replied: "I feel nothing." " Try to feel the same painful memory you had in your mind just a few minutes ago," I told her. "OK," she replied. She closed her eyes. I could see the movement of her eyeballs as if she was searching for that painful memory in her mind. "I can't, I... just can't feel the pain again, It's gone. It's impossible! I don't feel so sad for him anymore."

***

You have just read about one case out of the many women, men and children who suffered from grieving, anxiety, panic attacks, agoraphobia or other emotional disorders. They all had one thing in common. They reacted almost identically after being introduced for the first time in their lives to the effect of Palm Therapy.

What really happened? Is there a link between the hand and our emotions? Is it possible that somehow by stimulating certain lines in the hand it triggers some other processes in our brain/mind which eventually lead to an immediate relief?

Let's try now to understand what happened.

The following paragraphs will furnish you with some ideas for the link between the hand and mind as well as some hypotheses of how stimulation through Palm Therapy affects the human mind.

THE HAND/MIND AND THE PHYSICAL STIMULATION CONNECTION

Throughout the years, it has been proven and documented by researchers of the brain that stimulation for a few minutes in certain areas in the brain (directly and indirectly), can arouse emotions from overwhelming dread to pleasure and well-being. (See Bibliography at the end of the book.) Stimulation of an area in the brain called the *limbic system* and other areas, as well, proved to evoke sensations such as anger, hate, guilt and love; childhood memories arose, too, during the process.

With the use of electrodes implanted in various parts of the brain, researchers were able to turn these reactions on and off. The cause and effect relationship between the stimulation of the brain and the emotions or the behavior which preceded, were obvious.

There are many billions of nerve cells, or neurons, in the brain. The neurons have a spidery structure which enables them to form a network of interactions, forming gaps or synapses in this complex structure.

The neurons communicate with each other in various ways. Although they have been considered electrically excitable cells and the propagators of signals and signal processing within the neurons, they are significantly dependent on ionic current. They are known to communicate with each other mainly by a chemical communication called neurotransmitters—chemical substances that can be synthesized by the neurons. The neurotransmitters carry information to and from the brain. Your emotions, memories and desires are being manifested in every cell in your body.

Scientists found that often there can be a link between the

level of certain neurotransmitters in the synaptic gaps and the various mental states. Conscious or subconscious emotions, behavior and even mental disorders have been tied to the levels of these substances in the brain.

Clinical depression, for example, has been known to be related to low levels of the neurotransmitters serotonin and norepinephrine. A deficiency of the neurotransmitter serotonin also has been related to obsessive-compulsive disorder. Excessive levels of the neurotransmitter dopamine has been related to delusional states. Medications which lead to various chemical changes in certain levels of the neurotransmitters improve these conditions.

Moreover, scientists found that stimulation of the skin surface, such as rubbing, can lead to various rapid chemical changes in the synaptic gaps which are accompanied by pain relief and involve endorphines.

These findings may give us a clue as to why through Palm Therapy, a stimulation of the skin surface of the hand in areas which represent various mental activities and characteristics of the personality as seen in the hand, anticipated changes in the state of mind may be achieved rapidly. In this process, activation of certain lines on the palm can induce relaxation and an instant relief from stress, while stimulation of other lines may involve the release of childhood memories. Other areas of stimulation accelerate mental alertness, vitality, concentration, memory, talents, planning and decision making, and features which are vital for fulfillment and success. All of these may be possible as a result of chemical changes and other physiological processes that are achieved via a stimulation of the hand in certain areas which represent human brain activity and thinking patterns, in a similar way that researchers of the brain, were able to arouse rapid changes in thinking and behavior; from emotions of overwhelming dread to pleasure and well-being through the stimulation of certain areas in the brain.

Theoretically, since information from our brain is being transferred to and from any cell of our body, these results may also be achieved by the stimulation of any other part of the body. Why, then, did I choose the hand?

In the following pages you will read about some of the ideas that led me in this direction.

————

More about neurotransmitters:

Most of the neurotransmitters belong to the amino acids group which is divided into the excitatory and inhibitory groups. The other neurotransmitters that have been identified are the monoamines which are also divided into two major groups: the indolamines, and the catecholamines. The indolamines include melatonin and serotonin; and the catecholamines include dopamine, epinephrine and norepinephrine. The neurotransmitters functions for histamines which is included in the group of the monoamines are known as nitric oxide and purines. Another major neurotransmitter is the acetylcholine which has an important role in brain activity. Besides these neurotransmitters it has been found that some peptides function as neurotransmitters. For further, extensive information regarding the brain activity, please refer to the book: *The Molecular Foundations of Psychiatry* by Steven E. Hyman, M.D. and Eric J.Nestler, M.D., Ph.D., also to the related books listed in the Bibliography. (Remember that the study of the brain is proceeding rapidly. It is probable that during the process of publishing this book new findings in this area will be discovered.)

THE HAND—AN EXPRESSOR OF THE MIND/BRAIN IN SCIENTIFIC PALMISTRY

It is within the cerebral cortex, the layer of gray matter of the brain, which forms the surface of each cerebral hemisphere of the brain, that impulses are received and analyzed, where information is being stored, where thoughts are processed and memory formed, and voluntary actions of the hands and other parts of the body are initiated. Of course, more than one part of the brain participates in the processing of information and memory or the generation of emotions from perceptions and other functions. These parts may involve the hippocampus, the amygdala, the limbic system and others. Actually, information is being transferred to and from every cell in your body through the nervous system and other physiological processes.

Brain mapping reveals that the human hand, although relatively only a small section of the body, has a large area of representation in the cerebral cortex, both in the motor and sensory sections (Figs. 1a, 1b). This means that your hands, including your fingers, can perceive an enormous amount of information to and from your brain, which is a part of your physical body, and from the mind's thoughts and feelings as manifested in the various brain activities. We can say, then, that the hand is connected and influenced by your body and mind.

Frederic Wood Jones, who was a researcher and a professor of anatomy at the University of London, stated in his book *The Principles of Anatomy as Seen in the Hand* (Ch. 1, Page 4, publisher:J.& A Churchill, London):

"The hand as the expressor of emotional states affords a study in itself; it is a study that the physician cannot afford to neglect...The expression of the hand is a thing impossible to define, yet it is a very real factor. It is more easily noticed by its absence."

Apparently, information from our brain and mind mani-

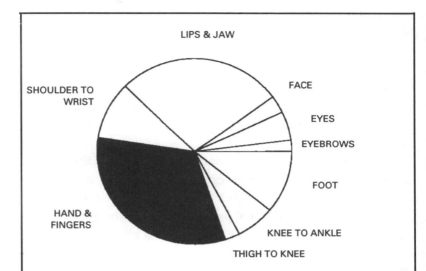

Fig. 1a   *The approximate degree of representation of the various body parts in the motor cortex of the brain.*

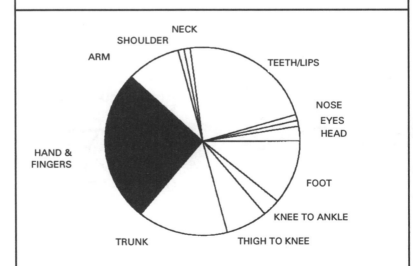

Fig. 1b   *The approximate degree of representation of various body parts in the somatosensory cortex of the brain.*

fests itself not only in the various gestures and postures of the hand, as part of the body language, but in the creases/lines of the palms, in our fingers, and in the general shape of the hand.

The hand, as an expressor of the emotions or mental activity, may provide us, then, with clues for the characteristics of one's personality including traits, talents and orientations, as well as some mental and physical abnormalities as seen in the medical field.

As you probably noticed, normally the palm of the hand at birth contains several flexion creases, two of which are transverse and separate from each other (the *heart line* and the *brain/head line*, in traditional palmistry). When these two form a single transverse crease, it is called a *simian crease* (Fig. 2). This crease may appear in a variety of developmental abnormalities (Taber's Cyclopedic Medical Dictionary 1984, Page 1331) such

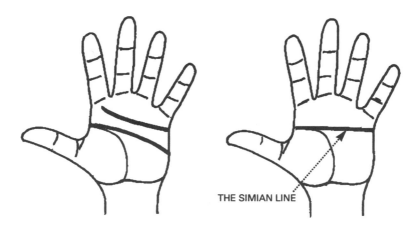

THE SIMIAN LINE

Fig. 2 *The palm normally contains several flexion creases. Two of them are transverse and separated from each other. The simian line may appear in a variety of developmental abnormalities (Taber's Cyclopedic Medical Dictionary).*

as Down's syndrome, also known as mongolism, with moderate to severe mental retardation, as well as in Turner's syndrome which involves, in some of the patients, impaired intelligence and amenorrhea. You may find it fascinating that the impaired proximal transverse palmar crease (head line) in palmistry represents intellectual difficulties or mental abnormalities. (The simian crease may appear in normal individuals as well. It is rare and it may appear mainly in only one hand. Again, this is only in a small percentage of the general healthy population.)

Another interesting fact from the medical field regards the drug hydantoin which was included in the etiologic factors of mental retardations (The Merck Manual, 1992, Ch. 191). Babies who were born to mothers who received this drug during pregnancy, suffered from the fetal hydantoin syndrome which involves distal phalangeal hypoplasia—a defective development of the tissue of the distal phalanges.

The fact that mental retardation appeared together with defective development of the tissue of the distal phalanges in those babies, reinforces the observations made in traditional and scientific palmistry which state that the distal phalanges of the fingers represent the logic and the intellectual development of the individual. (In the thumb it represents the will, used in deciding or choosing a thought or an act, as well as the power of controlling one's emotions or actions.)

Scientific researches into palmistry have been done throughout the years. Andrew Fitzherbert, the author of the book: *The Palmist's Companion*, 1992, Page 11-22, described various researches done by palmists. Among them were the following:

Charlotte Wolff, M.D., who was also a psychologist, revealed major findings after researches in palmistry. Her works were published in several scientific papers and in her books: *The Human Hands*, 1942, *Psychology of Gesture*, 1945, and *The*

Hand in Psychological Diagnosis, 1956. She made studies with children and adults from all sectors of life as well as with patients in mental hospitals. Her studies with schizophrenic patients confirmed other findings that showed breakages, islands, or other signs on the proximal transverse palmar crease (head line) in mentally disturbed persons.

Dr. Wolff was submitted to a blind test. She diagnosed hand prints of 25 people suffering from a variety of mental disorders. The results were remarkably accurate and correlated to the diagnoses of healthcare professionals who were in charge of these patients. Another research was conducted in 1982 by an Israeli psychotherapist, Ms. Yael Haft-Pomrock together with Dr. Yigal Ginat of Ben Gurion University. They studied the hands of some hospitalized schizophrenics and compared them with a control group of normal people. Their findings supported other studies in the field. They found prominent differences between the groups. The results of the research were published in the *Israeli Journal of Psychiatry in Relation to Science*, Volume 19, Page 5-22, Israel Science Publishers, 1982.

Besides these scientific studies, there were other less formal studies, and many books were published in this field. All of these scientific studies have confirmed the link between the hands and the personality.

Additional researches were conducted through the years with similar results. Books about scientific palmistry were published by many experts who dedicated their lives to this subject. Among them were physicians and psychologists such as William Benham, M.D., Charlotte Wolff, M.D., Eugene Scheinman, M.D., and others. (Please refer to the Bibliography at the end the book for a list of references.)

As we can understand by now, there must be a communication link between the human brain, the mind and the hand; a link which is more than merely the control of the hand's movements or the information that is transferred to our brain through the receptors, nerve endings of our hands: touch, pressure, temperature, pain, etc. The hand provides us with some information about various disorders and abnormalities such as seen in Down's syndrome and in people who suffer from schizophrenia or, simply, as seen in people with arthritis. It also provides us with information about talents and various characteristics of the individual. I believe that soon we will have more tools for the understanding of this communication link. The influence of Palm Therapy on the well-being, fulfillment and success of so many individuals could not have happened without it.

The following paragraphs will reveal to you another manifestation of the hand/mind connection.

THE HAND/MIND CONNECTION AND GRAPHOLOGY

Other fields which support the hand/mind connection are graphology, which is well-developed in Europe, and that of drawing counseling, which is practiced also in the U.S.A.

Graphology is also known as handwriting analysis. It is a way to analyze the personality or the unconscious disclosures made by one's handwriting. The Taber's Cyclopedic Medical Dictionary, 14th Edition, N.Y., 1984, describes graphology as a diagnostic tool in diseases of the nerves and as a means of analyzing the personality.

In Germany, for example, graphology is regarded as a branch of applied psychology and courses in graphology are an integral part of the academic curricula in psychology. (See Bibliography.)

Drawing, similar to graphology, has been used in the U.S.A. and other places in the world for counseling and as another diagnostic aid to the understanding of the mind. In the text-book for professional counselors *Counseling: A Comprehensive Profession* by Samuel T. Gladding, Macmillan Pub. N.Y., 1988, drawing is valued for its subtle unveiling of affective states. It mentions that various figures drawn by children displayed inner realities related to their social-emotional adjustment at school. This implies that, similar to handwriting, through the use of their hands on the paper they were able to convey some data about their fears, conflicts, anger and other parts of their inner realities.

A therapy method was developed from the field of graphology. This therapy is called graphotherapy and it is based on handwriting analysis. The basic assumption behind this therapy is that the circuit which is established between the brain and the graphic gesture by the nervous system is a two way circuit. In this therapy, handwriting patterns and signs which reflect flaws of the mind are consciously modified through repetitious "correcting" handwriting exercises, thus, giving a powerful suggestion to the subconscious to effect the corresponding character change. The technique is mainly known in Europe and is currently used successfully as a part of the work of psychotherapists in France. (See Bibliography.)

Our body and our mind try to communicate with us in various ways to get the help they need in order to let us achieve optimum potential and fulfillment in life. Handwriting is one of the manifestations of our inner realities that can be used to change those realities. If by changing a diagnosed by-product of the hand (such as handwriting activity) a modification of related traits of the mind occurs, then it makes sense that we can influence the mind and lead to corresponding changes in our lives through a direct stimulation of the first source of information to and from our brain and mind— the human hand.

A recent breakthrough in the field of neuroscience raises

another point of consideration that may reveal the other aspect of the hand/mind connection: The non-direct nerves communication.

THE HAND/MIND AND NON-DIRECT COMMUNICATION

Although the hypothesis of non-direct cells communication has been around for years in the metaphysical and other circles, it had never been scientifically proven. A breakthrough has occurred recently with a study done at Stanford University by Erin Schuman and Daniel Madison. This study showed that neurons can sometimes communicate with one another without a direct contact through the synapse (*Discover Magazine*, June 1994). That means that there is an additional type of communication other than the linear one (which involves chemicals such as the neurotransmitters).

If a nerve cell can transmit information to other nerve cells that are not connected to it, there is apparently a strong possibility that the nerve cells of the hand may transmit messages or information from the hand to the neurons in the brain and vice versa also in a non-direct mode.

The study is another vital reinforcement for the hand/mind connection theory. It may partially explain the mechanism that stands behind Palm Therapy and other skin stimulation techniques such as acupuncture, acupressure, shiatsu and reflexology. The study done at Stanford University helps us to scientifically consider the hand/mind connection and, actually, the intercommunication of all the cells in our body in addition to the physiological one. It may be the beginning for the consideration of additional ways of communication such as the telepathic phenomena and interconnection on a non-matter level—the energy level of our existence (which with future technology will be viewed just as matter is viewed today). I believe that following these findings, some aspects of the esoteric/metaphysical world will be gradually scientifically explained.

This topic naturally brings us to another connection mode which has been known for thousands of years but as yet has not been completely proven scientifically.

THE HAND/MIND ENERGY PATHWAYS CONNECTION

Various energy centers and pathways cross our body. They are interconnected and invisible to most people (although they can be seen with a special training). Special sensitive tools have been developed throughout the years in order to document this energy such as *Kirlian Photography* or *Electronographic Imaging*. Today, photographs of the body's aura, which is a reflection of some of these energy centers and pathways, are available. Some look at this radiation as the observed infrared aspect of the heat radiated out of the body or an object photographed. If it was only so, then this assumption cannot explain how the aura changes drastically while eating different types of foods of the same caloric value under similar conditions. This assumption does not completely explain why, by changing the brain waves activity from beta to alpha or to higher beta waves, which are equivalent to relaxation or anxiety states of mind, corresponding changes are seen immediately in the aura as well.

The aura, the body's subtle energy, was known for many centuries. The ancient people of India, for example, described the various main energy centers, called *chakras* (Fig. 3) the seven main *chakras*, the twenty-one secondary *chakras*, and the sixty-three peripheral *chakra*s. Traditional Chinese medicine emphasizes the work on the energy pathways known as the meridians of acupuncture (Fig. 4). Koryo hand acupuncture which was developed by Dr. Tae Woo Yoo describes the many meridians of acupuncture of the hand and the treatment of the whole body merely through the hand. Yet, other energy pathways which are used in reflexology of the foot or that of the hand are known as the meridians of reflexology. (See Fig. 5.)

Dr. Joseph Calligaris, M.D., 1876-1944, who was a scientist and a professor of neurology in Italy, described the energy pathways as a giant, netlike energy connection. Stimulation of various areas in this netlike energy generated a corresponding effect on the body and the mind.

By observing the flow of energy in the many energy pathways on the hands (Fig. 6) and body, I also concluded that the whole body is connected in an enormous, netlike energy path-

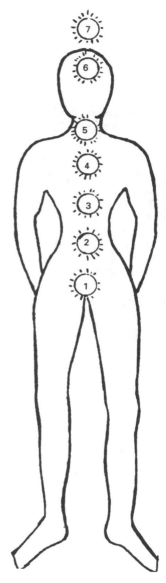

Fig. 3   *The seven main chakras.*

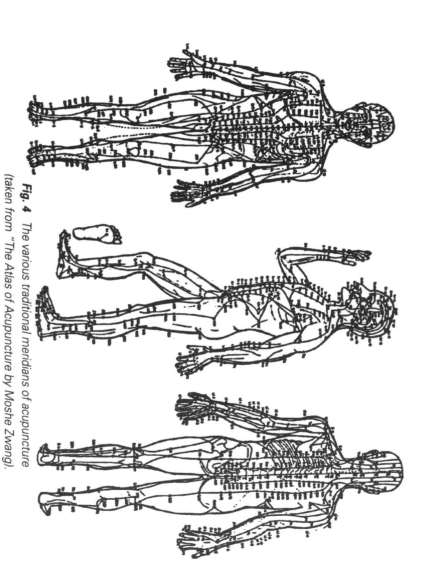

Fig. 4 The various traditional meridians of acupuncture
(taken from "The Atlas of Acupuncture by Moshe Zwang).

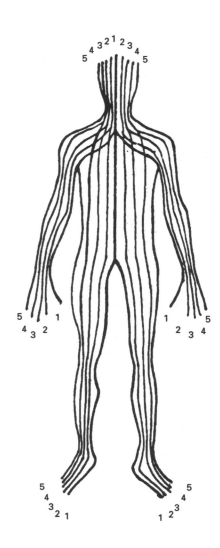

Fig. 5 *The meridians of reflexology
(taken from "The Atlas of Reflexology" by Moshe Zwang).*

way, but based on my experience, it seems that the hand, besides being connected to the whole body energy-wise, is also reinforced by additional types of energy paths to and from the brain. I call it: *The Super Hand Meridians System* (see Chapter 37). In the palm and the fingers, the major representatives of energy pathways are seen on the various palmar creases/lines and on the other minor lines, mounts and small signs. A stimulation of the hand in various areas leads to a balancing effect on the energy level which I assume is manifested in both the mind and body activity. I believe that advanced scientific technology will confirm this hypothesis which does not contradict, but completes, another aspect in the hand/mind connection and may confirm the various theories of acupuncture, reflexology, *chakra* balancing, kundaliny energy and in Palm Therapy.

THE HAND/MIND/SOUL CONNECTION

The Western scientific approach suggests that all human behavior including our emotions and thoughts are all brain functions. The extensive mapping of the brain done by the famous neurosurgeon, Wilder Penfield, was one of the many attempts to explain how the brain accounts for the mind. Neuroscientists have conducted thorough researches to prove that there is a physiological explanation to what we consider as the mind or psychological process. I do believe that the many extensive researches and the many tools that are developed for investigating the finer levels of the matter will eventually be able to explain psychological processes and almost any metaphysical phenomena with connections to the matter level. But do we have to ignore other levels of existence such as the energy level or the soul existence?

No. There are too many phenomena which, although they

See chapter 37
pg 587

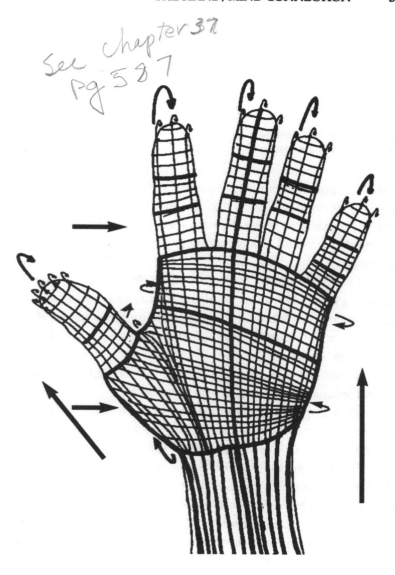

Fig. 6 *The Super Hand Meridians system of the palm
(discovered by Moshe Zwang, following the theory of Dr. Calligaris).*

cannot be scientifically explained yet should be considered seriously. Among them are telepathy, healing energy, out-of-body experience and near-death experience.

Now, let's discuss near-death experience phenomena: Near-death experience has been researched and documented throughout the years. Most patients of any age from little children to old individuals who came back to life after they had been pronounced clinically dead, amazingly featured similar details about their experiences over and over again; peaceful.... joy.... observing the body and the medical staff from above.... out-of-body travel, going through a tunnel.... seeing the light.... welcoming by dead family members and friends....encountering a being of lights....

Among the many documented works which all together included cases of hundreds of patients who had a near-death experience are the books: *Life After Life* by Raymond A. Moody Jr., M.D., and *Closer To The Light* by Melvin Morse, M.D., with Paul Perry.

Are all of these cases manifested by a specific brain activity that lets us feel as if we have left the body?

Many hypotheses were formed to try to explain this phenomenon. Some claimed that it may be a demonstration of a strong sixth sense or, maybe, it is the action of the defense mechanism of the body to feel better and as if it survived death. Others attribute it to the physiological effect of the many narcotic drugs which are given to seriously ill patients.

The latter book, *Closer To The Light* included documented near-death experiences of children, and a research conducted on the subject at the Children's Hospital in Seattle Washington. The findings with a control group showed that near-death experience was not reported by those seriously ill children who were given narcotic drugs and were exposed to the fear of being in the intensive care. They had some delusions and hallucinations but nothing as distinguishing as those who really were in a near-death experience. The descriptions of the phenomenon were repeatedly disclosed by all of those children who were really in near-death situations, such as those which had gone through cardiac arrests as a result of severe asthma, heart stoppages, surgeries, automobile and near-drowning accidents, etc.

Do these cases prove the existence of the soul? Techniques using different types of a gas therapy which were applied to try to improve the condition of mentally disturbed individuals led to the same phenomena. Morse and Perry, reasonably, commented that these individuals more than likely had gone through a near-death experience because of the gas that was forced into them. The same phenomena was also evoked in patients of Wilder Penfield, M.D. merely when he electrically stimulated a specific area in their brains. This area called the Sylvian fissure, is located in the right temporal lobe just above the right ear. But after devoting a lifetime experience into brain research, trying to prove that brain activity counts for the mind, Wilder Penfield, M.D., concluded in his final examination of evidence in this field that the mind is something different from the physical brain.

That area of the brain has been considered by some as the gap between psychology and physiology and the seat of the soul. It is very likely that the emotions and other feelings or thoughts we experience occur at various energy levels of our existence which include the mind and the soul. Once this energy is attached to the physical body it has the capacity of interacting with the matter and is manifested in the complex of the physiology including that of the DNA, the neurons, neurotransmitters, hormones and all the components of the body. Therefore, any therapy on the matter level can influence the energy level and vice versa. I believe that the stimulation on the matter level (the hand) done through Palm Therapy, although it probably will be explained by physiological processing, also affects the energy level of our existence via its attachment to the physical body, hence influencing body and mind.

THE HAND/MIND CONNECTION AND THE QUANTUM MECHANICS THEORY

The discoveries in quantum mechanics, the latest theory in physics, gives us another dimension to the explanation of Palm Therapy. In many experiments of quantum mechanics it has been proven scientifically that behavior of particles of light (photons) can influence similar results in a remote equal testing when there is observation of both. The observer, then, becomes part of the observation. Although the experiments are apparently very simple, the results affect every aspect of our understanding the universe and life including the fields of neuroscience and biology.

Based on these findings, and assuming that the hand represents the mind, it is very likely that by affecting the hand, the observer, in this case the Palm Therapist, affects the mind in a non-direct mode. In accordance with the quantum mechanics principle, since the effect of Palm Therapy may be directly on the brain/mind without a neural path or other systems of connection, it is unknown yet how the observer (the Palm Therapist) can influence the brain through the hand.

Researchers such as the physicist Roger Penrose, a professor at Oxford University and an expert in general relativity and quantum mechanics, developed a theory explaining the mind activity as a quantum consciousness in which the neurons firing signals could be quantum events. In my opinion, those quantum events can be influenced by the observer, the Palm Therapist, using the various hand/mind connections.

PALM THERAPY: DEFINITION

As in any mechanism or therapy that works, we naturally ask ourselves how and why it works, or what is the secret behind its effects. In this chapter I raised a few hypotheses as to the inner mechanism of Palm Therapy. Whether one or more theories apply, or perhaps some other explanations not yet discovered exist, time or history will tell.

Looking back to the past, I can remember how the idea of Palm Therapy was formed in my mind. It was at the end of 1985 in Israel. At that time, I worked as the head of the naturopathic clinic for the Vegetarian Association in Tel Aviv, Israel. And in the evenings or on weekends I used to conduct various courses, workshops and lectures in the fields of graphology and graphotherapy and other courses such as scientific palmistry, hand reflexology, foot reflexology, acupressure, acupuncture, seeing the aura, bioenergy (healing) and meditation. This knowledge together with the spiritual training and teaching contributed to the insight I had and to the formation of Palm Therapy.

If I need to define Palm Therapy after all these years, I would summarize it as follows:

Palm Therapy is the art and science of enhancing optimum potential, self-growth, fulfillment and success in all aspects of life through the stimulation of specific areas and lines in the hands which represent the various characteristics of the personality and brain/mind activities. Palm Therapy's stimulation sends direct suggestions to all levels of one's existence via the various hand/brain/mind connections and communications. This, apparently, bypasses the cognitive mind's critique and disapproval for new changes in thinking and behavior patterns. Therefore, it leads to rapid corresponding changes in mood, behavior and thinking patterns, potential, talents, personality and eventually in one's life. The process is done without effort or strain and can be enhanced anytime, anywhere.

Through Palm Therapy's stimulation, emotional pains such as grieving, anger, frustration, unhappy memories and the effects of negative experiences were relieved in a very short time, during the very first session of Palm Therapy. Cases of anxiety, panic attacks and various mental disturbances were improved dramatically. Symptoms of allergy as seen on the hand were overcome and neutralized; development of various higher brain/mind activities, such as the IQ, mental clarity, concentration, self-esteem, self-determination, awareness and stimulation of Success Energy, which are extremely essential for accomplishing goals in life, were effectively activated. Fulfillment, then, became an inevitable result of Palm Therapy as was reported by many persons from all walks of life on whom Palm Therapy was applied.

The stimulation of the hand through Palm Therapy initiates a rapid balancing effect on the state of mind which usually occurs within a few minutes of stimulation. This brings results that, otherwise, may take months or even years to achieve without treatment. But in order to help yourself achieve optimum potential, success and fulfillment, you need to overcome certain behavior patterns and emotional disturbances to which you have adapted yourself throughout the years and to activate maximum talents and the best characteristics for yourself. The reshaping of your personality and life through Palm Therapy requires more than merely a one-time stimulation in certain areas and lines of your hands. The duration of the therapy may vary from person to person, but in almost all cases the individual goes through the three stages of Palm Therapy:

> **First Stage : The Balancing**
> **Second Stage : The Release**
> **Third Stage : The Fulfillment**

The following section describes each stage of Palm Therapy. It will enable you to achieve a better understanding of the process involved in this amazing technique.

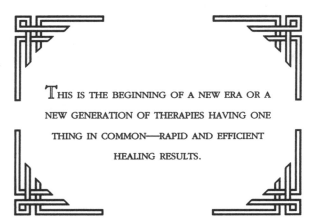

THIS IS THE BEGINNING OF A NEW ERA OR A
NEW GENERATION OF THERAPIES HAVING ONE
THING IN COMMON—RAPID AND EFFICIENT
HEALING RESULTS.

SECTION TWO

THE THREE STAGES
OF PALM THERAPY

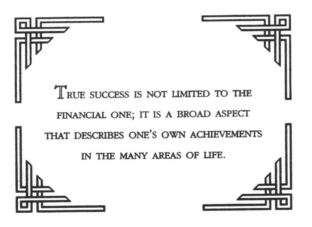

TRUE SUCCESS IS NOT LIMITED TO THE
FINANCIAL ONE; IT IS A BROAD ASPECT
THAT DESCRIBES ONE'S OWN ACHIEVEMENTS
IN THE MANY AREAS OF LIFE.

The Three Stages of
Palm Therapy:
Introduction

Do you belong to the group of the many talented people who find it difficult to control their emotions or to conduct a happy relationship, at work, at school, with friends or with people whom they love the most? Do you suffer from financial self-sabotage or procrastination or, for some reason, consistently fail to reach your goals? Do you suffer from fears and shyness, or forget that you also deserve to enjoy your own life?

Negative emotions can affect any normal person during the course of life; despairing mood, grieving, anger, guilt, shame, a sense of insecurity, fears, low self-esteem and frustration are just a few. Many of these feelings may interfere with your efforts or achievements in your daily activity. They gradually contribute to a high stress level which, if continued, can significantly affect your health and your life!

There are many reasons for the way you feel or act. They are rooted in your body, mind and soul. Some of them are due to the many events in your life. They may create negative thinking patterns in your mind which initiate or aggravate your problem. I assume that you are familiar with some of these stressors which can occur at anytime during one's life. They may be mild or severe, during your childhood or anytime later in life. They may include a change of school, a break up with a boyfriend or a girlfriend, a marital separation, a loss of job, a personal injury or illness, the death of a dear one, a war or a natural disaster.

There are things in your life that you cannot change— your childhood, your past and some genetic characteristics. However, there are many aspects in your personality, the ways you perceive or react towards the stressors in life, your emotional resistance, belief system, thinking patterns and energy balance, which can be helped and reinforced through Palm Therapy in order to activate fulfillment, success and happiness in your life... in a natural way.

It may sound unrealistic, but the results with many individuals who have experienced the power of this technique since 1985 are amazing. Some of their experiences are presented in the various case histories in this section.

We all are unique individuals with different expectations in life. Since each of us has a unique personality, our goals, needs and expectations may differ from others. Becoming successful is according to one's own beliefs, needs, dreams and level of awareness. True success is not limited to the financial one. It is a broad aspect that describes one's own achievements in the many areas of life. These are represented by the various parts of your hand and can be naturally stimulated through Palm Therapy. Some of the desired achievements include the development of:

Unconditional love and inner peace
Inner pureness
Faith
Intuitive powers/ESP awakening
Healing Powers

A better IQ
Mental clarity
Excellent memory
Power of concentration
New skills and talents
Achieving a degree

Creative problem-solving ability
Self-esteem
Self-motivation
Self-discipline
Positive self-image
Excellent loving relationships

Excellent physical health
Excellent body figure/beauty
Special achievements in sports
Special achievements in a career
Peak performance in any and all aspects
Magnetic personality
Charisma
Leadership abilities
Financial freedom/material wealth

Others (You may wish to pause now and think about
your own specific desires for achievement and success.)

These achievements and fulfillment of expectations can be developed step by step via the hand/mind connection with the three steps program—the three stages of Palm Therapy.

Let's review, now, each of them briefly.

1. THE BALANCING STAGE

In this stage the main concern is to help you feel good, emotionally balanced, calm, stronger, free of fears, and in control of your emotional state regardless of present difficulties and the symptoms of high stress or mental disorders which may disturb you in daily life. It may help you to accurately perceive various stressors and deal with them in a more realistic way. During this stage you will be prepared for the second stage of Palm Therapy. It is done by stimulating certain lines, signs, and shapes in the hands which trigger an immediate energy balancing which affects the mind. This stimulation also bypasses the cognitive mind's critique and disapproval of new changes in behavior patterns. Therefore, the initial effect is felt almost immediately.

Since the stimulation during the first stage of Palm Therapy is done for the purpose of inducing a balancing effect, you can experience the change in mood, especially if you are under stress or in emotional pain. Otherwise, if you are emotionally well-balanced, you will not experience any immediate change.

2. THE RELEASE STAGE

By stimulating certain areas in the hand which are related to your early childhood and the memory bank, but are not limited to childhood memories, you may start to release painful or traumatic memories as well as inner conflicts that limited you in the past. These may be responsible for a high stress level or certain mental disorders that you may have developed due to psychological or social stressors or other factors. This process is an essential part of the therapy and one that can free you from negative childhood patterns, anger, frustration, guilt and emotional pain. It serves as a tool to defeat self-sabotage and prepares you to achieve the best of yourself. The activation of a release process is triggered due to the bypassing of the cognitive mind's critique through the direct stimulation of the mind's energies and the memory bank as seen in the hands.

3. THE FULFILLMENT STAGE

At this stage, when you are already freed from the pain, conflicts or other negative emotions which stopped you in the past, you are naturally ready to anchor yourself daily in happiness and success. You will want to grow in all aspects of life and enjoy them as much as you can. In the third stage of Palm Therapy, stimulation of specific lines and areas in your palms triggers Success Energy in you, helping you to reach your goals in any direction you wish as long as they are reasonable and are leading towards a positive rewarding life.

The three stages of Palm Therapy, similar to the theories of Chinese medicine, are also tools to balance the mind and the body on an energy level. Once these energies are well-balanced with the help of Palm Therapy or other natural therapies, many of the emotional barriers that have limited you in the past will disappear. Then a stimulation of Success Energy, and other characteristics of human excellence which you choose to have, can be fully activated through the hand, leading to fulfillment, success and happiness in your life.

HOW LONG WILL IT TAKE ?

Despite the immediate balancing effect, the first and second stages of Palm Therapy may take from a few weeks to a few months. While the third phase, the Fulfillment Stage, can be stimulated as long as you wish to sharpen specific talents, qualities, and to accumulate more success in your life. Each one of us is special and unique with our own life experiences. Therefore, there is no specific time frame for the duration of Palm Therapy. In most cases the therapy may be as follows:

First Stage: The Balancing
1 - 3 months

Second Stage: The Release
1 - 2 months
plus about two weeks additional release, until all release signs disappear.

Third Stage: The Fulfillment
Up to the individual's needs. A life-time process of setting goals, achieving success, setting new goals, etc.

CAN WE APPLY IT ON OURSELVES ? *yes*

For the question as to whether we can apply Palm Therapy on ourselves, the answer is positive, but only after you learn practical Palm Therapy and are aware of all the aspects that were covered in the "Important Notice" at the beginning of the book and throughout the text. Actually, I had started the work of Palm Therapy by working on my own palms. However, we must be aware that the technique has to be precise when we do it. But suppose you would not do it so accurately. What happens then? Can any harm be done? The answer is no. If you don't apply it exactly as it has to be done, it won't have the effect of Palm Therapy. It just won't work since it can affect only when applied on some imbalances of the mind/brain's energies as seen in the hand or in places which represent specific characteristics that you want to activate. The good aspect about it is that if you miss the Palm Therapy's lines or areas in the palm, the stimulation, when applied, becomes then acupressure or hand reflexology, especially if the stimulation is applied on a painful spot on the hand. This may bring some benefits to the correspondent parts of the body represented in the hand. Therefore, my advice to you is: Don't worry if you are not sure yet how to apply it; do Palm Therapy anyway. In the worst scenario you would do a beneficial work as acupressure or hand reflexology. (See "Important Notice," first.)

Since Palm Therapy especially deals with the modification of certain lines, it is good to know that massaging the hands, working out, or doing any type of manual labor usually does not negatively affect the lines. You can safely continue massaging the hands and do any type of manual labor without worrying that some lines may be deleted or poorly modified. However, it is important to remember that any change in your emotional life or physical health can make changes in the palm patterns. This does not pertain to the dermatoglyphics which usually do not change during a lifetime. In order to detect deterioration or improvement, we need to compare hand prints which are taken periodically. I do recommend that you make a photocopy of both hands at least once per year. If you apply Palm Therapy on yourself, make a photocopy of your hands at every stage and compare with the previous ones. (See Chapter 6: "Hand Documentation.")

PALM THERAPY FOR INDIVIDUALS WHO SUFFER FROM MENTAL DISORDERS

You soon will read more about each stage of Palm Therapy. But before proceeding, I believe that some of you, being professional healthcare providers or being familiar with people who were diagnosed as having mental disorders (either mild or severe), may wonder if Palm Therapy can help them, too.

The answer is yes. Applying Palm Therapy can help since it works on balancing the energies that are related to various systems of the body and mind. It may help whether the energy imbalance is a response to psychological factors, social factors, or is due to heredity, biology, use of a substance, or a brain dysfunction. Palm Therapy can serve as a tool to help balance many diagnosed mental/emotional disorders. Among them are anxiety disorders, such as panic attacks (with or without agoraphobia), social phobia, or posttraumatic stress disorder. Other mental disorders include mood disorders (e.g., bipolar disorders, depressive disorders) and various disturbances that may have developed after some mild, moderate or severe life events/stressors.

A whole section is dedicated to various mental disorders and suggested Palm Therapy for each group of disorders. You may wish to review the various factors in the body, mind and soul which I believe to be involved in the development of a mental disorder. (See Section Five.)

It is assumed that many psychological processes, normal and abnormal, depend on brain functions. Some mental disturbances such as various types of anxiety disorders or of dementia are known to be caused by, or associated with, medical conditions or the use of a certain substance.

There are many medical conditions that can interfere with the normal activities of the brain. Among them are diseases of the brain or a systemic illness which secondarily affects the brain; endocrine disorders such as hyper-and hypothyroidism, hypoglycemia and other metabolic disorders. The use of certain substances can also interfere with the brain activities. These substances include alcohol, amphetamines, medications and others. They may disturb some brain functions or leave long-lasting damage that influences the central nervous system. Deficiency of certain nutrients is also involved in some of the medical conditions that may affect the way you think or feel. The symptoms of a deficiency may result in impaired functioning of the nervous system and may lead to certain mental disturbances. For example, vitamin B1 deficiency in delirium, or vitamin B12 deficiency in certain anxiety disorders are some of the well-known ones.

If you suffer from symptoms of anxiety, or of other mental disturbances, ask your doctor to give you a thorough physical examination before starting Palm Therapy because there are many medical conditions or allergies and chemical sensitivities to certain substances that may lead to the same symptoms of anxiety disorders such as panic attacks, phobias, obsessive/compulsive disorder and to mood swings such as depression and other symptoms.

Remember, Palm Therapy is not a cure-all technique, but since it deals with the energy level of the problem, it has a great balancing effect also on mental disturbances that are caused by an organic factor/s.

The next chapters in this section will take you further through the three stages of Palm Therapy.

2

The First Stage of Palm Therapy: The Balancing

You may start Palm Therapy at any phase of your life. It is always the right time to improve your life. No matter how old you are, or what life experiences you have had, any positive change in your personality, mental abilities, emotional resistance or level of awareness can open new doors for you.

In this stage, as stated earlier, the main concern is to help you feel good, emotionally balanced, calm, stronger, free of fears, and in control of your emotional state regardless of present difficulties, or the symptoms of high stress or mental disorders which may disturb you in daily life. It may help you to accurately perceive various stressors and deal with them in a more realistic way. During this stage you will be prepared for the second phase of Palm Therapy—the Release Stage. Balancing of your energies at this stage is very important for the continuation of the healing or improvement process.

No matter how strong your personality is, or how well you are aware of the various stages in this work, chances are that if you start directly with the second phase of Palm Therapy, the Release Stage, without balancing your energies, first, for a better emotional state, you probably will temporarily reexperience painful memories, fears, or conflicts from the past which can last from a few days to a few weeks. It depends on your past experiences and the intensity of the stimulation applied.

This is true of most healthy people. I have no experience of initially stimulating the second stage of Palm Therapy on individuals who suffer from various mental disorders. They probably would have different reactions from healthy people. (Remember, when you deal with any mental disorder, always do it with the cooperation and supervision of a mental-health-care professional.)

If you become a Palm Therapist, I advise you, as a general rule, always to start with the first stage of the therapy, the Balancing Stage, even if you are positive that your client is very stable and he/she is ready for the Release Stage.

If you practice Palm Therapy on yourself, which of course can be done, always remember to start with the Balancing Stage first, even if you believe you can skip it. Otherwise, the results may be that you will reexperience some painful memories from the past which, without being prepared and well-balanced emotionally, may cause you to withdraw from the therapy and discontinue the healing process. In this case please consult with a certified Palm Therapist.

Usually the first stage takes from one to three months, with one or two sessions per week lasting about twenty minutes each time. It depends on the severity of the condition or the general well-being of each individual. In spite of the length of time for the first stage, an instant relaxation is usually achieved. For some of you it may be an amazing experience.

THE FIRST SESSION

Again, let me repeat: To adequately rule out any medical conditions that could be initiating or aggravating your particular problem, have your doctor give you a thorough physical examination, including blood panel, and other tests as necessary (EEG, CT, EKG, etc.).

The Palm Therapist, after reviewing the questionnaire and the doctor's referral letter containing all the medical findings of the client, finds it is time now to review the personal history, complaints, and mental or emotional orientation. Then check these findings against the findings from the palms using scientific palmistry.

Next, it is time to work on the practical part of the consultation through Palm Therapy. Start with the first complaint mentioned which is usually the most important issue for that person.

Sometimes it is wise to work on relaxation first and then continue with the balancing of the first complaint through the hand.

Another possibility which is not recommended, but which is possible, is to work on the palm and balance the main lines and shapes even without an initial acquaintance with the case. I do not recommend it because in this way it is possible to overlook an important issue in the individual's life.

This stimulation through Palm Therapy bypasses the cognitive mind's critique and disapproval for new changes in behavioral patterns. Therefore, the initial effect is felt almost immediately. The first session usually leads to a deep calmness in the mood. Although, in some cases, some excessive emotions may be relieved first by tears. It can also be as a reaction to excitement of the changes in his/her life that a person feels he/she may go through during Palm Therapy.

We start the work by relaxing the client deeply, thereby alleviating anger, anxiety, irritability, depressed mood or other unpleasant negative feelings which may intrude on one's mind in daily life. Sometimes some physical pain should be released prior to dealing with any emotion. It can be done through reflexology, acupressure, hypnotherapy, bioenergy or any other natural healing method. This should be done only after a thorough medical checkup by a physician in order to avoid any complications due to undetected problems. Then you can proceed with Palm Therapy.

Once a state of relaxation is achieved, it is time to verify the deepness of the relaxation state by asking the individual to describe his/her feelings.

At this phase the usual response is: "I'm fine," or "I feel relaxed." If you ask the client to describe any change in his/her emotions other than normal relaxation, the usual answer is "I'm just fine." Only a few will feel a great change in themselves.

Next, we are going to let the client experience how strongly the change really is. Since this relaxation is induced in a very profound way through Palm Therapy, the client cannot bring up any negativity, worries, fears of stressful events in a way that usually could affect his/her emotions significantly prior to the first session. People at this phase can visualize the event or a recent stressor such as a significant loss, a major life change, fears or difficulties in reaching their goals, but they usually feel emotionally relaxed, even if they try very hard to provoke negative feelings.

In the next few pages you will read about Bob, John, Peter and Melissa. Although each one of them started with Palm Therapy sessions for a different reason, they all shared a similar reaction during their first session.

BOB'S CASE: POSTTRAUMATIC STRESS DISORDER—THE EARTHQUAKE

Bob, a 23-year-old, was one of the many people who experienced the 1994 California earthquake. When I asked Bob for the reason for his visit, he didn't talk much, but he said that he was very irritated lately. In his case I had decided to initiate relaxation first through Palm Therapy.

After about two minutes, Bob started to open up and reported that for the last six weeks, since the major earthquake that had hit his living area, he had became very irritated and his inability to concentrate at work was noticed by all of the other workers. Thoughts about the terrifying moments when everything in his little apartment shook kept intruding on his mind. He told me about his attempts to avoid those thoughts, but with no results. They even bothered him at night. Bob had difficulty falling asleep. His sleep was usually disturbed. Occasionally he used to wake up a few times a night feeling as if there was another earthquake. He used to turn on the TV in order to check the magnitude, only to find out that there had been no report about an earthquake at all.

Bob felt very tired during the day. He stopped going out

with his friends. He, also, dropped a course which would entitle him to a promotion at his work place; "Life is short," he commented. His hands revealed a lot of stress. We concentrated on the balancing of his emotional state. After working on his hand for a few minutes, I asked Bob to concentrate on his earthquake experience:

"Tell me, how do you feel about it now?"

"It does not feel so bad now...I think I can handle it...interesting!" he replied.

We kept working on the Balancing Stage. In the third session, Bob reported that he felt much more relaxed and had better sleep at night. He also reported that he was much more focused in his work.

In the fifth session, Bob told me that he had decided to rejoin the next course so that he could be promoted at work as previously he had planned. His social life improved as well. He enjoyed going out with his friends just as he had used to do.

After a few more sessions, Bob reported that he was regaining control over his life. We continued to work on other subjects that he raised; among them was the acceleration of his learning abilities and his memory power. The results were manifested in the course that he took later. Bob was graduated successfully. He was promoted shortly after that. By overcoming his stress, Bob obviously improved his life!

***

When stress is left uncontrolled, it may further complicate an existing problem or initiate a new one. It may influence any system in your body. These can take the form of endless symptoms from merely headaches to back pain, neck pain, stomachache, stomach ulcers and many others.

JOHN'S CASE: HIGH STRESS LEVEL AND THE NECK PAIN

Palm Therapy is a great tool for inducing relaxation especially in stressful situations that, if continued, could lead to further complications.

John, a 42-year-old, was a successful business man. Lately he had been involved in a legal case and his business started to slow down as well. John was stressed but was not really aware of his intense stress. The only thing he felt was fatigue and neck pain. He was checked by his doctor who referred him to me mainly for that neck pain. Because John had heard about my work with Palm Therapy, he asked if I could help him to relax as well. While observing his hands, I could see the stress in him. Since he also experienced a neck pain, I released that pain first.

After relieving his neck pain, I applied Palm Therapy for a complete relaxation. Within a few minutes of work (3-4 minutes), I asked him how he was feeling. His response was: "I'm fine, but I don't feel any special change."

This is another perfect case for testing the therapy. I inquired about any event or situation in his life that might have led him to worry or to be in stress about it. In his case he said that he was being sued by a client and was worried about the court decision. I asked him to focus on that event and feel again his fears or anxiety as he had normally felt just before we started with the therapy. To his surprise, he could think about the case, but he couldn't experience any stress, anger or other negative emotions that used to rise when he had thought about it before. He described it as if the whole incident had happened to someone else, but not to him personally. He still knew that he would have to face the court, of course, but emotionally he was totally relaxed and strong, feeling that no matter what the results would be, he was going to overcome the event.

Since John was a very logical person, he immediately

explained that he was just feeling relaxed, therefore he didn't really want to worry about the court and the results. Then I asked him: "Please try with all your power to bring these worries again, try to feel the anxiety and the fear again." To his great surprise he couldn't do it. No matter how hard he tried, he just couldn't bring up any stress or negative feelings, but, somehow, he wasn't convinced.

In this phase some of the clients may be very stubborn mainly because it could be difficult for them to believe that worries and even painful events that they carried for a certain period of time could be relieved within a few minutes simply by stimulating various lines or areas on their hands.

In cases like that, I sometimes ask the clients:

"Fine, since you don't want to bring these worries up, as I understand, what if I will bring them against your will ?"

Next, I ask their permission to do so, for just a very short time, and I assure them that I will relax them again.

Since John was sure of himself, he agreed to my challenge. I worked on his hands stimulating the release of the event. Within a few seconds I noticed that John's body turned tense again. The look on his face changed, hardened, and shortly after, he said: "I can't believe it. It is amazing! Please stop it."

Naturally, I immediately started to work on a deep relaxation and balancing through his palms building hope and calmness in him.

As in the first case, we established a program that would initially work on the first stage, the Balancing. This stage is essential for strengthening of resistance and endurance as well as for keeping the relaxation state. I also gave him some explanation in regards to the second stage of Palm Therapy, the Release, cleansing of the past, and how it leads to the third stage, the Fulfillment.

In John's case, a physical pain (neck pain) accompanied his high stress level. Sometimes, as stated earlier in this section, a physical problem may lead to an emotional disturbance. This is why it is important to be thoroughly checked by a healthcare provider before proceeding with other therapies. The physical problem may be a mere allergic reaction or a more complicated problem.

PETER'S CASE: DEPRESSED MOOD, LACK OF ENERGY AND THE ALLERGY

Peter, a 52-year-old, was referred to me by his doctor. For the past five years, Peter had complained about experiencing a depressed mood and being very tired during the day even when he had had a good, full night's sleep.

The change in his mood occurred with no apparent reason. His medical history, physical examination and all the laboratory findings revealed no medical problems.

His life was stable. He had a lovely, caring wife and three grown-up children of whom he was very proud.

Observation of Peter's hands revealed well-marked allergy lines on both hands. They were unusually dominant in color. They looked as deep as the main creases/lines on the palm. (You will learn about the lines in Section Three.) I decided to stimulate various lines on Peter's hand to increase his vitality first.

In the next session, I checked Peter for allergy with applied kinesiology technique. At my request, Peter brought with him small samples of various foods he usually consumed throughout the day. We found out that he was reacting to eggs, coffee and wheat.

I explained to Peter that through Palm Therapy we could help him overcome the allergy reaction and its symptoms, but that it didn't mean that consuming these food every day, especially the eggs and the coffee, would help him in the long run.

I stimulated and balanced the lines which were related to his condition. Within a few sessions, Peter reported that his depression subsided significantly and he generally felt much better. After two more sessions, the symptoms completely disappeared. Peter told me that he felt younger and with much more energy than he had had before. In the last session, Peter announced that he and his wife had decided to join the nearest gym and to exercise there regularly a few times a week. Peter came to visit me a few months later. He looked happy, full of energy and much younger than he had the first time I met him.

Controlling his allergy with Palm Therapy's stimulation not only relieved him from the depressed mood but provided him with more vitality, well-being and happiness.

***

Palm Therapy is a great tool to accelerate more happiness, well-being, personal growth, awareness and fulfillment in your life. You should work on these aspects regularly since nothing in life is static. Everything flows. This is a law of nature. Whatever you achieve today can accumulate or change tomorrow. Although you are the one who should control your life, there are other influences from unexpected events and from people you love or with whom you share your life. Emotional attachment, for example, can be the most wonderful thing in your life, but if it ends for any reason, it may be a very painful experience.

Grieving is one of the worst emotional pains that you may ever experience during your lifetime. It is an emotional reaction that follows the loss of a loved one.

How long does it take to overcome such a pain? It depends on the many components of your personality and the support you get. Without any help, it may last for a long time. Some of you may have carried such pain through a lifetime.

MELISSA'S CASE: THE GRIEVING

Melissa, a 26-year-old, could barely walk when she came into my office. She was physically supported by her best girlfriend. Her eyes were puffy from lots of crying. It was obvious to me that she was in a state of significant emotional pain and sorrow. When I asked her about what had happened to her, she could hardly speak up. I found out that her husband had left her suddenly without any notice.

Melissa was left with their child and with no means of support. Above all, she also was shocked because she loved him so much. That had happened three days prior to her visit.

This kind of situation and other painful emotional conditions may enable one to realize how powerful the effect of Palm Therapy can be.

After checking both of her hands, I stimulated certain lines in her palms for about five minutes. The look on her face gradually changed. She was more relaxed; the relief from pain was obvious as she repositioned herself softly on the chair, now looking more comfortable. When I inquired about her feelings, she replied with a surprised look on her face: "It's gone! The pain is gone!" Then I asked her to describe her feelings toward her husband. She became bewildered and said that she didn't care so much about him anymore and expressed her wish to rebuild her life in a better, more rewarding way.

***

Of course, the whole therapy period should continue after the immediate relief (in Melissa's case overcoming the grieving phase). The first session is just a beginning of the strengthening and the balancing of the personality. The goal in the first stage of Palm Therapy is feeling good regardless of present difficulties.

As we can see, this stage is of utmost importance to anyone. But in spite of the immediate results which are usually achieved in the first session it is a slower process to train and transform the mind to regularly keep a positive emotional state. It takes several sessions until the mind accepts the new "state of mind" as part of its own reality.

In general, the first stage of Palm Therapy can help you to feel calm and to be able to adjust yourself in a relaxed way to the various circumstances or stressors in life. After this stage, you may feel so well that you will probably want to ignore the other stages of Palm Therapy. Because the state of mind is balanced for a while, nothing seems to bother you. But you must remember that without the release part, all the negativity is still there, and may affect you at a different time in the future.

To the professional therapist it will be interesting to note that this work can be speechless. I had a few clients who, besides having their medical history reports, didn't want to discuss their problems at all, yet they achieved a relaxation state and were benefitted simply by Palm Therapy. We don't have to create a verbal session in order to get results. If you practice any therapy including hypnotherapy, you can combine your therapy system with this work. (See Section Six and Appendix B.) Palm Therapy may induce, if needed, a very deep alpha state, so you can proceed and combine other therapies and get the most out of them. But if your therapy system cannot be combined with this work, you still can be very effective by applying just Palm Therapy as needed, inducing relaxation and preparing your client for the second stage of Palm Therapy—the Release Stage.

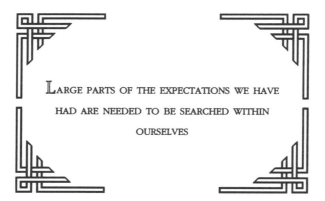

LARGE PARTS OF THE EXPECTATIONS WE HAVE
HAD ARE NEEDED TO BE SEARCHED WITHIN
OURSELVES

CHAPTER 3

The Second Stage of Palm Therapy: The Release

The Release Stage is a very essential part of Palm Therapy. During this stage negative memories from the past are being released. By stimulating certain areas in the hand, which are related to your prenatal life, early childhood and the memory bank, you may start to release painful or traumatic memories. Inner conflicts which have limited you in the past or which may lead to certain mental disturbances, including those that were developed due to psychological or social stressors, may be released. This process is an essential part of the therapy and one that may free you from negative childhood patterns and from self-sabotage.

    Any events or trauma that couldn't be dealt with positively

may leave an emotional scar which can influence one later in life or interfere with the physical health. Sometimes, as strange as it may sound, positive experiences in your past may be related to some of the negative behavior patterns you have in the present. It is also possible that a specific medical condition has initiated your symptoms. The Release Stage is recommended whether your present feeling and behavior patterns were initiated by psychological or physiological aspects.

THE MOST COMMON QUESTIONS AT THIS STAGE

Before we continue, let's review some important questions that are often raised when dealing with the Release Stage of Palm Therapy.

-When should we start with the Release Stage?

The Release Stage should start AFTER you have been balanced/reinforced by the first stage of Palm Therapy and you feel better.

-What is the difference between the balancing effects of the first stage and the balancing effects we achieve in the second stage of Palm Therapy?

The second stage of Palm Therapy also deals with energy balancing, but the difference is that in the first stage we balance the various negative emotions or symptoms that interfere in normal daily life without really dealing with the causes that initiate or maintain the various emotional symptoms. In the second stage, after the person has gone through the strengthening and balancing period of the first stage, the individual is ready for the release of deep, painful memories and the unresolved events which stand as barriers in his/her life. For example, fears/phobias are not that easy to release. Even if the person is aware that his/her avoidance of driving on the freeway is due to a fear of death which might be as a result of an accident or of a drive-by shooting, still the fear is there preventing the individual from driving on the freeway (specific phobia). Through Palm Therapy the fear is neutralized during the first stage by balancing and relaxing the individual, then it is released from the source at the second stage.

In many cases of panic disorder with agoraphobia, the fear is of being in a place or a situation from which escape might be difficult, even embarrassing, or in which help may not be available during such a panic attack. Here, as well, Palm Therapy helps to balance the phobia in the first stage of Palm Therapy. Then it works to release the deep-rooted negative memories, including fears, conflicts and other morbid thoughts, in such a way that the individual may be free from fear, can visit or be anywhere, or do anything he/she wanted to do previously, but could not do due to his/her condition.

-What do we feel at the Release Stage ?

As we stated before, at the early phase of this stage, you may reexperience painful memories that you had stored in your memory bank or subconscious; changes in your mood are felt, too. In spite of the release of many negative events which may be irritating to a certain degree you may feel strong and in control because you already have gone through the balancing period of the first stage of Palm Therapy. You have the awareness that it is a temporary process which may free you from many of the symptoms you had experienced before you started the therapy.

You may start experiencing the release process either a few hours later or few days after the first stimulation in this direction. It can be during your sleep through your dreams which sometimes are very direct dreams related to negative events or traumas in the early childhood. It is not an unusual experience to have some nightmares that, at first glance, appear to have no connection to the past. Symbolic dreams are often experienced in normal life and during this stage in particular, especially whenever one's moral code, belief system, or fears prevent him/her from dealing directly with the real issue.

During this stage, the mind has the tendency to release the most painful memories first and not necessarily in chronological order. In most cases, significant fears or a phobia were released first. You may experience some other negative emotions such as fears, depression and nightmares. But, as mentioned above, these are temporary. The feeling is that when being in a state of negativity or in a depressed mood, still there is a sense of well-being, control, and the confidence that everything is OK.

-Why do we need to deal with old painful experiences and memories? Isn't it better to leave the past where it belongs, in the past, and not to bring it up?.

The Release Stage is an important one. During this stage, you can get rid of inner conflicts that have limited you in the past, and break through the fears that are blocking your fulfillment. You may release negative childhood patterns, procrastination and self-sabotage.

Some theories in child development imply that from birth, and even before, we develop emotional or chemical imbalances of the brain. Of course, from birth on we accumulate experiences partly positive and partly negative. While positive experiences are usually reinforcement stimuli, negative ones may sometimes develop into sorrow, sadness and fears, or left as an emotional trauma which may affect your life later on, whether you are aware of these emotions or not. They are stored in the mind's bank and can arouse as a problem that may seems unrelated, usually affecting the system in which you are most vulnerable.

The basic assumption is that whenever your mind is loaded with some negative experiences, unsolved events, or when it has to deal with conflicts, taboos and prohibited thoughts—these excessive emotions, if unsolved, are being stored in the memory bank of the brain or subconscious mind in order to avoid letting them interfere with daily life. According to the Chinese theory, when these excessive emotions are overloading the memory bank of the brain, some of the emotions are being stored in the various body organs such as the liver, kidneys and the stomach, thus affecting the person physically and emotionally and which may be manifested as physical or mental disorders and diseases.

The Chinese theory of the human tendency to store various emotions in the different organs of the body is not well-accepted in the West. The Western scientific approach is to classify every activity only when it can be measured or documented as such. These kinds of stored excessive emotions are not yet documented as physical activity or chemical activity, therefore, from the Western point of view they do not exist as storage in the various organs.

Chinese medicine accepts energies as a form of matter, therefore they accept the idea that excessive emotions which can disturb normal daily life are stored in the various organs of the body. The problem is that, in the long run, these unsolved events, negative emotions or conflicts, do disturb the physiological functioning of the various body systems.

Since, in Palm Therapy, the balancing of the energies of body and mind functions is done in a systematic way through the various lines and mounts on the palms, you don't really need to checkup or to diagnose emotional storage in the various organs of the body, as it is done in Chinese medicine. But, as mentioned earlier, you may need to see your doctor if you have any symptoms.

By releasing the energies of these excessive emotions from the body and the memory bank in the brain, a spontaneous healing may occur both in the physical and mental aspects. After this process, you may experience an enormous relief, a better mental clarity, and you will probably be well-prepared to put most of your energy into growth and fulfillment that can be stimulated in the third stage of Palm Therapy.

-Is it dangerous to deal with the subconscious mind?

Except for specific cases of mentally ill individuals, there is no danger in dealing with the subconscious mind (or, according to Chinese medicine with other storage of memories as well) through Palm Therapy. Since Palm Therapy is a natural way of dealing with the subconscious mind through the hands, the healing process can safely proceed. We don't really force anything out. The mind, in its various parts, is powerful enough to release some emotional pain or negative memories when it feels it is safe to do so. More than that, it is better to release some negativity from the subconscious mind than to do nothing about it at all. We really can not measure the importance of even a slight release versus none. But we assume that it is to the advantage of any person to release even a small amount of pain from his/her memory bank.

You must remember that Palm Therapy is a natural way to stimulate the Release Stage. It works in accordance with the holistic theory of detoxification. Detoxification is a natural process of body cleansing that takes place after any holistic therapy method is applied. During this process the body releases toxins and healing is taking place. It is a natural and a positive process that accelerates the healing of the body.

The mind can heal itself once we provide it with the triggering to do so. Palm Therapy is one of the triggers which stimulates a spontaneous healing process of the mind in a natural way. The analogy for this release process, as stated previously, would be the healing of the body. Once we let it heal itself by providing it with healthy food and the avoidance of toxins as much as we can, or by using natural methods of therapy, the body may start a spontaneous healing process which may be as follows: Initially the individual feels great. Then a process of release takes place in which most of his/her ailments' symptoms are temporarily reexperienced in a reverse order until the reexperiencing of the ailments of his/her childhood. After this body cleansing process the person usually feels healthier, full of energy with joy and a feeling of well-being.

If, for example, you had suffered from asthma during early childhood, and overcame it, then you developed a chronic headache and then an arthritic condition, the healing process will probably be as follows: First, you will reexperience some of the symptoms of the arthritic condition, then the headaches, then the asthma. After this temporary process of releasing the body ailments you will probably feel physically balanced, energetic and free of the symptoms of these diseases.

The mental healing is very similar to the physical one.

However, this time everything happens in the mind. The release of the negative memories may not occur in a reverse order such as in the body release process. The most traumatic or painful memories usually are being released first.

Any release through Palm Therapy will be beneficial to the healing process of the mind. The toxins of the mind (and I don't mean, the chemical ones) are the traumas, the fears, the guilt, the shame, the anger or any other negative emotions and conflicts which for whatever reasons, you could not deal with successfully. They are inscribed in your memory bank.

Most of your learning and behavior patterns are based on positive or negative memories. Whether they were stored before or after birth is questionable. Many of your failures or blockages in life are the result of unresolved issues or negative memories that have accumulated continuously during your life. (For other factors, see Section Five/Chapter 20.)

The Release Stage balances one's energies and, in this case, balances the energies of your memory bank in such a way that most fears and traumas diminish, thus the process results in a focusing on the daily life and future planning. The Release Stage is a very important one. It leads to the building of a happy and joyful future.

-How long will this stage take?

This stage may take from a few days to 1-2 months depending on your age and various life experiences. As you proceed with this stage, the reaction after each session is less profound until you reach a state where, although you continue to stimulate the Release Stage, no negative reactions are being noticed. The reason is that once the mind's energies are well-balanced you cannot reach more than that at the Release Stage.

Therefore, one can assume that most of the work has been done at this phase. However, since the ability to detect minor emotional traumas is limited to some degree, when reaching this stage, it is better to continue the release for about one-third more of the time that was needed for this process, but at least for two additional weeks.

-What if the release is too strong or too painful and you wish to stop the process? Perhaps you have a special event at which time you want to be at your best without the effect of the Release Stage. Can the release be blocked when needed?

The Release Stage is an essential part of Palm Therapy. This stage may be irritating to a certain degree, mainly if you have suffered from severe emotional imbalance most of your life. This imbalance will probably be evident in your palmar flexure creases/lines as severe breakages of the energy flow.

Sometimes, the release takes the form of sadness or depression which usually is experienced in the mornings. If these feelings are too irritating or overwhelming, it is a sign that you have jumped too early into the second stage of Palm Therapy. In this case, you have two options which are up to you to decide:

> **a.** To go back to the first stage, the Balancing Stage and block the release. This is mainly done by stimulating the lines that you had stimulated in the first stage. Continue with it until you feel that you are more ready for the second phase.
>
> **b.** Continue with the release, but in a less intense manner.

It is comforting to know that if you have a special occasion when you need to have a peak performance or to be at your best, the release process can then be stopped and the balancing process can be applied instead. This is the great benefit of Palm Therapy. You may block the release process at any time. It may be stopped almost completely, temporarily or for a longer period.

However, sometimes, even after blocking the process, one may still realize that the healing forces of the mind, once they have found out that the release is a form of healing, may continue to activate the process to a very limited degree.

If this happens, remember that no harm whatsoever occurs. On the contrary, through the release and the balancing of the mind's energies with Palm Therapy, the healing process of the mind is activated. Therefore, it is not like losing control. It is gaining control of the mind's healing center. But even so, you may block it by imprinting some crossing, longitudinal lines on the transverse lines which were stimulated for the release process. (That is, crossing mainly the proximal and distal transverse palmar creases, the head line and the heart line. See Section Three and Section Four.)

If necessary, while in this stage, there is also a way to apply Palm Therapy for the stimulation of some specific aspects, such as Success Energy, improving self-esteem, reinforcing the memory, preparing for an examination, improving the vitality and energy and improving the intuition. These aspects will be dealt with later in this book.

Practically it is not recommended to work on two stages at same time. I found out that the best results are achieved when we focus on one stage at a time. The explanation is that during this healing process, one's energy should be focused on one direction at a time. It becomes less effective to stimulate both stages simultaneously simply because it divides the energy into two separate currents. But, as mentioned above, some aspects can be temporarily stimulated when needed.

Now, that you are more relaxed and you know what to expect during the second stage of Palm Therapy, you may wish to read the experience of Janet's Release Stage.

JANET'S CASE : PANIC DISORDER

Janet, a-38-year-old married secretary with no children, was diagnosed as having had panic disorders for the last 15 years. Almost every month she used to have a panic attack during which she felt shortness of breath and dizziness with nausea. Her heart would pound so fast as if she was going to die or go crazy. Those attacks occurred suddenly and without any reason that she could relate to. Janet was fearful. After each attack, the fear about having the next one grew constantly.

For a few years, Janet was sent for many medical examinations to find out if there were any medical causes that may have triggered her panic attacks. She was first checked by a cardiologist. Then was sent for endocrine disorders tests to rule out the possibility that she was suffering from hyperthyroidism or other endocrine related disorders. Janet was also asked if she was taking any drugs such as amphetamines, cocaine or consuming an excessive amount of caffeine. She went through many other tests but they all proved negative. Observing Janet's hands, I detected clear marks of emotional suffering during her early childhood. I started to work on balancing her with crossing lines on her radial longitudinal palmar crease (life line in palmistry) at the location representing her early childhood. The first stage took about six weeks before we proceeded with the next stage.

From the very first session, Janet was surprised by the relaxation state she experienced during the session. After the first two weeks of Palm Therapy, Janet reported that she wasn't so worried about having the next panic attack. She felt stronger; it was more than a month since she had had an attack. We continued the balancing stage for another four weeks. Janet didn't experience any panic attacks for the next two months.

At that phase we decided to proceed with the Release Stage. I explained to Janet that during the second stage she was probably going to experience some painful memories and emotions from the past and that she might even have panic attacks as well.

Janet was very cooperative and determined to heal herself. She commented that if there was a chance that the temporary stage was going to help her overcome her panic disorder, from which she had been suffering for the previous 15 years, it was worth it.

During her Release Stage, Janet kept having childhood nightmares. She usually woke up feeling frightened just as she used to do as a child. Sometimes, in her dreams, she was back as a little girl at her parents' old house. Some vivid events that seemed unrelated to each other were repeated in those dreams. Until that time Janet had no clear memory of her early childhood. Next, she would experience some memories, especially feelings of being helpless. She would experience the pain when her mother left their house storming and never came back. At the very young age of three years Janet felt that her mother, the only person who gave her some feeling of security, actually didn't care much about her.

During the first few weeks Janet reported that beside her dreams, she spent her free time thinking about the past. She also experienced sadness, especially in the evenings. We continued to work on the release for about two more months. During that period Janet noticed a reduction in the number of these dreams. Next, Janet reported on a fundamental change in her life. She could enjoy things like never before. It had been five months without panic attacks. She also stopped experiencing fears of having another attack. Janet became relieved and emotionally balanced. For the first time, after so many years, she had full control over her life and enjoyed the freedom it provided her.

***

If you are going through the various stages of Palm Therapy, it is recommended mainly in the Second Stage that you write down all of the dreams that you can recall in this stage. It is interesting to note that after you are relieved, it will be reflected in your dreams, too. They usually become less frightening or threatening and, in some cases, less violent until they become pleasant.

CAN POSITIVE EXPERIENCES LEAD TO UNWANTED BEHAVIOR ?

As in Janet's case many individuals who feel emotionally imbalanced did go through some hard times in their lives that predisposed them to these disorders. But there is another aspect to deal with which is complementary to the release process. It may sound absurd, but some negative or unwanted behavior in the present time, may be the result of some successful experiences in the past which set or encouraged specific negative behavior patterns in the present. The initial cause/s is not always rooted in early childhood; it may start at any age. It can relate to something you experienced yourself or to something that you witnessed. From feelings of pleasure, joy, love and pride it may develop into a guilt, fear, anger or frustration in certain situations without any apparent reason.

Since the initial experience was a positive one, you may wonder if the Release Stage should be stimulated in such a case. The answer is yes. You do need to stimulate the Release process in order to balance blockages or negative behavior patterns from the source, whether they were initiated by positive or negative experiences in your past.

MERRY'S CASE: INTERPERSONAL RELATIONSHIP—THE SILENCE WEAPON

Merry, a 30-year-old secretary in a law firm, came to my office with a broken heart. After a separation from her beloved boyfriend, her world came apart as if she had no reason to live. There was a complete emptiness of feelings besides the dominant and persistent emotional pain she felt.

Merry sadly told me about her many boyfriends of the past. None of them stayed with her for more than one to two years. She wanted a steady life, but it didn't happen. She felt that something was wrong with her. Many of her girlfriends were already married or had stable relationships.

In the first session, I applied Palm Therapy for relaxation in order to let her overcome the emotional pain she was experiencing. The relief was fast and enabled her to continue with her daily life without being so heartbroken.

After a few sessions, when Merry was much more balanced, she confessed that whenever she had gotten angry with any of the previous boyfriends her reaction would be to avoid talking with them until they would comply with her expectations. Actually she wanted to communicate with them very badly, but she felt that something was causing her to keep silent until they would comply, or ask her to break the silence.

Within the first month of the therapy, Merry reported feeling better and emotionally stronger; her ability to concentrate at work had improved significantly.

It was time now to start the second phase of Palm Therapy, the Release Stage. While I was triggering certain parts in Merry's palm during one of the sessions, she commented that, at a very early age, she had learned that by avoiding talking with her father, he would do everything to please her. It became a rewarding experience and a tool to get her way.

After a few sessions of the Release Stage, Merry started to release memories from the past. She experienced some guilt feelings about the way she had treated her father. Sometimes she woke up feeling distressed while at other times she experienced happy dreams. At that period she also had some mood swings during the day. I explained to Merry that those experiences were only temporary. She decided to continue. After all, it was not as hard as she had thought it would be.

Four months later, she reported experiencing a great relief like never before. The distress feelings and the mood swings disappeared.

Merry had a new boyfriend. For the first time in her life she focused on full, open communication with him even in stressful situations. It became, by now, natural and easy for her. Obviously, she didn't feel the need for the silence weapon anymore.

We continued stimulating the release for an additional month's period (for releasing some minor problems). Then we proceeded with the third stage, the Fulfillment Stage.

***

IS PALM THERAPY A PSYCHOTHERAPY?

No. it is not. The Release Stage can be performed in other ways, too, such as by hypnosis as well as various methods in psychotherapy.

Psychotherapy is the treatment of disorders by psychological methods. In most cases the emotional release process of various techniques is considered psychotherapy. The release of emotions is one of the main aspects which many psychotherapists encourage in order to help their patients live a better life.

Since the results of the second stage of Palm Therapy are somewhat similar to those of psychotherapy as well as to the effect of certain psychotic drugs, it might confuse some of you with the feeling that a psychotherapy work is involved. Since in Palm Therapy we don't have to talk at all, and the work is mainly physical (pressing or marking lines and other sections on the hands), it should be very clear to all that this work is different. It is a physical activation of certain lines, marks or areas connected to the brain's energy via the energy pathways. Therefore, it is actually a combination of a massage therapy, acupressure and hypnotherapy through the hand!

My findings, through Palm Therapy, are that by balancing the energies as detected on the palms of the hands, we provide an emotional balancing of many disturbances, or "homeostasis" of the brain and the mind energies. Through the hand, we actually bypass the critique of the conscious mind which usually resists changes. That's why Palm Therapy is not dealing directly either with mental disturbances due to psychological stressors or due to a physical/medical condition.

In Palm Therapy it is not necessary to know what is being released. It is necessary to know what lines and areas of the hands should be triggered in order to balance the energies in the various parts of the brain and mind, including the short- and long-term memory. By balancing the energies of the brain and mind through Palm Therapy, these centers have the ability to improve, or heal themselves from many unwanted conditions.

Chinese medicine deals with the energy imbalance as well. A treatment for mental and emotional problems will be through the balancing of the meridians. The difference between Palm Therapy and acupuncture or acupressure is that through Palm Therapy we rely on the various aspects of the mind in a visual way (palmistry). Because the mind presents itself very much in detail through the hands, more than just problems or imbalance of the energies can be detected. Through the hands you can see the character, the present emotional situation, talents, goals and qualities such as self-esteem, determination/willpower, as well as career inclination, and the level of success the person experiences at the present time. Through the hands you can also detect many of the flaws which interfere with the achievement of goals and life fulfillment of an individual. Applying Palm Therapy can assist in making a real change in one's life. It is a safe method which, I believe, should be applied (by a certified Palm Therapist) to any person who needs it, from the newborn to the very old.

Can Palm Therapy substitute for psychotherapy?

The answer is NO. Palm Therapy cannot substitute for psychotherapy or for any verbal therapy because besides balancing the negative emotions that limited you, releasing problems from the past and triggering your talents to achieve your success, a skilled psychotherapist will teach the patient some ways to deal with life. The nature of Palm Therapy is a process for the inner balancing, cleansing, improving or positively predisposing one's basic skills such as learning, memory, concentration, the development of self-esteem, readiness for success, goal oriented personality, etc. Still, some of these have to be gained by learning and experience.

The analogy can be a car in which we exchange the engine for a bigger and stronger one and the transmission to a better one (the new stronger engine will be acquired through Palm Therapy). To drive the car, we need additional things such as gas, oil, water, air and electricity (these are the learning skills that we have to refile constantly. We can refile them by life experiences, studying and psychotherapy of any kind). To maintain the strength of the new engine, again we use Palm Therapy.

We always have to remember that exactly the same as an engine needs constant treatment, so does our mind. It is clear to all of us that a strong and healthy body does require constant exercise or physical activity. We all understand the importance of physical activity, but very few of us are aware that the mind needs a constant stimulation in order to stay sharp and to improve the mental skills. Therefore, once we finish the second stage of Palm Therapy, which has a limited time according to the individual case, the third phase in its various aspects is really unlimited.

Because the third stage of Palm Therapy is the triggering of success and fulfillment, it is the stage of increasing our skills and talents, and of setting and achieving goals. It is the stage of supermental, emotional growth, and if you wish to stimulate it, also, of spiritual development and higher awareness. This stage is unlimited in effect and in time. It goes on as long or as far as the person wants to grow, thus, increasing Success Energy and fulfillment in all aspects of life.

To the certified Palm Therapist:

Remember, Palm Therapy isn't a psychotherapy. Therefore, unless you are a licensed healthcare provider, I urge all of the Palm Therapists to work in conjunction with a psychotherapist or other healthcare professionals of the mind. Palm Therapy is a great tool, but it is not intended to be a substitute for a medical treatment, psychotherapy or of psychiatric treatment. You should never be in conflict with other healing systems. You should cooperate and work as a team with the various therapists whom the client may have at that time, for the benefit of your client and for your peace of mind.

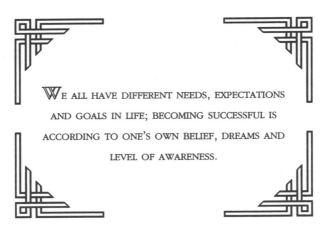

WE ALL HAVE DIFFERENT NEEDS, EXPECTATIONS
AND GOALS IN LIFE; BECOMING SUCCESSFUL IS
ACCORDING TO ONE'S OWN BELIEF, DREAMS AND
LEVEL OF AWARENESS.

CHAPTER 4

The Third Stage of Palm Therapy: The Fulfillment

At this stage, when you are free from the pain and conflicts or other negative emotions that stopped you in the past, you are ready to anchor yourself daily in happiness and success. You will want to grow in all aspects of life and enjoy it as much as you can. In the third stage of Palm Therapy, stimulation of specific lines and areas in your palms triggers Success Energy in you, thus helping you reach your goals and actually change your life.

INCREASING HUMAN POTENTIAL

Many therapies are dedicated to solving the emotional problems which prevent many individuals from fulfilling their lives.

There are only a few techniques that have dedicated themselves to the increasing of the human potential by searching into the development of the IQ, talents, skills, creativity, concentration, spiritual growth, prosperity and success. Palm Therapy is actually oriented towards improving these aspects and many others to the maximum potential one can achieve.

During the third stage of Palm Therapy, you will reinforce and stimulate your mental, spiritual and physical abilities to their fullest potential. You will stimulate and sharpen any talents you may have and, the best of all, trigger the energy needed to fulfill your goals. You will activate these aspects through the stimulation of various lines and areas in your hands.

Since this stage of Palm Therapy is one of truly personal growth and development, it is virtually endless both in magnitude and duration. Exactly like in sports, the more you work and exercise your body correctly, in a better condition you will be.

The same applies to personal growth and success through Palm Therapy; the more you apply Palm Therapy at this stage the better results you will have!

This is true, especially, if you want to reach goals by using your talents. Since the various activities of your brain and mind are represented in the hand, you can detect them and stimulate the qualities you wish to improve or initiate in yourself.

For example, if you want to become a writer, work on both: your ability to write and the ability to become successful. Both can be accomplished by the stimulation of the various aspects of the mind as seen in your hand. It is necessary to activate the right places in order to achieve the results you want to have. Therefore, you need to learn what qualities, talents or characteristics are represented by the various components on your hand. Since the various activities of the brain and the mind are represented in the hands, you can detect them and stimulate the aspects you choose. This is one of the most powerful and simplest aspects of Palm Therapy!

Actually, I started Palm Therapy in 1985 by working in this direction. I stimulated the energy pathways related to the increasing of the IQ. The results were very clearly seen and felt after a few months of working on the hands. You may want to stimulate other aspects. It may be a better self-esteem, leadership abilities, intuition, willpower, persistence, excellent learning abilities, money making orientation, warm loving personality and much more. As we stated at the beginning of this section each one of us has a unique personality. We all have different needs, expectations and goals in life, so becoming successful is according to one's own belief, dreams and level of awareness.

This stage of the work will help you achieve your own personal growth and fulfillment, thus leading to satisfaction and well-being.

ACTIVATING SUCCESS ENERGY

One of the main powers behind the ability to achieve your goals in this stage is _Success Energy_. Stimulation of Success Energy is actually one of my greatest findings in Palm Therapy.

By imprinting certain new lines or reinforcing existing lines on various areas in your hands you may increase the energies of what I call *the department of success* in the mind and in other levels of your existence, hence triggering naturally the flow of success within yourself.

Since, after the Release Stage, your energies are well-balanced, you are naturally ready and open to the unlimited flow of Success Energy. The stimulation of the certain areas in the hands accelerates its flow. Success Energy does not teach you how to be successful, but it removes the fear of success; it builds up higher expectations and a better capacity to learn new skills, to become successful, and to subconsciously act and behave in a way that draws more success to you. The changes usually come rapidly and more effectively than ever you imagined possible. Sometimes, they are a combination of very small changes in your life-style, work and social activity which all make enormous differences in your destiny. New directions open suddenly and become more available to you. Many of you may notice some changes already at the first stage of Palm Therapy, since just by eliminating negative emotions and having positive ones instead, you may start drawing more positive energy to yourself.

In the following paragraphs you will read about the positive changes in the lives of Jim, Sara, and Dave. The changes in their lives occurred while in the process of Palm Therapy.

JIM'S CASE : FROM FRUSTRATION TO FULFILLMENT

Jim, a 32-year-old, is a real estate agent. Jim was very frustrated the first time that I saw him. He claimed that he had hardly sold any houses in the preceding months. Jim was considering the necessity to file for bankruptcy if the situation was to continue.

In the first session, I worked with Jim on relaxation and the balancing of his emotional state. Jim's hands revealed a lack of self-esteem. We worked on this aspect for a few more sessions through Palm Therapy.

After the sixth session, Jim reported that he felt more energetic, had talked to more people and had made important contacts. At the eighth session Jim excitedly reported that, during the preceding week, he had put two houses in escrow. He was very anxious to continue with the therapy sessions. We proceeded with the various stages of Palm Therapy. Jim had gone through many changes during that period, and as he described: "I feel like a new me." Shortly after we stimulated the Success Energy, during the third stage, Jim became one of the most successful agents in his real estate office.

SARA'S CASE: A PROMOTION AFTER 12 YEARS

Sara, a 54-year-old, was a worker in the food department of one of the department stores in Los Angeles. She had worked in that department store for over twelve years with little recognition for her devotion and dedication to the work. Balancing of her emotions and financial situation came first, because these had led her to lots of depression and feelings of helplessness. After one month of Palm Therapy sessions, Sara was promoted to be the head of the mini-restaurant of that department store. Sara also was given an award in recognition of the dedication to her work. Her salary was increased. Now, she felt the need for a more balanced (emotional) life. We proceeded with the Balancing Stages of Palm Therapy.

As you can see, sometimes depending upon the case, you may be able to go directly to the achievement of greater results in daily life and then do the whole basic work of Palm Therapy. (The basic work of going through the three stages of Palm Therapy usually promotes more stable results.)

DAVE'S CASE: FEAR OF SUCCESS AND THE ENTERTAINMENT INDUSTRY.

Dave, a 28-year-old actor, married. Dave was very depressed in his first visit. He saw himself as a gifted, talented actor, but in reality his best acting time had been when he played in high school shows. As a professional actor he had played a minor part in a movie just once in the previous seven years of his long struggle with this career. He constantly took acting classes at different schools to improve his skills and went to many auditions but was never selected. He was spending hardly any time with his wife and their 2-year-old girl. When he was at home, he preferred to stay undisturbed. That frustrated his wife and threatened their happiness.

The first thing he asked me was : "Do you think I can be a successful actor? I have dedicated my life to this profession, but somehow I have never made it."

Looking at his palms it seemed that he was talented, but with fears which were blocking his ability to become successful in this profession. During the Balancing Stage, an improvement was noticed. After clearing the fears and blockages through the Release Stage of Palm Therapy, we proceeded with the third phase, the Fulfillment Stage. In Dave's case it was to become a successful actor.

I worked with him on the Success Energy for two months. Initially, he started building high expectations as to becoming a successful actor.

After about two additional months of stimulating Success Energy, he was accepted for a major role in the entertainment industry as one of the stars. His life improved drastically, not just money wise. Although he had much less free time now, he always found time to enjoy being with his beloved wife and their child. He learned to get and give more love to his family and to himself.

Success is according to one's expectations and beliefs. The main characteristic of real success is the enjoyment of and the love of what you do. Money and recognition will come in most cases when people love what they do, become professionals and persistently go for their goals.

"KEEP FIT"

The work of the third stage of Palm Therapy, initially, should be at least once or twice per week. Then once you reach your main goals, you have the option to either continue towards other goals in your potential skills, or like in sports, mentally "keep fit" by stimulating your specific skills at least once per month for the rest of your life.

To some people, the idea of continually going through a therapy for the rest of their lives may seem absurd, but not if you understand that skills and talents must be practiced for as long as you want to keep at your best with a specific talent. For example, the greatest violinists in the world who are obviously mastering their skills as musicians must practice a few hours per day everyday for as long as they intend to have peak performances. Palm Therapy can provide the extra edge in that direction by increasing your potential. But just as the musicians do, you must train and stimulate your mind's energies continuously through your hands. At this stage you may be skilled enough to continue the stimulation of your specific skills by yourself once or twice per week. When you enter this stage in life usually the appetite or the motivation for growth and success is very high in all of your activities.

In most cases, people feel a great improvement, but as the time goes on, the feeling of improvement is less noticeable. The reason is very simple. When a specific talent or energy is totally off balance, restoring the balance makes a significant change. As time goes on and the person is getting more and more in shape and in balance, the improvement to near perfection is usually as slow as it is in the mastering of most skills or talents. The final is usually the hardest and longest to achieve, but with each small change you can make an enormous difference.

AWAKENING TOWARDS FURTHER EDUCATION AND TRAINING

Very much the same as mastering skills and polishing talents, initially you may feel a great improvement in the situation. Then you will probably reach a kind of plateau during which the expectations are very high, but it seems that no change occurs.

At this time you may subconsciously be motivated to start looking for new skills or ways to push yourself higher, either by joining some type of educational system such as a college, courses, workshops, religious training, institutes of any kind or associations. The eagerness to learn more is usually the result of the Success Energy's stimulation.

The mechanism goes as follows: Initially Success Energy pushes the individual to become successful with his/her own knowledge and level of training. But, since we continue to stimulate Success Energy through the palm during the third stage of Palm Therapy, the expectations grow beyond the skills, knowledge or training the person actually has at that time. Subconsciously and consciously, people understand that skills should be acquired at some type of learning facility. It is very possible that this thinking was always there, but without any motivation or triggering to act. At this point, they feel the urge from within to go and join some training or learning institutions that they suppose will help them to fulfill their expectations and, eventually, their goals. Some people may feel as if the Success Energy doesn't bring them success anymore. Actually the stimulation should be continued because the motivation to act as they do is triggered by Palm Therapy. This urge is especially appreciated by people who started Palm Therapy with a very low motivation for success or with a lack of goal orientation.

It is hard, sometimes, to understand the ways of Success Energy at certain periods of this stage. However, we should remember that there is nothing mysterious in Palm Therapy. It is a simple way to increase the human skills, potential and motivation for success. Thus, you will have the urge to learn, to acquire specific skills, or to do the right things that will bring you the type of success or accomplishment you wish to have, whether it is in business, social life, academic studies or other fields.

It is not always a matter of learning new things, but sometimes it is manifested in using your knowledge in a new creative way or reaching new levels of awareness. It may take the form of an insight, a discovery or an adaptation to other's ways of doing things successfully.

CONSISTENCY BRINGS RESULTS

The feelings you have at this stage may be in the form of a need to discover the world and to know more about life or about the specific way in which to be successful. Even if you feel that at this stage there is no change or no significant improvement while working on the hands, it is very important to pass this plateau.

Keep stimulating Success Energy and the specific talents you choose until you see results. In almost all cases, after the plateau comes a giant step forward into success or achieving the result the individual is reasonably seeking.

Remember, you must be patient and persistent with the work until you get the results you are waiting for. Keep working on the hands. The results will manifest in many ways and aspects of your life. Also, please keep a written record of your fulfilled expectations and achievements. (If you wish, you may write and inform me about them. I'm always glad to hear from people as to how Palm Therapy has helped them to improve their lives.)

Since Palm Therapy, at the Fulfillment Stage, is the work of improving your skills, talents and success, it is a lifetime asset that you build throughout your life.

SUCCESS ENERGY AT ANY AGE?

You may start Palm Therapy at any age. You can and should improve yourself at any stage of life. It is never too late. But of course, like in sports or in studying, the earlier you start the better chances and results you get, yet you can grow and fulfill your life at any age.

Balancing of energies in the first stage of Palm Therapy and releasing of emotional pains at the second stage can be done at any age, the earlier the better. The third phase, the Fulfillment Stage, also can be stimulated any time during your life although the approach and expectations at an older age will be different from those of a young child or a young adult.

For people who are retired, success usually means good health, peace of mind and a secure income. These can be stimulated through the various representations of those aspects in the hand. Many people at their retirement age have started a hobby, dated again, or even found an additional source of income as a result of Palm Therapy. A new vitality source has been opened to them. Their feelings change all of a sudden to: "I want to enjoy life, I have the energy and the urge to do so !"

Remember, whatever your goals are, they can be reinforced and facilitated with the help of Palm Therapy at any age.

CHILDREN AND PALM THERAPY

Since their rational minds are not fully developed, the emotions in young children are dominant. For them success is first of all being loved by others (actually we all want that as grown-ups, too), getting all their needs fulfilled rapidly while enjoying and loving themselves, exploring their surroundings and fulfilling

their natural curiosity. Through Palm Therapy you may stimulate their full emotional and cognitive growth which will positively influence their physical growth as well.

In young children the potential is unlimited. The challenge to bring their utmost capacity in terms of their happiness, self-esteem, IQ, specific talents and the natural curiosity and love to study is much greater.

While working with young children, I saw the growth, happiness and success they have achieved at their level. I believe that all of the children in the world deserve the chance to grow up secure and happy, to reach their optimum human potential, and to create a better destiny for all. You can help them with Palm Therapy!

SUMMARY

The third stage of Palm Therapy, the Fulfillment, is the stage of setting goals and fulfilling them. It is a stage for personal growth in almost any direction you may wish, including mental, emotional , material and spiritual growth.

Success Energy is triggered in this stage to help you achieve your goals. Success Energy is one of the most interesting aspects of Palm Therapy. It does not teach you how to be successful, but it removes "the fear of success." It builds up higher expectations and a better capacity to learn new skills, to become successful and to subconsciously act and behave in a way which draws more success to you. It pushes your desires to succeed in a specific area of your choice to higher levels, and stimulates you to fulfill these desires as well. It may take the form of frequent positive coincidences in your life. For some individuals, it may seem as miracles or as just being lucky, but it is actually the work of your mind's energies which turn your expectations into achievements and success.

The Fulfillment Stage is a lifetime asset. The stimulation in this stage should be continued regularly as long as you want to fulfill new goals, draw more prosperity to youself and experience further personal growth.

At this point I would like to show you how to apply Palm Therapy for the various stages; where to stimulate in order to balance your emotions, where on the hand to trigger the release process and which line/s to reinforce for the activation and strengthening of various qualities of your personality and for achieving your success. In order to do so you will need some knowledge of palmistry. You will need to recognize the lines and forms in your hands. The next section will provide you with this information. It also incorporates some vital information on Palm Therapy and my new discoveries in palmistry.

To the certified Palm Therapist:

I recommend that the work with children should be done only in the presence of their parents or guardians. It gives the child a better feeling that he/she is safe while doing the work and, also, it may prevent misunderstandings and will help the parents to cooperate with the young child and continue the work at home between sessions.

If the work of Palm Therapy is for other than improving skills the supervision of a licensed therapist is mandatory.

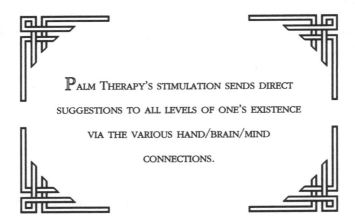

Palm Therapy's stimulation sends direct
suggestions to all levels of one's existence
via the various hand/brain/mind
connections.

SECTION THREE

PALMISTRY

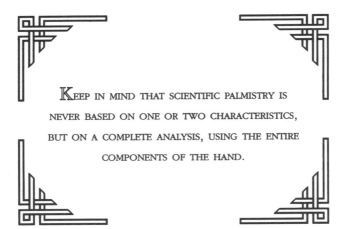

KEEP IN MIND THAT SCIENTIFIC PALMISTRY IS
NEVER BASED ON ONE OR TWO CHARACTERISTICS,
BUT ON A COMPLETE ANALYSIS, USING THE ENTIRE
COMPONENTS OF THE HAND.

Palmistry:
Introduction

In order to apply Palm Therapy effectively, we need some knowledge of palmistry. This section will introduce to you the wisdom of traditional and scientific palmistry, including my findings in the field. In the first chapter of this section (Chapter 5), you will read about the history of palmistry, about some of the authors and researchers of palmistry and their contributions to the field. In Chapter 6, you will acquire some practical knowledge of how to prepare hand documentation which is essential for the professional Palm Therapist or anyone who would like to document the changes of lines and areas in his /her hands periodically. It proceeds with general suggestions of how to diagnose the various components of the hand.

Throughout this section, I will share with you my new findings in the field of palmistry which I discovered during my work to develop Palm Therapy. At the end of Chapter 7 which deals with the traditional hand types I included a new classification according to the *yin* and *yang* aspect of the Chinese theory. Chapter 8 describes the various mounts. Those of you with some background in palmistry will probably notice that I have discovered four additional mounts. I named them: Earth, upper Uranus, lower Uranus and Pluto. You will also read about the synergy of the various mounts in our hands, total of 14 mounts on each, and about the characteristics in your personality they represent. You will also discover the prenatal life and the natural process of addictive behavior patterns as seen in the mounts. Information about Palm Therapy's stimulation of the mounts, and some hand exercises to accelerate different aspects of the personality is added in Chapter 8, too.

Some vital data about Palm Therapy is incorporated in the chapters about the various lines as well as some of the suggestions for improvement and change. This includes stimulation of certain lines and creation of new lines.

In the last few chapters of this section, you will find additional information about some components of the hand which are not considered as the main factors in hand diagnosis but which can help you in the basic diagnosing through palmistry. Among them are: the nails, flexibility of the hand, changeable colors in the hand, the dermatoglyphics and even the postures and gestures of the hand.

Keep in mind that scientific palmistry is never based on one or two characteristics, but on a complete diagnosis, using the entire components of the hand. As stated earlier, in order to effectively apply Palm Therapy for reshaping the personality, you need some knowledge of basic palmistry because your main goal should be to restore/improve the various lines and shapes of the hands that represent specific behavior patterns and characteristics of the personality. Read this section thoroughly. Then you can use it as a reference, especially when you deal with the sections of the book: "The Application of Palm Therapy" and "Palm Therapy for Mental Disorders." Do not start stimulating your hands. First read the suggestions and warnings at the beginning of these sections and throughout the book.

I hope you will enjoy reading about the fascinating field of palmistry and by the time you are done with it, you will have the basic knowledge necessary for you to understand Palm Therapy.

This section is a brief introduction to palmistry which will enable you to understand Palm Therapy. But in order to fully master the wisdom of palmistry, further study is mandatory. The Bibliography will provide you with the names of some of the books on the subject. For a more complete list of books on palmistry, their value and uniqueness, refer to the excellent work written by Andrew Fitzherbert: *The Palmist's Companion—A History and Bibliography of Palmistry,* the Scarecrow Press Inc. Metuchen, N.J. and London 1992. Also, in the future, you can refer to our additional, extensive book, dealing with scientific palmistry as the foundation of Palm Therapy by Moshe Zwang, Yaron Swery and Diana Zwang, Ultimate Mind Publisher.

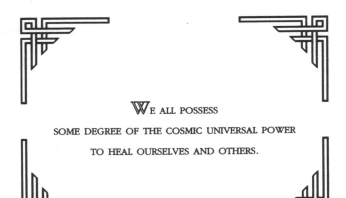

WE ALL POSSESS
SOME DEGREE OF THE COSMIC UNIVERSAL POWER
TO HEAL OURSELVES AND OTHERS.

CHAPTER 5

The History of Palmistry

You may wonder why, for centuries, various sections of the hand were named after stars, planets, or Greek goddesses. The reason for that was simple. Astrology in ancient times was a dominant prediction and diagnostic tool. Palmistry was less-developed and people knew less about it. The various components of the palm were initially named after animals. I believe that to get more acceptance or uniformity between these two ancient diagnostic tools, the ancient palmists in the Western part of the world changed the various names of the lines and the mounts of the hand from the animal kingdom to astrological terms. They corre-lated the various components of the hand to the planets, stars and their symbols as they were described in astrology. Therefore, the fingers and the various sections of the palm and the mounts, are named as Jupiter, Saturn, Apollo, Mercury, Neptune, Moon/Luna, Venus, etc.

There are recorded data on palmistry which passed from generation to generation. One of the first known written documents on palmistry was dated from about 2000 years B.C. (from the Vedic period) in India. Since that first documented information there were many ancient cultures such as Egypt, Aram Naaraim (Iraq and Iran today), Greece and many others which developed palmistry. We don't know much about their knowledge or theories, but we can guess that it was mainly the lines and the mounts of the hands which were referred to as animals and astrological signs.

It is unknown whether the information or knowledge on palmistry was transferred from one country to another or developed in various places by different sources. We can only assume that such sharing of information was part of the ancient trade. There was an established trade route and the road to India was open to the Greeks, as well as to the Arabs.

The Greeks were exposed to many aspects of the Indians' culture and knowledge which probably had an influence on their palmistry as well. One of the most famous Greek philosophers, Aristotle, wrote several treatises on palmistry. (This is a claim on which we don't have evidence of its authenticity.) Aristotle's work on palmistry was dated from about 350 B.C. It is considered to be one of the oldest treatises on palmistry that has a logical explanation with some references to the theory about the hand and the lines. His work was translated into English and it drew the interest of many researchers and students of palmistry. Aristotle included in his work ways for the diagnosis of personalities through the face—physiognomy. When the Romans conquered Greece the knowledge of palmistry was passed to them.

The ancient Hebrews, with the mystery of the Kabbalah

(Cabala/Qabala) mentioned that information in a different way. They described the different lines with astrological names according to the Hebrew letters called *Alef Beith* (ABCs).

The Chinese also viewed palmistry as a very ancient tool for divination long before Aristotle in Greece. From these short references we can see that palmistry was well-known in the ancient world of the East as well as of the West (including the Middle East).

The oldest palmistry manuscript in English is the *Digby Roll IV* in the Bodleian Library. According to Fred Gettings in his book: *The Book Of The Hand*, it is a summing up of different characteristics in palmistry. This manuscript was written probably before 1440 B.C. All the old manuscripts were short and hard to study. They were mainly based on intuition as the main tool for reading with a little reference to the lines or the shapes of the hand.

Throughout the centuries, many authors have left written testimonies on palmistry. During the dark ages, palmistry, as well as astrology, physiognomy and other fortunetelling methods were believed to be part of witchcraft. An accusation of practicing witchcraft lead to a death sentence by the Church. Therefore, most of this wisdom was destroyed and those who practiced it never had the opportunity to study seriously. Rossell Hope Robbins stated in his book: *The Encyclopedia of Witchcraft & Demonology* Page 210, Bonanza Publ. NY, 1981 edition, a declaration that was made by a Church Council at Melun in 1579 and that can summarize this point:

"*Every charlatan and diviner, and others who practice Necromancy, Pyromancy, Chiromancy, Hydromancy, will be punished by death.*" (Chiromancy, originally, pertained to divination through the lines of the hands.)

In Europe there was a great revival of interest in palmistry during the 16th century. John Indagine was one of the remarkable Renaissance men whose work in palmistry emphasized the practical application for the various aspects of it. There were many more who published similar works in the field.

In the 17th century, palmistry received a more scientific approach, thanks to Dr. John Rothman, a German physician, who formed a system of the principles of hand reading through a set of rules rather than intuition. He also tried to combine, as many others had, the principles of astrology with those of palmistry.

During the 18th century, not many works on palmistry were published. Those that were published were mainly repetitions of the knowledge that was known up to that century. Lavater (1741-1801), a Protestant minister, who wrote several books on mysticism, was known for his observations. He suggested that the hands of man are equally diverse and dissimilar as are their faces.

The next 100 years were marked with many famous palmists who wrote about their works and experiences. Among them were two great Frenchmen whose works changed the study of palmistry, D'Arpentigny, 1798, and Desbarrolles in 1801. D'Arpentigny rejected the astrological theories and the Kabbalistic approach to palmistry. He disregarded the lines of the hand. He was more concerned with the general shape of the hand and features such as texture, shape and color of the nails. He observed and classified many hands all over the world. His research led him (according to Fred Gettings *The Book of The Hand*) to distinguish six basic types of hands and another one which he called: *the mixed hand.*

Desbarrolles (1801-1886) published several works and books in the field of palmistry and graphology in France. His research was in the Kabbalah (the mystical part of Judaism) and scientific data connected with the nervous system. He also corroborated the findings of D'Arpentigny in the field of chirognomy. He claimed that intuition should not enter into the interpretation of hand reading. On the other hand, he redefined the *astral light* of the Kabbalists, or the *chi* of the Chinese, as a magnetic electricity which he believed surrounds us as well as the whole world at large. According to Desbarrolles the changes occurring in the lines of the hands are actually the tracings produced on the ultrasensitive surface of the palm by the vital current of electricity that is constantly passing over it. The nervous impressions made upon the individual are responsible for the changing in the width and color of the lines. His theory influenced almost every palmist for the next hundred years.

This was, so far, the Western approach to palmistry until the last century. But palmistry was not neglected in the Eastern side of the world as well.

In the Far East, Chinese researchers and sages of the centuries developed their own style of understanding the personality and health from the hand. The book called: *The Four Books* was the basic philosophic approach of the East. (It consists of the four main works: *Confucian Analects*, *The Great Learning*, *The Doctrine of The Mean* and *The Works of Mencius*.)

Fortunetelling, according to the *Book of Changes*, the *I Ching*, was well established during the centuries. The principles were taken into palmistry as well. Although they had a very accurate reading system through the hand, it is hard to call it a scientific palmistry.

Some authorities related the Chinese palmistry to the Indian influence on palmistry, as well as to the Buddhist religion in China.

Others believed that palmistry was known in India and China for many thousands of years before Buddhism or even before the earliest Taoism religion. As we mentioned before, with the Western approach to palmistry, the Chinese, or more exactly, those on the Eastern or Northern part of Asia, developed their system of reading the hand many years ago. The way they viewed life was a much more symbolic approach than that of the Western doctrine. The Chinese sages developed a correlation between the *macro- and microcosmos*, between man and nature and between the palm of the hand and the human body. Balance in life meant living according to the laws of nature. This concept was the whole truth in religion as well as in health. The hand as a representative of the body and path of life was an important tool of diagnosis.

The Chinese were geniuses in symbolism. Their ideas were a very imaginative way of thinking. In every sign on the hand they looked for a symbol representing one aspect of life. Their readings, as I mentioned earlier, were accurate. By understanding that humans and nature are one, finding the various representatives of nature as seen in the hand made it an incredible system.

Palmistry, as is Taoism and as are many other doctrines in the Chinese philosophy, is based on the concepts of *yin* and *yang* and the *Five Elements*. These concepts are being taught in detail to the students of Chinese medicine and acupuncture. The major elements for diagnosing the hand are relatively very close to those we study in acupuncture.

The various factors are reflected on the hand. A skilled Chinese doctor, who knows Chinese palmistry, can use it as a medical diagnostic tool (in addition to the Chinese methods of pulse diagnosis, tongue diagnosis, ear diagnosis, abdominal diagnosis, etc.). The Chinese reading actually combines the face and the hand in the same reading.

Japan, later in years and up to present day, has been influenced by the Chinese doctrine of palmistry. Therefore, the Japanese palm reader works very similarly to his/her Chinese colleague.

The Jewish/Hebrew Kabbalah presented another method

THE HISTORY OF PALMISTRY

of palmistry. The Kabbalah described it in a series of 23 books named *The Zohar*. In the "Portion of Yitro," Page 18 up to Page 60, *The Zohar* describes the various techniques of diagnosis through the palms. It mainly consists of face reading and palmistry. Most of the readings were done intuitively. The readers were expected to work a lot on their ability to understand the human nature as well as to develop their ESP, especially their telepathy, in order to be able to read the face or the hands. The clues for reading in *The Zohar* were, as mentioned earlier, taken from the Hebrew *Alef Beith* (ABCs) in a series of printed letters and hand written letters which were called *the secret of the letters*. For example, Page 37 in the "Portion of Yitro," Part 138, describes the secrets of the Hebrew letter *Zain*. It refers to the lower case and the capital letters and has some foundation in numerology which in Hebrew is called *gimetria*.

For example, it is believed that a person who has three longitudinal lines and three transverse lines, has a sure sign for success. If you wish to translate it to modern palmistry, we can say that the three longitudinal lines, consist of one fate line and two Apollo (success) lines. When having two clear success lines we can assume that the person will be successful. The point is that in traditional palmistry, according to the Kabbalah, there is no reference to a fate line. Yet, the reading by those who practiced Kabbalah was usually accurate and with an ability to predict the future. We have to remember that the Hebrew *Mekubal* (a practitioner of Kabbalah), had to study traditional religion most of his life, and only after the age of 40 could he start with the learning of the secrets of the Kabbalah. In so many years of praying, meditation and learning the secret of the higher self, he developed his ESP skills and could read the hands mainly by intuition and telepathy. This factor alone made powerful readings. The Hebrew writings on palmistry and face reading are very short and to the point. If one tries to read about it in order to master these kinds of techniques by himself, he will probably fail because of the way it is written. It can be understood only after an intensive learning of *The Zohar*. Various translators and teachers tried to explain and teach *The Zohar* to the students of Kabbalah. One of the famous ones was the great Rabbi Yehuda Lieb Halevi Ashlag, who wrote the *Sulam Explanations*. It contains a very comprehensive explanation (in Hebrew) for *The Zohar*. But even with this explanation it is not enough for those who didn't learn the basic principles mentioned in that book. *The Zohar* also refers to astrological elements in palmistry, but the main point is the intuitive reading which makes it so convincing to the lay person.

The Egyptians had their own system of reading, but they, too, worked mainly on intuitive reading.

In the last 100 years, together with the technical and scientific revolution, palmistry has received a deeper look from researchers in the West who left the traditional palmistry for a more systematic and scientific approach. The pioneer of that approach was Dr. William G. Benham, who published in 1900, the book: *The Laws of Scientific Hand Reading*, one of the most complete books in the field of palmistry. His book describes the various personalities according to the mounts and the lines of the hands. It is considered as a must for any serious student of palmistry. Benham examined thousands of patients and criminals. He tried to get away from any mystical or metaphysical aspects associated with palmistry. However, he did believe in the existence of the soul which is a form of energy that enters into the body. His assumption was that the soul enters into the body through the hand of the fetus. He described the life energy as the Chinese described the *chi*. William Benham established a whole new systematic concept on palmistry including a theory as to why it works. Although his basic work was based on D'Arpentigny, Desbarrolles, and others, his research and methodical approach gave to palmistry a deeper understanding.

Count Louis Hamon, known as Cheiro, is considered to be one of the most remarkable palmists in his history. He published several books on palmistry including the book: *Cheiro's Language of The Hand*. In this book he described the various types of hands. His ability to foretell was legendary.

Part of what we see in Cheiro's work was taken from the Gypsies. We don't have much of their work, because in the dark ages those who dealt with palmistry were considered as practicing Black Magic or Witchcraft and, as mentioned earlier, had a death sentence if they were caught dealing with palmistry.

Others who lately contributed to palmistry were Noel Jaquin, who wrote a few books about palmistry. His main contribution was his research into the small patterns of the skin on the palms and feet called dermatoglyphics. Through these small patterns or papillary ridges, Noel Jaquin could detect many diseases in their early stages. According to his finding, the dermatoglyphics of the palms are the mirror of the health balance. In many aspects he was also one of the pioneers of scientific palmistry.

Another great discovery of scientific palmistry was made by Charlotte Wolff. Her point of view was that the different shapes of the hand were influenced by hormonal development. Her work was very unique and added another dimension to the field of palmistry. Dr. Charlotte Wolff also focused on the hands of children who were mentally ill as well as on the normal types of personality for clinical diagnosis.

There were, of course, others who were pioneers in this field and we acknowledge their contribution to palmistry. Unfortunately we don't have enough room to write about their unique works in this book.

Throughout the centuries various terms were designated to describe the field of hand analysis. Some of them have the same definitions.

Since Palm Therapy (Dec. 1985) is a breakthrough in scientific palmistry—from hand reading to actually balancing one's state of mind and stimulating optimal potential of various aspects of the personality for success and fulfillment, I have added new terminology to this field while developing the technique. Most of them can be found throughout this book (new mounts, new lines and new concepts).

The following are some of the various well-known old and new terms. You don't have to memorize them in order to understand how Palm Therapy works.

Next to each term you will find the definitions as they appear in the dictionary or those that are well-known in traditional palmistry. This list includes some of the terms that I added during the development of Palm Therapy. The sources are marked with star signs as follows:

*   Webster's Third New International Dictionary's definitions of the various names related to the palmistry. (If only parts of a term are defined by the dictionary, a separate star sign appears before each one of them).

**   Various authors of Traditional and Scientific palmistry related certain aspects of the study of the hand to specific terminology.

***   Moshe Zwang's new definitions

The terms are organized in an alphabetic order as follows:

Chiroglyphics / Cheiroglyphics
*Chir: hand

*Glyphics from Greek, Glyphein: to carve
**The study of the small skin patterns (papillary ridges) on the hands and feet.

Chirognomy / Cheirognomy
*Chir: hand + Gnomy: science, art, or means of judging;
**The art or practice of reading a person's character or aptitude and especially his past and possible future events from the general characteristic shape of his hands, fingers, lines, forms (mounts) and marks.

Chirokinesics / Cheirokinesics (Moshe Zwang, 1991)
*Chir: hand
*Kinesics, from Greek, kinesis: motion; A systematic study of nonlinguistic body motion in its relationship to communication.
***The study of the spontaneous gestures and postures of the hand in order to diagnose one's present mood, feelings and intentions, as well as basic characteristics of the personality.

Chirology / Cheirology
*Chir: hand
*Logy: science, theory, doctrine
**Another term to describe palmistry. The study of the hand through the whole art and science of palm reading which includes all the features of the hand: shapes, fingers, nails, mounts, skin texture, colors, flexibility, thickness, lines, marks, skin patterns, etc. (chirognomy, chiromancy, dermatoglyphics and onychognomy) See palmistry.

Chiromancy / Cheiromancy
*Chir: hand, Mancy: divination;
Divination by examination of the hand.
**a. The reading of the character, personality and events in one's life mainly through the study of the various lines and marks on the hand.
   b. A medical approach to study and interpretation of the various physical variables of the hand.

Chironomy / Cheironomy
*from Greek: Cheironomia,
Cheir/Chir: hand + Nomia: management
A method of directing the singing of Gregorian chant by hand gestures indicating the rise and fall of the melody.
**The study of ritual and spontaneous hand postures and gestures in order to diagnose one's character, personality, mood and feelings.

Chiropsy / Cheiropsy
*Chir: hand
(The whole term is not defined by the dictionary.)
**The study of the hand through its general shape, fingers and nails.

Chirosophy / Cheirosophy
*Chir: hand, Sophy: science or study of; same as chiromancy: Divination by examination of the hand.
**The whole field of palmistry (see below).

Dermatoglyphics
*Derma: skin + from Greek Glyphein: to carve
 Skin patterns, patterns of the specialized skin of the infe-

rior surfaces of the hands and feet; the science of the study of skin patterns

**The study and interpretation of the various small skin patterns (papillary ridges on the hand or soles of feet) for the diagnosis of one's personality and potential, events and general physical condition. According to some authorities it related to one's Karma.

Kinesics Therapy (Moshe Zwang 1991)

***The art and science of balancing the state of mind and reshaping one's personality by conscious modification of certain hand gestures, postures and total body language which represent specific moods, characters, intentions and the personality in general (based on kinesics, body language, chironomy, chirokinesics). This therapy form has not yet been published.

Onychognomy

*Onych: nail of the finger or toe

*Gnomy: science, art, or means of judging

**The study of the nails for learning about one's character, personality, events and general physical condition.

Palmistry

*(Palm + Mastery)

The art or practice of reading a person's character or aptitude and especially his past and possible future events from the general characteristic shape of his hands, fingers, lines, forms and marks.

Unfortunately, another definition for palmistry in the dictionary is as follows:"dexterity or trickery (as pocket picking) involving use of the hands." No wonder then, why some authorities who continued to research into the hand's small patterns, dermatoglyphics, stayed away from the total concept of palmistry.

**a. The study of the hand through the whole art and science of palm reading which includes all the features of hand shape: fingers, nails, mounts, skin texture, colors, flexibility, thickness, lines, marks, skin patterns, etc, and gestures and postures of the hand (chirognomy, chiromancy, dermatoglyphics and onychognomy) traditionally for divination or character reading.

b. The art or science of studying the hand (as above) in order to learn about one's character, personality, aptitude, goals, major past events and possible future events which is mainly based on one's personality, goals, talents and attitude as seen in the hand.

Palm Therapy (Moshe Zwang, 1985)

***Palm Therapy: The art and science of enhancing optimum potential, self-growth, fulfillment and success in all aspects of life, through the stimulation of specific areas and lines in the hands which represent the various characteristics of the personality and brain/mind activities. Palm Therapy's stimulation sends direct suggestions to all levels of one's existence via the various hand/mind connections and communications.The stimulation apparently bypasses the cognitive mind's critique and disapproval for new changes in thinking and behavioral patterns. Therefore, it leads to rapid corresponding changes in mood, behavior and thinking patterns, potential, talents, personality and, eventually, in one's life. The process is done without effort or strain and can be enhanced anytime, anywhere.

(Palm Therapy's stimulation leads to a remarkable relief and a change in mood which usually occurs within a few minutes of stimulation, but the whole therapy which may change one's personality and life, goes through the three Stages of Palm Therapy—the Balancing, the Release and the Fulfillment. The duration of the therapy may last for a few months or longer. It depends upon one's general well-being, needs and expectations for success.)

THROUGH THE HANDS
YOU CAN DETECT MANY OF THE FLAWS WHICH
INTERFERE WITH THE ACHIEVEMENT OF YOUR
GOALS AND LIFE FULFILLMENT.

6

Hand Documentation and General Instructions for Hand Analysis

Hand documentation is an important tool for the Palm Therapist and those individuals who apply Palm Therapy for self-help. It helps to direct the various necessary moves according to what is seen in the hands, as well as for follow-up and comparison of the positive changes in the course of the lines, marks and mounts of the hand. Any clinical Palm Therapy work with individuals should be based on hand documentation and comparison of improvements periodically.

Traditionally, hand documentation was done by covering the palm with a special thick ink with the help of a small hand roller, then imprinting it against the surface of a white paper which was lying on a sponge surface. In this way all parts of the palm could be imprinted.

Today, there are alternative ways to that basic method of hand ink imprinting, yet, it is ranked among the best ones.

In this chapter you will learn about the traditional ink hand print documentation and some of its advanced alternatives.

TRADITIONAL METHOD OF HAND DOCUMENTATION

Ink Prints

The tools you need are:

1. Roller: The kind that is/was used in photography. You can find it at any art supply store.

2. Ink: The kind you should use is thick pasty ink not a liquid one. This thick ink is the same kind that is/was used for fingerprinting by the police or the Department of Motor Vehicles (DMV) in the U.S.A. although today computerized scanning techniques replace its use in many places.

3. Paper: White 20-50 lb, paper size 8.5" X 11" or any other size that can accommodate the entire hand of an adult male is needed (you print one palm on each sheet). Take into account that you will need 2-3 sets of each for your observation. During the work, you will notice many times that this approach lets you detect more details which were not clearly presented in the first imprint. The reasons are many:

Uneven or too much ink on specific areas of the palm may cover some of the fine lines. The different amounts of pressure on the palm, while imprinting, plays a role, too. It takes some experience. The stretching of the fingers and general hand posture, while imprinting, can also result in a better or worse result. And the last reason for making more than one imprint is simply because the ink left on the palms after the first imprint lets you have another which is many times of a better quality.

4. Sponge: A soft sheet of rubber sponge, in the size of the paper or larger, to be placed underneath the paper. This will help to expose the depth of the center of the hands and ensure that the entire palm is printed. (If you practice Palm Therapy, take into account that you will need to give one set to your client as well.)

5. Writing tools: You can use a pen or a pencil for contouring the entire hand after the imprint is made. Special attention should be made to mark the actual tips of ladies' fingers who have long fingernails.

6. A smooth surface: You need any small glass or metal smooth surface to pour the ink on (on this surface you will roll the roller). It is essential for an even, thin coat of ink on the palm and fingers.

7. Cleaning materials: Any cleaning material such as soap and water, baby wipes, a cleaning paste based on vaseline and citrus essential oil, and paper towels.

The procedure of hand printing is as follows:

1. Put a small quantity of the ink on the a smooth surface, then roll the roller on the ink until the roller is evenly coated.

2. Place a clean sheet of paper on top of the rubber sponge.

3. Coat the entire palm, fingers and the sides of the palm evenly with the help of the roller. Special attention should be given to the fingers and the sides of the palm, including the semi-circular depression (the mount of Earth) located between the thumb and pointer. This part is slightly extended towards the back of the hand

4. The hand (fingers slightly open) should be placed on the top of the paper firmly and without any movement. You may gently press evenly on the back of the hand. Then contour the entire hand with a pencil; carefully lift the hand, rolling it to the ulnar side of the palm (side of little finger), so that the side is pressed against the paper. This is essential for the documentation of the three new mounts which are located on that side (you will read about them later in this section). Then, lift the hand gently from the paper, turn it to the other side, and imprint the semi-circle depression on the radial side, just between the thumb and pointer finger. With some experience you can do it easily.

5. Repeat the palm prints of each hand a few times. Make at least three of each. (The back of the hand cannot be well documented with ink. You may wish to use the new alternatives for the traditional hand prints.)

6. After imprinting, you need to write on each imprint the date also any special characteristics of the hands such as: left/right, color of the palm, flexibility, viscosity, shape of nails, etc. (These aspects are covered in the various chapters in this section.)

The Palm Therapist should also add the client's name, telephone number, birth date, special events which were verified by your clients, as well as specific negative patterns. Remember, that even if you have a photographic memory, you may forget important details after years and thousands of printing. So write immediately. Don't delay!

7. It is a good idea to imprint the hands before and after each stage of Palm Therapy, so that you (or your client) can observe the differences on the palms. Make at least one additional imprint of the hand every year for evaluation.

8. The Palm Therapist should file this hand documentation with the questionnaire and any additional data you may get from your client's health practitioner. Next, when you are done with the observation of the hands you need to add your findings, too.

NEW ALTERNATIVES FOR THE TRADITIONAL HAND PRINTS

Photocopy
Set the photocopy machine on medium-light tone. Place both palms on the photocopy surface, or place one at a time. Cover them with a white sheet of paper so that the background will be clear. Then photocopy in the same way as you would photocopy a document. (See "A few words about radiation" below.)

It is a very quick and easy procedure, but you need a good quality photocopy machine. It is recommend to make three different copies of the same posture (front, back and sides of the hand). All the information then should be written as soon as you can (refer to # 6-8 above).

Photograph with a Camera

Another good and an accurate way to imprint the hand is with the help of a high quality camera which has special lenses for near photography. With training, this method is fast, clean and easy.

The disadvantages are that you need an expensive camera to start with; you don't see the result immediately, and you can't write detailed information on the print itself.

Write all details as explained above, (# 6-8) on a separate sheet of paper. Again, you should make at least three different sets of prints of the same posture (front, back and sides of hands).

Computer Imprints

With today's technology, we can scan pictures and some items into the computer. The palms of the hands can be documented that way, too. If you have such equipment, then you can scan all sides of the hand (front, back and sides) store it on a disk and watch it on the computer's monitor .Then you can add all details as explained above (# 6-8) and save the disk. (See "A few words about radiation," below.)

A few words about radiation:

The new methods of hand prints may concern some of you. To what degree the exposure to light is harmful is presently unknown. It is assumed to be safe (until some researches will prove it otherwise). For those who are concerned about it, I recommend that they try the other methods of imprinting or take extra anti-oxidant and anti-radiation supplements such as niacin and minerals. You may also consider coating the palms with solar protection ointment. Let it dry before processing. The decision is yours. Use your own common sense.

GENERAL INSTRUCTIONS FOR HAND ANALYSIS

Although the handprint will supply you with vast information, as part of the hand documentation, you will also need to add some of the findings from the hands' observation in writing.

Palm reading can be done in many ways, each technique has its logic and value. The diagnosis can be done by observing the items that have changed most recently: first, for example, the postures and gestures of the hand or the various colors in the hand. The reason for checking the posture, gesture and changeable factors first is simple. They provide us with an instant approach to the feeling and behavior of a person at the present time.

Others prefer to start with a more sound observation and diagnosis by checking the more basic characteristics proceeding to the more changeable ones.

I'm used to working and analyzing the hand in both ways since both are very logical approaches. But, for the novice who would like to establish a sound pattern of analysis, I suggest making the observations according to the following order:

- The general shape of the hand according to the Seven Hand Types and the Classification of the hand according to the *yin* and *yang*.
- Consistency of the hand

-The various mounts, starting with the most dominant
to the least dominant.
- The fingers in general and each one of them
individually.
- The nails
- Flexibility of the hand
- The major lines of the Palm
- The minor lines
- Small signs
- Changeable colors in the hand
- The basic derma patterns of the hand
- Hair
- Texture of the skin
- Posture of the hand
- The aura/energy of the hands (for those who have
learned to see it)

I believe that all components of the hand should be considered when studying the personality. In the proceeding chapters of this section, you will obtain some information about each one of the components (not in the order listed above, see "Contents").

REPETITIOUS TERMS TO REMEMBER

In the description of each hand and its various components, I use the anatomical terms: radial, ulnar, proximal and distal (Fig. 7). These are mentioned in Appendix A: "Anatomy of the hand," but to make it easy for you to remember them, I give you some hints that are related only to the hand's descriptions as follows:

Radial: The side of the thumb (or the radius bone)
Ulnar: The side of the little finger (or the ulnar bone)
Proximal: Closer to the wrist (nearest the center of the body)
Distal: Away from the wrist (farthest from the center
of the body) towards the fingertips

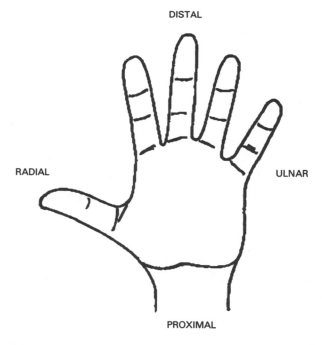

Fig. 7   *The radial, ulnar, proximal and distal sides of the hand.*

WHEN CONSCIOUS ALTERATION
IS DONE CONSISTENTLY THROUGH THE MANY EXPRESSOR WAYS
OF THE MIND—THOUGHTS, SELF-TALK, FACIAL EXPRESSIONS,
HANDS' POSTURES/GESTURES, HANDS' LINES/SHAPES,
HANDWRITING, TONE OF VOICE, GENERAL BODY LANGUAGE AND
THE LIST IS LONG—IT CAN LEAD TO A TRANSFORMATION IN
ONE'S PERSONALITY AND LIFE.

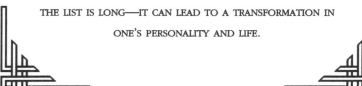

CHAPTER **7**

The Seven Hand Types

The diagnosis through the general shape of the hand is a method which was adopted by many professional palmists all over the world. The method of classification according to the *seven hand types* was originated in the last century by D'Arpentigny, a French palmist, who used it as a tool to diagnose the various personalities. The various hand types were described by Cheiro in his book: *The Language of the Hand.*

There are other good methods of classifying the various hand types. Among them is the classification according to the Four Elements: Water, Earth, Fire and Air as described by Fred Gettings and others. These methods are not included in this book (refer to the Bibliography for further reading).

At the end of this chapter you will find a new classification for the seven hand types which I based on the aspects of the *yin* and *yang* of the Chinese tradition.

131

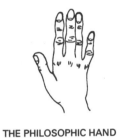

THE ELEMENTARY HAND

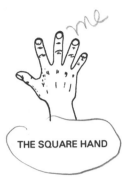

THE SQUARE HAND

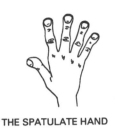

THE SPATULATE HAND

THE PHILOSOPHIC HAND

THE CONIC HAND

THE PSYCHIC HAND

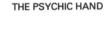

THE MIXED HAND

Fig. 8 *The Seven Hand Types.*

Palm Therapy uses mainly the lines, signs and the various areas of the hand for stimulation and modifications. Nevertheless, the seven hand types can provide you with some information for the basic characteristics of people.

Following are the seven hand types (Fig. 8) each of which represents, in general, a different type of personality:

1. The elementary hand
2. The square hand
3. The spatulate hand
4. The philosophic hand
5. The conic hand
6. The psychic, sensitive hand
7. The mixed hand

Most of the hands that we are going to observe during our life are a combination of more than one type. So, in a way, we can say that most of the hands will fall under the seventh category—the mixed hand. In order to understand this principle, we should describe each of the first six hand types individually.

It is well worth noting that there is no such a thing as a positive or a negative hand type. Each hand type represents different aspects of the needs of the human race—they are all essential to the balance of humanity. Also, the hand type may change during one's life, and more than once with proper documentation you can observe it yourself.

HOW TO MEASURE THE HAND

In order to differentiate between some of the hand types, it is necessary to measure the basic shape of the palm and the fingers

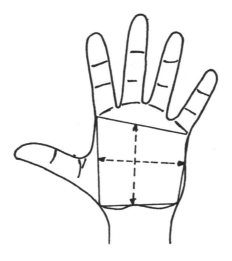

Fig. 9 *Measuring the palm.*

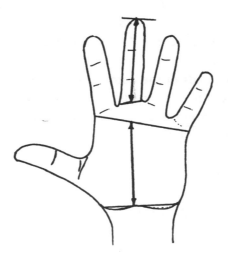

Fig. 10 *Finding palm to fingers ratio.*

(Figs. 9 and 10). You need to measure the length of the palm by drawing an imaginary line from the radial border of the palm (the side of the thumb) to the ulnar border of the palm (the side of the little finger) starting at the base of the second finger towards the base of the little finger. Then measure from a mid-point at the wrist's distal bracelet (the one which is closer to the palm) to a mid-point on the imaginary line.

To measure the width, draw an imaginary line from the base of the second finger to the wrist's bracelet (the one which is closer to the palm). Then measure from the mid-point on that imaginary line to the ulnar border of the palm. Comparing the sizes will give you an idea of the basic shape of the hand.

When you measure the fingers you need to measure the middle finger which is called the finger of Saturn and then compare its length to the length of the palm. You will find more information about this subject in Chapter 9.

THE ELEMENTARY HAND

The elementary hand (Fig. 11) usually shows the most primitive or lowest type of mentality. This hand is thick, coarse and clumsy. The whole appearance of the hand is of heaviness, especially heaviness of the fingers. This meaty hand can not usually handle sophisticated themes. The feeling is that the only thing this kind of hand can hold is an ax, a shovel or other tools which are used mainly to perform physical work. It is estimated that in the agriculture profession, among those who do the main physical labor, a large group of people would have this kind of hand. Their fingers are usually thick and short. The fingernails are short as well and tend to be unclean. The hand is wide, indicating physical activity and strength.

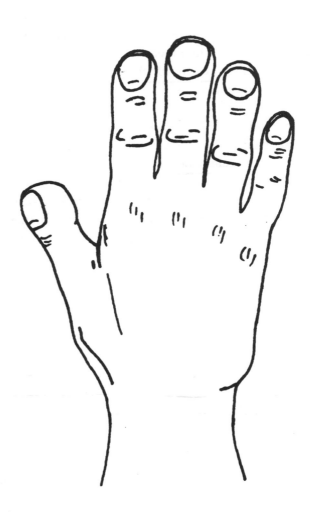

Fig. 11 The Elementary Hand.

Looking at this type of hand, we shall notice the main lines—the basic flexure creases. The veins of this hand are, in most cases, not seen clearly if the work that this type is involved with is done mainly with the help of muscles other than those related to the movement of the fingers, and vice versa. It is usually more of a "meaty hand".

The character of this type is one who cares mainly for the basic things in life. The people who possess this type of hand tend to obesity later in years. They become angry very quickly, but most of the time they are calm and simple in their needs and way of life. They are considered as brutal people and coarse in their behavior. They are capable of brutality if their desires are not met, but less of cruelty. The idea that the people who have the elementary hand are mainly violent and have a high temper is partly true. They prefer to deal with things in their life in a physical way rather than a mental one. Their reasoning is more basic, therefore they are considered by other people around them as not having reason at all.

Usually, if you find this type of hand, it will be mainly without combinations of any other type of hands. The owners of this shape of hand are usually interested, as mentioned, in the very basic and down to earth needs such as food, sleep and sex in the simplest form. On the other side, these persons make the perfect believers of any religion or of the authorities with whom they grew up. Usually, they tend to be very superstitious but, unless educated, they refuse to believe in palmistry or anything that is not accepted by those with whom they were reared. Their mental capacity is mainly low but, sometimes like an animal, they can be very shrewd. They are usually far from the appreciation of painting, music or other art. However, they might be fascinated by the power and beauty of nature. They are most adapteds to living in rural places and within nature's basic demands. They don't read much, but do accept the TV (where it is available). The rapid changes of civilization seem to pass above their heads without much influence on their lives. They are by far the workers, physical laborers for others. It is very rare to see them in capacities of control or success and if they do, it is always a sure sign of a combination between the elementary and other hand types. Usually these people accept authority and try to live in peace. They can be very loyal to the place in which they live and, in a way, have more stability than the other hand types. They can live for years in the same way and same location without much change or improvement. Their needs for stability, security and a place of their own is greater than others.

Their need for love and affection is like that anyone else has, but because it is hard for them to express themselves, they mainly expect others to express their feelings and explain what has to be done.

As we shall see in all of the hand types, there is no negative or positive type as a whole, but within each group of hands it is possible to find positive and negative people.

To determine a positive or a negative attitude of personality, we have to look at various factors in the hand. The color of the hand, for example, white or pale color means a stressful personality. Very dark reddish palms denote a hot temper with the possibility of aggressiveness out of passion or anger. The balanced hand would be the one with a pinkish palm (in any race or origin). The color of the hand can also change from minute to minute according to one's mood and various factors such as exposure to cold or hot temperatures and to mechanical pressure.

But the color is only one of the factors that we have to look to in this hand. The other components that we need to

check are the mounts, especially the mounts of Mars for aggressiveness and the mount of Venus for human warmth, sexuality
and vitality. You will learn about the mounts later in this section. The fingers should also need to be observed. In this type of
hand we expect the thumb to be short and of high setting, an
indicative of a lack of logic and of willpower.

Can an elementary hand of a child change into another
type? In the past, experts in palmistry viewed the various hand
types as final types, meaning that those who were born with a
certain type of hand cannot change that fact. However, after
years of observing many individuals who possessed the elementary hand, I found that education and environment can change
the character/fate of a person. During this natural process of
adapting to new life patterns, one's hand will change, too.
Except for the dermatoglyphics in the hand as well as those in
the soles of the feet everything else does. The hands change
constantly according to the various factors of life. Therefore, a
child with this kind of hand can easily change to a different type
and vice versa. It is a very interesting aspect that these people,
although they usually don't possess a high IQ, after special
training and education may undergo a specific transformation of
their lives and hands. Although some people are born and stay
with the same shape of hand most of their lives, it is not a rule
or a law, but the way things usually happen.

Please remember, when examining the hands, we need to
take into account the possibility of a changing process.
Therefore, although those people seem to be primitive at a first
glance, they might be in a process of self-growth. We all possess
this ability for improving not only our quality of life, but our
mentality as well.

THE SQUARE HAND

There are many combinations with this basic type. The square hand has a square palm or one that is wider from the radial side to the ulnar side than its length (Fig. 12). The wider the hand, the stronger the person is. Usually the fingers of this type are rectangular in shape and their width is equal from the base to their tips. The nails may be square-shaped or rounded.

We consider the classic square hand as the basic builder or technician. This person has the ability to create and to deal with technical and mechanical things better than any other hand type. In a way, we can say that this type of hand builds the world as we see it today.

People with a square hand are usually punctual, have good self-control and a good eye-hand coordination. As children, we can watch them playing and building more often than those with the other hand types. At school they do better with mathematics, physics and other analytical and technical subjects. It is not necessarily the hand of the genius, creator or inventor, but it is the hand of those who support and build our technology from the simple things to the most sophisticated ones. Some of them love to improve their homes and are great at any labor including housecleaning and any home repairs.

We can find people with a square hand type in a variety of professions. They are indeed everywhere. The classical type with square hands and square fingertips are, as mentioned above, the technicians of our world. We can see many orthopedists with this kind of hand. Other professions in which we can find the square hand are anything from scientists to agriculture workers, seamen, pilots, engineers, electricians, mechanics and the like. Actually, in all professions, the most practical ones will be those who possess the square hand.

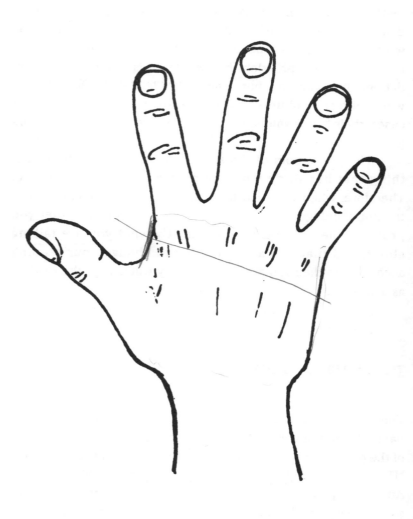

Fig. 12 The Square Hand.

The hint as to what direction the person goes would be in the fingers, the mounts, and the lines. They are practical and methodical in their thoughts and habits and usually prefer to deal with matter rather than with ideas, religion or the esoteric world. If we find this type dealing with religion or the metaphysical world, the impression they will leave is of ideas with foundations. It is amazing, but some of the leaders in the religious world of many cultures possess the square hand, but in most cases, their hands will be mixed with philosophic or pointed fingers.

The possessors of the square hand, usually, ignore anything that has to do with the esoteric world or New Age. Therefore, when you read the hand of such, be precise and to the point and ignore the initial rejection they radiate. After you prove to them that you know exactly what you are talking about, and that you are not going to change your reading according to their remarks, usually they will accept the reading as a science.

THE SPATULATE HAND

The spatulate hand (Fig. 13) is the hand in which the width of its palm next to the base of the four fingers is wider than the width of the palm as normally measured in the middle of the palm. (See "How to Measure the Hand" at the beginning of this chapter.) Another type of spatulate hand is one with a square palm and spatulate fingers. In this case, the fingertips are wider than their base. Both types can be considered as the spatulate hand. The

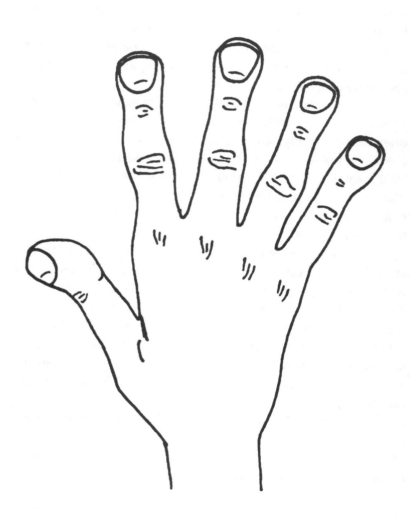

Fig. 13   *The Spatulate Hand.*

first one, with spatulate palm, is the classic one, and the other one is a combination. Another shape of hand which has a wide base next to the wrist and slender next to the base of the finger is also considered by some authorities in palmistry as spatulate hand, but in my opinion this hand should be classified as the conic hand. If its fingers are with broad spatulate tips, then it should be considered a mixed hand.

The spatulate hand is usually a strong hand, hard and firm. This type of hand indicates practicality, energy, activity, a goal oriented personality, working hard; one with a high temper. The classic spatulate hand is the more profound type with a need for a mental activity. The other type, the square palm with spatulate fingers, is more of a technician than a creator. He/she might be restless, energetic and creative, but to a lesser degree than the basic spatulate hand.

This hand can be named "the active hand" since it demonstrates restlessness and the need to do things. The owners of this hand are usually at positions in the military (high ranks). They are the practical explorers of nature, the scientific/laboratory researchers. They look into reality of things in a different way from the common. We can also call it "the inventor's hand" or "the hand that puts a new face to old things," but even the inventors who possess the spatulate hand will focus on practical ideas.

If the spatulate hand is soft and flabby, the possessors are attracted to arts rather than to science, also to the exploration of the unknown/spirituality which is part of science that cannot be understood today with present knowledge.

As with the possessors of the square hands, since they are suspicious in nature, when working with them, you must establish an initial trust by talking about their past and special events as seen in their hands. They will try to discourage you at least in the beginning. Then, after you establish trust with them, chances are they will accept everything you say.

THE PHILOSOPHIC HAND

The philosophic hand (Fig. 14) is a hand with a rectangular palm and long, knotty fingers. The interphalangeal joints of the fingers are well-pronounced which makes it the main characteristic of this type of hand. People who possess this hand have a more philosophic outlook on almost all aspects of life. They tend to look at life from the questioning point of view, trying to understand the world in their special way of thinking. They prefer thinking over acting. They are satisfied by understanding the reason behind things and may accumulate a lot of knowladge and wisdom in their lives.

The philosophic hand creates many philosophic ideas and philosophers, professors in colleges, researchers, theologians and so on. Nevertheless, many of the people with philosophic hands work as mechanics, electricians and at other manual jobs. If these people work as technicians, they usually go deeper into the questioning and understanding of their work and of their life in general. They love the details and have the ability to discuss things either with themselves, if their little finger (the finger of Mercury) is especially short, or with others, if this finger is long. (See Chapter 9: "The Fingers.")

One of the main characteristics these deep thinkers have is love for the unknown; the esoteric and metaphysics of any kind. They prefer to deal with the unknown and discuss it as long and as detailed as their deep philosophic thinking goes.

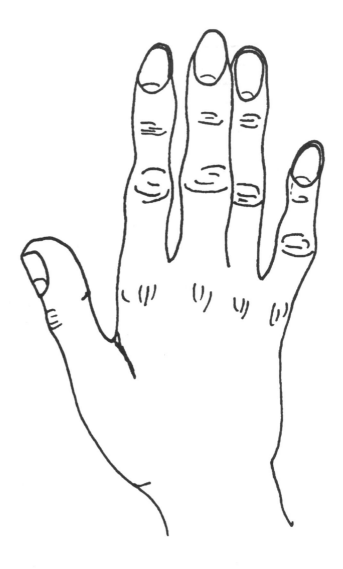

Fig. 14 The Philosophic Hand.

Another aspect of the philosophic hand is that, although they are inclined to be silent, careful and analytical in their expressions and thoughts, they possess great abilities to get involved in long hours of discussion well into the night. Therefore, if you deal with someone who possesses the philosophic hand and you want to avoid an argument, you can either agree with the point of view of the possessor of this hand, or do not enter into it in the first place.

Throughout history there were many great philosophers and leaders who possessed the philosophic hand. The book: *Cheiro's Language of the Hand*, mentions people such as Abraham Lincoln, Cardinal Newman, Cardinal Manning and others. During my life, I have met many major clairvoyants all over the world. Many of them had the philosophic hand. Their love to discuss the unknown is one of the characteristics of their philosophic hand.

THE CONIC HAND

The shape of the conic hand (Fig. 15) is, as its name implies, a conus. It is also referred to as creative hand, artistic hand, or cone-shaped hand. The base of this hand, next to the wrist, is wider than the width of the palm next to the base of the fingers. The fingers form a tapered cone at their tips. The basal phalanges are wider than their tips. In a way, we can say that the conic hand is the opposite of the spatulate hand. The conic hand is, usually, a soft and fleshy hand type, but it can be narrow in shape as well. Although it is never as narrow as the psychic hand (described later in this chapter), still it lacks the power and persistence of the wider hand types such as that of the square hand.

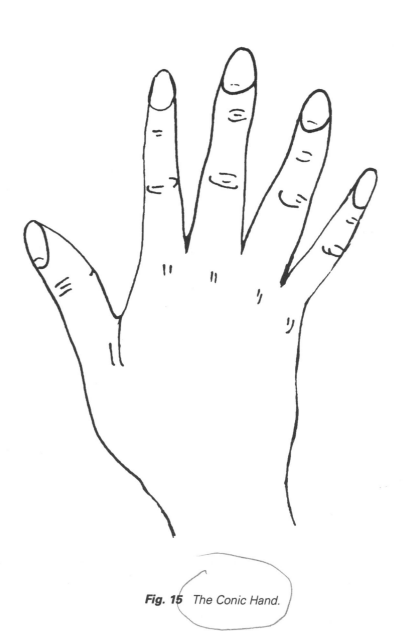

Fig. 15 *The Conic Hand.*

The basic characteristic of the conic hand is sensitiveness. The possesor of this hand is moody, open to impressions, influence of intuition and impulses. He/she is usually a weak achiever who is more inclined toward enjoyment, pleasure, love of beauty, luxuries, art and imagination.

Many times the conic hand is also referred to as the artistic hand which may imply that the owners of the conic hands are great artists or possess beautiful hands. My observation shows that those who have the conic hand are esthetes, love beauty and art, but are not necessarily artists. They may be good consumers of art, but they just lack the power and strength to achieve the things that the square or spatulate hands can do, unless their hands are firm, wider in the base, and the veins are prominent on the back of their hands.

In understanding the concept of the types of personalties according to the shape of their hands, we must remember that the wider the hand the stronger the personality is.

If the conic hand has knotty fingers, where the joints are well-pronounced, it indicates a combination of the conic and philosophic characteristics which lead to a more philosophical thinking.

THE PSYCHIC (SENSITIVE) HAND

The psychic hand (Fig. 16) is the most sensitive type of hand. The shape of the hand is delicate, thin and fragile. The fingers are usually long and thin with almond-shaped fingernails. This hand is considered to be the most beautiful of all hand types, but also the most impractical one. The owners of this hand, usually, dream a lot but achieve very little. They live on the mental and spiritual planes rather than on the material one.

The name of this hand denotes its tendency to living in their own psychic world. It does not mean that those who possess this kind of hand are real psychics. It does imply that they are too sensitive and therefore live in different dimensions. In the extreme cases, we can find these people in mental institutions. Many of them, young or adult, usually live with their parents. Sometimes they seem to find it so painful in dealing with the cruel reality of this world that they prefer to isolate themselves. They may stay in their room and avoid social life or any career at all. The outside world seems too rough for them to handle. They feel that they are the victims of life (many times it is true). People who live with them feel the urge to help them because they are so weak and delicate (males and females).

We need to consider that by being passive, they become indirectly in control of others. It is a powerful way of convincing their surroundings to do more for them and support them. For many others it seems a weakness, and those who possess this hand type do feel weak, helpless and in constant need of help.

The thinner and narrower the hand, the weaker the person is. It is more often seen in females than in males. If we consider the *yin* and *yang* characteristics and symbols we can understand this fact (see "Yin and Yang" concept in the following pages). The ultimate *yin* represents the female, while the ultimate *yang* represents the male or its characteristics.

When the hand feels stronger but the shape is still of a psychic hand, it may denote more practical qualities. Such people may be dealing with the esoteric or mental aspects of life including art and beauty. When we see this type of hand, we get the reaction or feeling of a person who cares for the welfare of the world, justice and the more ethical aspects of life.

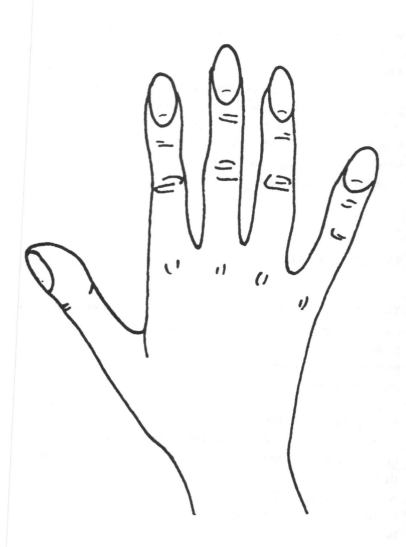

Fig. 16 *The Psychic Hand.*

Those who possess the psychic hand are excellent for conversation, poetry, songs, music and storytelling. Their imagination is great. They also tend to educate themselves in the many aspects of life. Therefore, they are very interesting to talk to.

As Palm Therapists, when we encounter people who do possess the psychic hand, it can be helpful to show them, or recommend to them, hand exercises to strengthen their hands. It is interesting to note that by changing the structure of this hand we do change the character as well. Of course, the younger the person is, the better results we shall have.

THE MIXED HAND

The mixed hand (Fig. 17) is the most common hand of all. As the name implies, it is a mix of a few hand types. The most common combinations of hand types are of two shapes which are close to each other in terms of characteristics. For example, the elementary palm with the square fingers, the square palm with conic fingers, or square palm with philosophic fingers, also the conic palm with square fingers, or the spatulate palm with square, conic or philosophical fingers. There are endless possibilities of mixed hand combinations. There can be a combination of two, three or more hand types when each finger is of a different type, but once we understand the characteristics of each one of the six basic hand types, we can figure out how to analyze the mixed hand.

When observing the palms remember, the wider the palm, the stronger the personality is, the slenderer the palm, the more sensitive the person is.

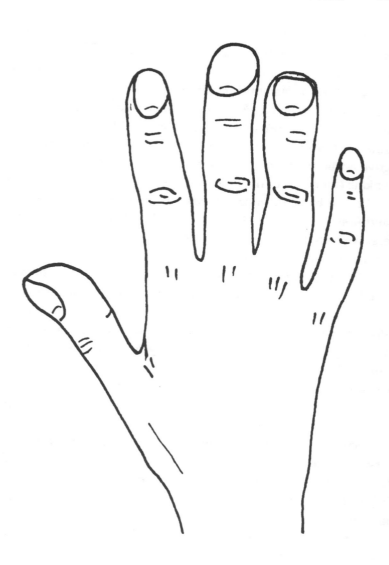

Fig. 17 *The Mixed Hand.*

In regard to the fingers, each type (conic, square, knotty and spatulate) represents a different perception of life, from the intuitive to the cognitive thinker, from the philosopher to the practical creator. As a rule, short fingers represent a more practical personality and a less theoretical approach, while long fingers represent a more intellectual style but a less practical attitude. Square/spatulate fingers are the more technical and active, while the pointed or knotty fingers represent theoretical thinking (more about the fingers in the chapter 9).

In the basic diagnosis, focus on the general shape of the hand first, next on the shape of the palm, then, that of the fingers. We have to ignore other features at first, such as the lines, fingernails, hairs and so on,

To examine the hand, check it from the root to the top, i.e, from the base of the hand next to the wrist to the tip of the fingers. Like a tree, more changes will take place in its upper parts. Fingers, especially, may undergo changes according to the changes in the personality and physical condition. On the other side, we have to remember that all components of the hand are important in the process of diagnosis.

Now, with these rules, you can figure out how to observe the various possibilities of the mixed hand.

Some conflicting combinations may occur, but they are very rare and you usually will not encounter them. If you do, you may probably find out that the owner of this hand was diagnosed as mentally ill. For example, the elementary type of palm with psychic type of fingers. The elementary hand is heavy, thick, strong and of a hot-tempered type (extreme *yang* type, see below). While the psychic hand is extremely delicate and weak (extreme *yin* type, see below). They do not match together, but, when you find such a combination the hand looks so irregular that you cannot ignore it.

In my whole career of observing thousands of hands of my students and clients, I found only one single case like that. The female was 28 years old, mentally retarded, with no ability to take care of herself. The hands looked as if they had undergone a deformation; a very wide palm of hand, thick and heavy (elementary type), with five thin, weak fingers separated from each other (psychic type). She was obese with no signs of femininity development. In the literature, I didn't find such a combination at all, but at least I saw it in reality.

YIN AND YANG, ANOTHER APPROACH TO HAND CLASSIFICATION

Another way to classify the seven hand types, including the mixed hand, is according to the *yin* and *yang* aspect of the Chinese tradition.

Since part of my findings in Palm Therapy are also based on the Chinese philosophy and medical theory, I developed an integration of *yin* and *yang* concept to the seven hand types. The *yin* and *yang* theory can be a basis for any other theory or approach and there is nothing new in the yin and yang basics. The innovation applies to the application for the various hand types.

Another classification, a more detailed one, could be by the *Five Elements* of the Chinese traditional philosophy plus their *yin* and *yang* properties. This can give us ten different hand types instead of seven. Since the purpose of this work is Palm Therapy, I didn't include the Five Elements theory of the hand types in this work.

The yin and *yang* are the symbols of the universe in the Chinese philosophy. The theories of *yin* and *yang* were the way to view nature in ancient China. According to some authorities these theories were established over 2000 years ago, and according to others, over 5000 years ago. The exact age or the foundation of this concept is unknown, as are the roots found in the various legends of the Chinese concepts about the world (macro- and microcosmos).

The theory of *yin* and *yang* indicates that every subject or phenomenon in the universe consists of two opposite aspects— the *yin* and the *yang*. They are in conflict but depend on each other, supporting each other and transforming from one object to the other. If we give it some thought, we would find out that in every *yin* there is a *yang*, and in every *yang* there is a *yin*. This relationship between the two is the universal law of the material, energy, and metaphysical worlds. The *yin* and *yang* is the principle and source of existence of meridians and the root cause for the flowering and perishing of things.

The ancient Chinese sages applied the theory of *yin* and *yang* and the other theories of the Five Elements as a way to understand nature, the human body and mind. This theory was so complete and sufficient that it holds until today. In today's schools of Chinese medicine and acupuncture in China and in the U.S.A. these concepts are being taught as the basic theory to understand acupuncture and its various components. The theory of *yin* and *yang* is extensively used in traditional Chinese medicine and is the basis for the explanation of the physiology and pathology of the human body. It also serves as a major guide in diagnosis and treatment in the clinical work.

Chinese chiromants use the same principles for analysis and fortunetelling.

The following table lists part of the characteristics and aspects of the *yin* and *yang*:

YIN	YANG
earth	heaven
female	male
night	day
moon	sun
low	high
heaviness	lightness
falling tendency	rising tendency
movement inward	movement outward
relative stasis	clear action
interior	exterior
front	back
lower section	upper section
bones	skin
inner organs	outer organs
blood	*chi* /energy
inhibition	stimulation
deficiency	excess
negative	positive
dark	light
weak	strong

Fig. 18   *The symbol of the Yin and Yang— the unity of opposites.*

The *yin* and *yang* can be summarized as the law of the unity of opposites (Fig. 18).

Personalities, as well as nature, are classified according to this concept. Each person is recognized by the way he/she looks, acts and thinks.

The Ultimate Yang Type of Personality

The most *yang* type can be a person who probably does not exist. In reality only few of these characteristics are present in one person. From all hand types the elementary hand is closer to his characteristics. He is a male with all the masculine properties. He has a very hot temper, his behavior is brutal, violent, full of energy and quick to fight. His blood pressure is high and a dark reddish color is dominant in him. Usually he does not take care of his body. He has the ability to think or focus only on one subject at a time.

He could go as deep as his IQ permits, but only in one profession. He is the classic extreme narrow-minded one. His main concerns are for the basic needs in life. Everything with him is in excess. He eats a lot, he is busy with sex and conducts physical activity above the average. He is quick to act physically and mentally towards any stimulation. He may be very educated in his field and totally focused on his goals.

The *yang* quality is like the sun, always hot, active, expanding, radiating and entering all of his surroundings. The *yang* type of person acts the same. Since this type of person possesses some of the characteristics of the square hand type we could think that he may own this kind of hand, but he usually possesses an elementary hand type. While being too *yang* he is lacking the refinement which the square hand has. (Refinement is a *yin* property.)

Working and acting is a *yang* characteristic, while sleeping is a *yin* one, hence, the ultimate *yang* type will not sleep at all. Therefore it doesn't exist.

The Ultimate Yin Type of Personality

As in the *yang* type, the extreme *yin* type should be someone who does not exist, or if very close to this type, probably has spent one's life in a mental institution. In terms of hand type, it should be similar in shape to that of the extreme psychic hand—very thin, whitish or pale and with a transparent type of skin. The veins can be seen, but they are never prominent on the skin. The hand is smooth and extremely soft, flexible, cold, lacking vitality and energy. It is narrow, weak and very fragile. The mount of

Venus is extremely small. The head line curves into the mount of Luna in extreme. (You will read about the mounts in the next chapter.)

The ultimate *yin* type usually belongs to a female. By nature, this female lacks in energy. She mainly lives in her imagination and is unable to perform a practical work. This type of person is very thin and never mature enough to support herself. Mental help and certain exercises to strengthen some muscles of this hand, including other techniques of Palm Therapy, may change the situation only if the person who possesses this type of hand is willing to cooperate at all.

As mentioned above, I divided the hand types according to the *yin* and *yang*. The following scale presents the classification of the different types of hands according to their *yin* and *yang* characteristics. Numbers 0 to +10 represent the yang characteristics, where the ultimate *yang* is represented as number +10 and the ultimate *yin* is represented as number -10. In practice, ultimate *yang* or *yin* personalities do not really exist, therefore, number +8 can represent a very *yang* personality, or the elementary hand, and number -8 in the scale will represent an extreme *yin* personality or the psychic hand (Fig. 19).

The elementary hand which represents extreme *yang* appears almost at one end of the scale. Then comes the square hand, and the spatulate hand. In the *yin* part we can see first, the philosophic hand, then the conic hand, then toward the other end of the scale, we can find the psychic hand which represents extreme *yin* characteristics. The mixed hand can be considered, in many cases, as the balance of the *yin* and *yang* characteristics; it is found in the middle of the scale.

Different authorities subdivide the various personalities into ten different categories, some into seven, others into three

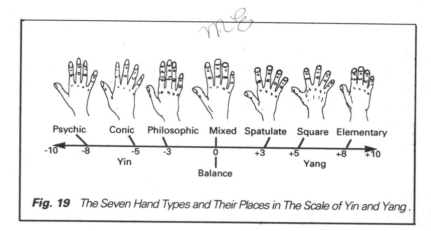

Fig. 19 *The Seven Hand Types and Their Places in The Scale of Yin and Yang.*

or four. Remember that there is not a real classification of the *yin* or *yang* types of hand. It is only a tool for easy study and comparison of the various hand types. There are no good or bad types. Also, each hand type may be a male or a female. A balance is in accordance with the personality.

CAN WE CHANGE THE GENERAL SHAPE OF THE HAND?

The general shape of the hand goes through some major changes from childhood on. It usually continues to change slowly throughout one's lifetime. As an adult your hands are different from the basic shape of hand you had as a child. It gets harder, more practical and usually with better abilities to perform in life. You may wonder what is being changed first, your character or your hand shape? I believe that both processes may naturally occur simultanously, and each change influences our entire future.

The same as in your body, you may be able to shape some parts or the general shape of your hand by practicing certain hand exercises. There is a way to gradually modify the hand type with Palm Therapy's special instruction and exercises. It applies to the hands the same as it applies to the whole body, although you may not realize it because you use your hands and fingers daily and you are not bothered by extra fat to burn or lean muscles to develop in that area. But through specific exercises you may be able to initiate certain basic, desired characteristics in your personality. Whether enhancing the flexibility in the *yang* type of hands by stretching and flexing movements of the fingers and palm, or the opposite, strengthening the weak *yin* type of hands by gradually exercising all fingers to develop the muscles of the whole hand and widen the palm. The process is usually slow, but any change in the hand, consequently, indicates a change in one's character, too.

To the certified Palm Therapist:
Before suggesting any exercises through Palm Therapy, make sure that your clients understand the process of the gradual change which may take place in their personalities and, eventually, in their lives. Ask your clients to consult first with their healthcare providers in order to make sure that their physical condition allows them to conduct repetitive exercises of the palms and fingers for few minutes once a day for a period of months or years, depending upon the case.

CHAPTER 8

The Mounts: Reflection of the Various Aspects of the Personality

The fleshy part of our palm is formed of muscles and the fascia as well as other components responsible for the elevated or depressed shapes found on our palms. These topographic shapes vary in size and radiation from person to person and represent specific characteristics of the personality. In palmistry these areas are called "mounts" although some areas in the hand which are referred to as "mounts" may be flat or even depressed.

The mounts were traditionally named (Fig.20) after animals or Greek goddesses. Later on, according to the astrological planets and their characteristics which were attributed to each mount.

The following are the names of traditional and new mounts

1. Earth	6. Lower Mars	11. Luna
2. Jupiter	7. Middle Mars	12. Upper Uranus
3. Saturn	8. Upper Mars	13. Lower Uranus
4. Apollo	9. Venus	14. Pluto
5. Mercury	10. Neptune	

The work to develop Palm Therapy and the counseling of people from all cultures and walks of life enlightened new areas of discovery to me in the field of palmistry as well as the human mind. Now I'm going to share it with you. In the following pages I'll take you through the harmony and relationship of the various mounts and their special ways of describing your life and personality. I'll also introduce you to the new mounts which I named: Earth, upper Uranus, lower Uranus and Pluto (Fig. 21 and Fig. 22). They supply us with vital information about inevitable addictive patterns in our lives which have to do with our survival as human beings. This information, when understood, can serve as a tool that can help many people all over the world.

You will also learn some ways of reshaping your life, talents and personality through the stimulation of the various mounts. The mounts on the palms of the hands represent, similar to the hand types, the personality, preferences, behavior and modalities in one's life. The difference is that the seven hand types show us the personality in general, while the mounts represent each aspect of the personality in particular including the needs of the individual.

In the past some researchers used only one of these

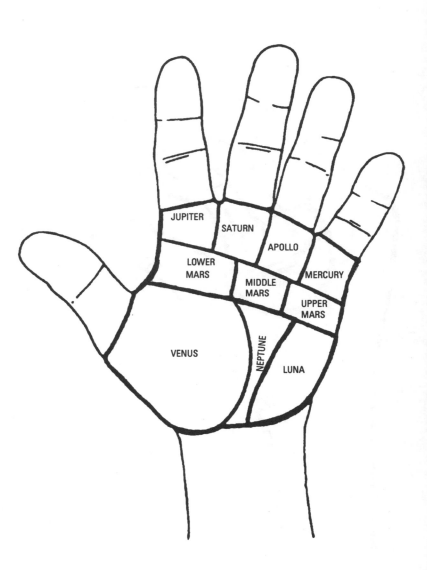

Fig. 20 The Traditional Mounts.

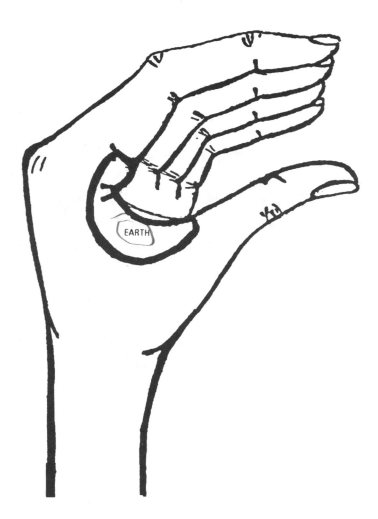

Fig. 21 *The new mount on the radial side of the hand:*
The Mount of Earth.

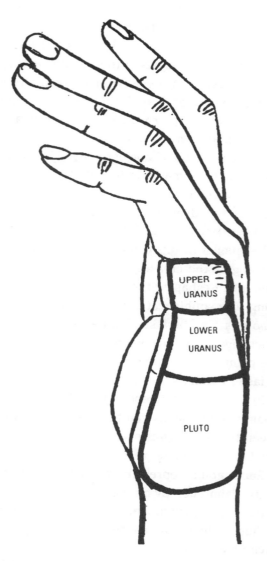

Fig. 22 *The new mounts on the ulnar side of the hand:*
The Mounts of Upper Uranus, Lower Uranus and Pluto.

modalities to diagnose the characters. Since both modalities have their own justification in evaluating reality, I recommend the inclusion of both observations for diagnosing. First to generally examine through the basic seven hand types, then to have a thorough analysis of the mounts as they appear on the hand. I believe that these two methods, although originating back in the Victorian Period, still have their validity.

In the last chapter we covered the seven basic hand types and their characteristics. Through various exercises you may gradually change the shape of the hand. A change in the general shape of the hand may lead to a change in your personality and the way you perceive life.

I didn't go deeply into my findings on the reshaping of the hand types because of the slowness in achieving results and the fact that similar results can be achieved faster when stimulating and changing the creases/lines of the palms or the activity of the mounts. Reshaping the hand takes special instructions and training. The sophisticated methods of reshaping the quality of the mounts may be faster and easier to gain, thus leading to deep changes in your personality. The stimulation of the lines of the palms, which is the main topic of this book, can lead to even faster results.

In terms of effectiveness, the stimulation of the mounts on the palms of the hands can be ranked somewhat in the middle between the hand types exercises and the creases/lines stimulation, but when changes are made they are significant.

Each mount represents a main characteristic of the personality. Palm Therapy on the mounts can increase or decrease the intensity of each mount's energy and its special characteristics, thus leading to a change in personality, thinking patterns, behavior and mood.

For those of you who may be interested in this profound

part of Palm Therapy I included at the end of this chapter a brief method of how to activate the various mounts.

I hope that by the time you finish this chapter you will gain some knowledge of mastering various parts of your personality and developing new areas in your life through stimulation of the mounts.

If you are familiar with various alternative healing methods you may wonder whether a stimulation on a region (mount) of the hand activates some acupuncture/acupressure or reflexology areas?

Yes. It may be so, but Palm Therapy is applied differently. Although it works on overcoming allergy symptoms, and can affect the well-being of body and mind, it is mainly concentrated on the mental changes and abilities of the personality rather than on the physical relief or stimulation such as is done while applying reflexology, acupuncture or acupressure.

As you will see during the reading of this book there are a few differences that were mentioned earlier. The main ones can be summarized as follows:

a. The stimulation through Palm Therapy works mainly on the balancing, healing and strengthening of personality, behavior patterns and many emotional, cognitive and spiritual aspects, while in reflexology, shiatsu, acupressure or acupuncture the main focus is on the balancing of physical disorders, and to a lesser degree of mental disorder and not at all into achieving success in life.

b. The focus of Palm Therapy is on visual lines and shapes or mounts as seen in the hand, rather than feeling the sensitive areas or specific points such as in reflexology, shiatsu or acupressure/acupuncture.

c. With Palm Therapy you imprint a line until it can be clearly seen (see "Important Notice" at the beginning of the book and throughout the text). There is no such attempt in the other healing methods mentioned above.

d. The direction of the stimulation on the hand which is mainly the imprinting of a longitudinal line or a very light-touch circular stimulation to specific areas is totally different from what is done in acupressure, reflexology, or shiatsu, for example.

LOCATING THE MOUNTS

In order to stimulate or reshape the various mounts for achieving results, it was necessary for me to define their properties, range of influence and their borders.

The mounts on the palm have, traditionally, very definite and clear borders and characteristics, but according to my observation this is not so. There is some overlapping and influence which is carried from one mount to its neighboring mounts. I came to this conclusion by checking literally thousands of hands and comparing the data obtained from what their owners expressed about themselves, their history, their feelings, behavior and thought patterns.

Also, I went further to check boundaries and the center of each mount with other methods such as the stimulation of the mounts in various ways. Then I examined to see the changes in feelings immediately after the stimulation, then after a week's time, a month's time, and a year's time of therapy. I found, as mentioned earlier, that the boundaries of the mounts are not clear, and there are some overlapping areas between the mounts. The energy of the hand seems to be in a constant flow which is reflected in the mounts as well as in our moods and personalities.

I continued with different types of observations. Among them the use of a pendulum, very much as it is done with Radionics. (Radionics and similar diagnostic methods are not accepted by Western scientific medicine as valid diagnostic or treatment methods. Radionics is an esoteric alternative type of diagnosis and treatment which uses the pendulum as a tool to verify and diagnose diseases and problems. For more information about Radionics please refer to the book: *Report on Radionics The Science of the Future,* by Russell W. Edward 1979, Neville Spearman Publ., Great Britain, and to other books on Radionics in our Bibliography.)

I went through all this checking in order to have an additional point of view while defining the borders of the various mounts. According to my findings the real borders of the mounts vary from person to person. There is no clear line which cuts between the mounts. In some people the separation, or the imaginary border line between the mounts, is far from those described in traditional palmistry. In my drawings I still continue with the traditional borders of the mounts simply because in this way it is easier for the beginner to remember the location of the mounts. In reality, I recommend to go case by case and find the actual borders and the center of each mount before applying Palm Therapy for the activation of the characteristics represented by the mount.

Before we continue with the description of the characteristics of each mount and its location, let's define the quality of a mount:

> -A weak mount is indicated by flatness of the fleshy part which normally can be elevated as well, and by a pale color of the area of that mount.
>
> -A strong mount is indicated by a well-developed raised region of the fleshy part of the mount and is characterized by a reddish or darker color compared to the surrounding mounts.
>
> -For those areas that we call mounts, but which are actually planes or valleys, such as the middle Mars (also called the plane of Mars), we should pay attention to the color of the region. Pale or white represents weak activity, while reddish or darker color denotes a stronger activity of the area.
>
> -The viscosity and the texture of the skin should be considered; high viscosity means a stronger mount, low viscosity indicates a poor mount.

Now, let's learn about each mount.

THE MOUNT OF EARTH

Throughout the years, the sides of the hands were given very little consideration in palmistry. My interest in these areas started

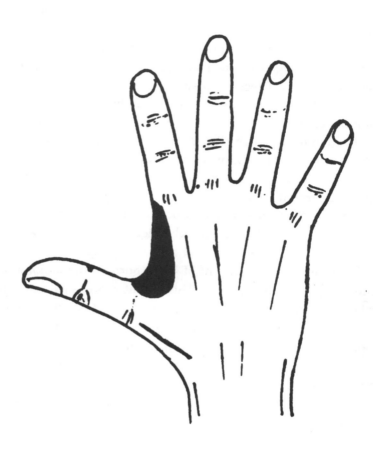

Fig. 23 *The Mount of Earth.*

with the work of releasing allergies and addictive patterns through Palm Therapy. Allergies are represented in the ulnar border of the palm nearest to the wrist. By examining the ulnar border of the palm you can get some vital information about various aspects of life, such as positive or destructive addictive patterns not excluding love, attachment, belief system and addictive behavior patterns. These are manifested by the new mounts on the ulnar side of the palm which are actually influenced by the mount of Earth.

The mount of Earth (Fig. 23) is located in the outermost radial border of the palm, in the folded skin of the hand between the thumb and the pointer. Its area can clearly be seen (when you stretch your thumb) as a moon shape that occupies the area of the folded skin. Its border on the back and the side of the hand is where the dermatoglyphics end, as well as at the basal crease line of pointer and at the basal phalanx of the thumb. In the palm, the mount of Earth borders the mounts of Jupiter and that of lower Mars. This mount represents the prenatal period which may leave a long-lasting effect on one's life.

While continuing with the pattern of hand documentation, I realized that the initial imprinting of life, as a fetus before birth, is manifested in the same direction of the general flow of energy or the influences that shape the hand; from the radial to the ulnar side of the hand and from the proximal to the distal part of the hand.

The flow of energy from the radial side continues to the ulnar side. Then it parts into two. Part of the energy encircles through the back of the hand to return to the radial border, and the rest of the energy flows from the ulnar side back into the center of the palm somewhere between the mounts of Saturn and Apollo, which then radiate out of this area. This forms a main energy center, or what we know as the secondary *chakra* (center of energy) of the heart *chakra*. It increases the energy in the mount of middle Mars which affects various so-called paranormal phenomena such as bioenergy (healing) through the hands, telekinesis, etc.

Another energy stream, which flows in a longitudinal direction, radiates along with the acupuncture energy paths, the meridians. This energy flows from the proximal region towards the fingertips. Then it continues on the back of the hand from the fingertips towards the wrist, shoulders and further.

Another subcurrent of this longitudinal flow, not described in acupuncture, returns from the fingertips towards the center of the palm. This focuses on the center of the palm with some additional deeper currents towards the wrist.

The various main flows of energy eventually form the *netlike energy pathways* of the palms of the hands.

Since, traditionally, the whole palm was mainly categorized by the various planets, I continued the tradition by naming the new areas as planets.

In astrology the planet Earth is not considered as a planet. But since it represents the prenatal life, or the real birth of the person, the name Earth mount or mount of Earth is the most appropriate one (although the area that represents this mount does not really look like a mount). As mentioned in the Bible (Genesis): "And the Lord God formed Man of the dust of the ground". In the Hebrew language the word "ground" also is called "Earth".

The mount of Earth represents the center of the more primitive brain and the limbic system. It represents the total self-content, self-interest, self-care, self-centeredness life of the fetus. Tremendous changes and influences occur during the prenatal period. They are marked with the various transverse or longitudinal lines seen on this mount. The lines appear and disappear, demonstrating the various changes and influences of the other basic parts of the brain. The first stage of the development of the fetus represents the whole process of evolution of the human race; from a few cells to the full complex of a person. These changes and rapid growth hold the attention and energy of the fetus at those stages. Therefore, we can see on the Earth mount events which occurred to the individual during prenatal time. We don't see trends of personality or character. These are marked on the palm of the hand at various places.

The prenatal period is an extremely important one. It determines the person's self-assurance, self-secureness, self-contentedness and the feelings of being loved and cared for. This period is responsible for the setting of a lifetime addictive or attachment patterns which can appear on all three levels of existence.

-emotional/spiritual

-cognitive/behavioral

-physical(substance)/ chemical

These three levels will be widely discussed later in the chapter dealing with the mounts which appear on the outermost ulnar side of the hand: the mounts of upper Uranus, lower Uranus and Pluto.

If the fetus perceives the feelings of love and a secure environment and receives all his physical needs in the womb as well, then he/she grows there in a relaxed atmosphere that helps him/her to acquire optimum development, self-esteem and self-worth. After birth these babies will usually exhibit normal, positive growth patterns. They will consume and behave in a moderate and well-balanced way through life, also when encountering stressful situations.

If the fetus does not have all his/her needs in a relaxed and safe environment due to his/her mother's environment and stressful life, his/her behavior will be more desperate. After birth this individual will tend to be more insecure and his/her needs to protect oneself on the various levels of existence may be stronger than those who had a better start in the prenatal life. Individuals who did not receive all their needs in the prenatal period will have various degrees of insecurity, with a tendency to consume more, save more, and look for more protection during life. The basic feeling of "not enough" may be carried for the lifetime.

The mount of Earth also represents many diseases and disorders that are attributed to genetic or prenatal factors. One of the main assumptions is that by conducting researches on twins who grow up in different families, we can check some specific genetic factors. Assuming that if both twins have the same disorder or disease, it is an indication of some genetic, hereditary factor. But, can it be that those so-called genetic/hereditary disorders actually originated during a stressful prenatal period?

My assumption is that both cases are possible. Whether some occurrence happened during the prenatal life to one or both twins at the same time, or it was a genetic predisposition of some kind, both are represented in the mount of Earth.

The initial events, as a fetus, are described in the Earth mount. The upper section which stretches from the basal crease line of the second finger to the beginning of the head line (the proximal transverse palmar crease or an imaginary continuation of it) represents the brain, thoughts, feelings and emotions of the fetus, and events which influence his/her personality or this part of its body. The rest of the body is marked below the head line and covers the whole section of the folded skin between this line and the thumb's metacarpal. It represents various aspects of health and events in the life of the fetus.

Question: Can we reverse hereditary, genetic or prenatal disorders with the help of Palm Therapy on the mount of Earth?

Answer: No. It is unlikely, but some emotional traumas which were passed by stressful periods or situations can be alleviated by Palm Therapy as it is also done with the help of other alternative therapies such as hypnosis and past-life regression. (We assume that the fetus's prolonged dreaming states documented by rapid eye movement, REM, associated with a dreaming state has to do with its own growth and development, current events of his/her mother and may be his/her own memories of previous lives events.)

When practicing Palm Therapy on the mount of Earth, a special attention should be applied to some of the transverse lines other than the beginning of the head or life lines (the proximal transverse palmar crease and the radial longitudinal palmar crease) which extend to the palmar side of the hand. The little transverse lines (Fig. 24) on the mount of Earth demonstrate the influence of addictive patterns, stressful situations and emotional traumas that passed from the mother to the fetus. This part is of special importance when dealing with individuals whom you know from their history that their mothers were on drugs or alcohol, had accidents or experienced stressful situations during their pregnancies. These could affect the embryo/fetus at any prenatal period from 0-9 months and later in life. (Note, in the medical terminoly, the child in the utero from the third mount to birth is called *fetus*. Prior to that period it is referred to as an *embryo*.)

In some of the more stubborn cases of emotional disturbance or self-sabotage, the results dramatically changed once I imprinted longitudinal lines on the Earth mount where the transverse lines appear.

To analyze or to apply Palm Therapy to this area, the thumb should be opened maximum (90^0 or wider) so that the

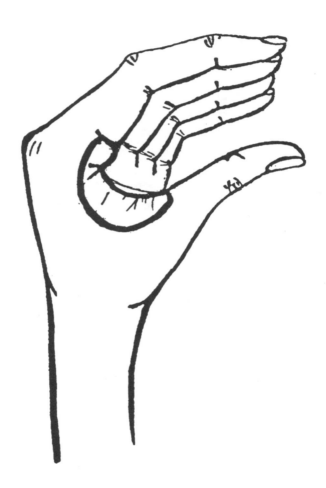

Fig. 24 *The little transverse lines on the Mount of Earth.*

folded skin between the thumb and the Jupiter finger is fully stretched and enables us to view the whole mount.

The thicker and larger the Earth mount is, the better start in life the individual had. The more transverse lines on this part that an individual possesses, the more difficulties were experienced as a fetus. The deeper towards the back of the hand these transverse lines stretch, the younger was the fetus when these stressful situations occurred.

As I have mentioned above, the fetus is totally self-centered. The fetus can not distinguish between traumatic events of his/her mother which influence its emotional and physical development in the womb and later during life. While checking with hypnosis, I found that there is a possibility that the fetus has very basic extra sensory perception (ESP). According to this suggestion, the fetus may be able to identify him/herself with various emotions and events that his/her mother goes through. The link between the mother and the fetus is more than just the caring of the fetus in the womb and the feeding through the umbilical cord. Her feelings and thoughts about the fetus and about herself or the surrounding world affect the fetus's emotions during the prenatal period. The mother's thinking patterns, as well as some sounds or music, may have long or lasting effects after birth. It is difficult to follow the exact root of these marked events on the mount of Earth which are also marked on the dermatoglyphics patterns. But the importance of this short period of nine prenatal months to our lives is demonstrated by the relative large area of this mount. Although this area may seem to be small, there is no other place in the palm of the hand that shows so much in detail for such a short period of time.

The birth is indicated on the edge of the folded skin between the thumb and Jupiter finger. After birth the focus passes to the palm of the hand.

The border between the back of the hand and the dermatoglyphics represents the first months of existence or the fertilization process. It is not clear according to the hand observation. It may indicate that the real life, as we know it today, is not clear-cut in the fetus's life but a process of some time, which from that point on the self-awareness, or if you wish, the soul, enters the body of the fetus. I assume that this happens at about 4-6 weeks of prenatal age.

What lies behind the dermatoglyphics border towards the back of the palm is a question to which I have dedicated a lot of time. The actual skin patterns of the back of the hand have some minor lines and the skin patterns remind one of a netlike pattern. Is it the imprinting, in a different format, of a previous life/lives? It is likely so. More research should be done in this unknown area in order to find out past-lives events and how they are connected to present lives. Our current knowledge about the back of the hand is mainly based on reflexology, traditional acupuncture, Koryo hand acupuncture and the enormous netlike meridians. These reflect some physical and mental aspects, but we still miss the personal/event story which the back of the hand has to tell. My conclusion on this topic is not yet definite. I will dedicate more research to it and publish the conclusion when I complete it.

THE MOUNT OF JUPITER

The mount of Jupiter (Fig. 25) is located under the finger of Jupiter (pointer). The mount of Jupiter represents the parts of the personality that drive the person to interact with others, either on a social basis, work or activity. If this mount is weak, it represents a tendency towards withdrawal from society by iso-

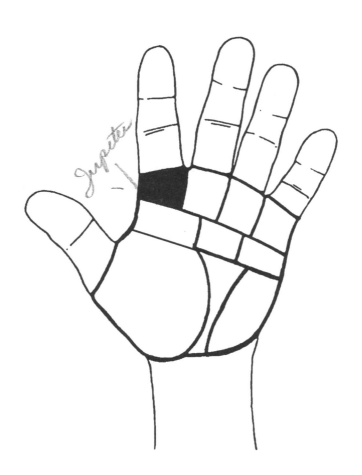

Fig. 25 *The Mount of Jupiter.*

lating oneself. If the mount is a little stronger, the person interacts with others, but on a passive basis. When this mount is well-developed and of reddish color it represents a high intensity with strong characteristics of the mount which denotes high interactions with others. Such a person is a leader in a certain field or of high rank among his/her peers.

Traditional palmistry recognizes this part and look at the mount of Jupiter as the leader's mount.

According to my findings, this mount may change its intensity and influence many times over one's lifetime according to the changes in interaction with others.

Jupiter mount is the explorer of others and their reaction towards oneself. It is the self-esteem part in relation to being accepted or not accepted by others, and the need to socialize, to influence or be influenced by people with higher intensity. It represents the ability to give and accept authority.

Other aspects of this mount are satisfaction from the outside world including sex, enjoyment of eating and drinking, stimulating activities and gratification in general.

It seems to me that after birth and the interaction with the surroundings, the young person continues his/her needs for others to satisfy the many levels of interest and activity. It is in this mount that we see social activity. In general, there is more information in each mount because the personality and its segments are compounded by layers of different activities and needs. Sometimes the underlying traits of the personality in that mount are the opposite to the ones we see. The more deeply we go, the more we may detect different aspects of each mount's characteristics, including, of course, the mount of Jupiter.

Question: Can we increase characteristics such as leadership, self-esteem, self-value and the feeling of being loved by others—the qualities represented by this mount?

Answer: Yes. With Palm Therapy we can increase the intensity of the mount and, in doing so, increase the qualities which are manifested by this mount. A change in the quality, size and color of the mount may naturally occur also if you work in methods other than Palm Therapy to increase your self-esteem, leadership ability and other characteristics which are represented by this mount. Palm Therapy accelerates these characteristics via a direct stimulation of the mount.

By stimulating the mount with a circular, light massage with *yin* or *yang* mode, according to the case, we can experience a great release of inhibitions, blockages or negative feelings that have prevented the optimum manifestations of qualities represented by the mount of Jupiter. (You will learn how to stimulate the mounts at the end of this chapter, see also Section Four.)

THE MOUNT OF SATURN

The mount of Saturn (Fig. 26) is located right under the middle finger which is the finger of Saturn. While the mount of Jupiter represents the person's interaction with the world, the influences one receives from or gives to others in order to enjoy life, the mount of Saturn represents another aspect of the personality—the dealing with oneself; the interaction is between the "ID", the "Ego" and the "Super Ego", according to S. Freud. In other words, the constant fight and negotiation between the "I want it here and now" approach, and the various social conventions, goals, orientations and demands of society to which we adapt, so we can be, or consider ourselves as better people.

The mount of Saturn deals with the belief systems; the way we see and accept ourselves and how we perceive the sur-

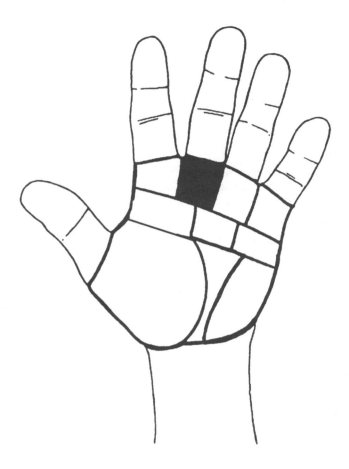

Fig.26   *The Mount of Saturn.*

rounding world. This mount is related, therefore, to the issues of soberness, wisdom, satisfaction, love and joy as well as to negative thoughts and emotions such as depression, sadness, anger, hate, superiority/inferiority complex and frustration.

The mount of Saturn also represents the philosophical approach to life; religious aspects of the personality, esoteric and metaphysical parts of life. This mount, when well-balanced and strong, represents a lot of satisfaction. Deficiency of this mount has been detected in many of those who suffer from depression and sadness. Therefore, I believe it is important to stimulate the mount of Saturn if nothing else that we do works.

Personally, I prefer to start the reinforcement of positive qualities of the personality and emotions through the lines of the palm, simply because of the fast results we can achieve. While stimulating some of the lines on the palms, the mount of Saturn becomes more radiant and intense even without any direct stimulation of the mount itself. This is another way to see the interaction between the various components in our hand.

THE MOUNT OF APOLLO/ SUN/ SUCCESS

The mount of Apollo (Fig. 27) is also known as the mount of Sun or the mount of success. It is located under the finger of Apollo (the ring finger) and is the base for great qualities and characteristics. It represents the stage of fulfillment and it is the seat of success, achievements, brightness and the ability to enjoy life and its beauty. Traditionally, talents of art were known to be part of the main characteristics of this mount.

When checking the flow of energy of the entire palm, I noticed that most of the energies flow toward the center of the

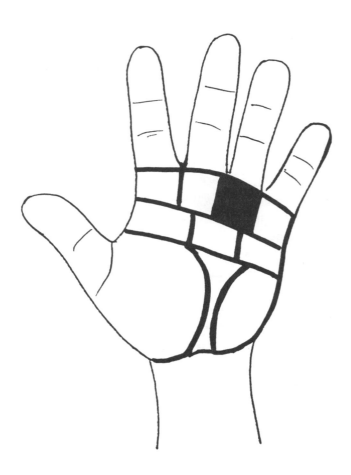

Fig. 27 *The mount of Apollo/Sun/Success.*

hands. The palmar flexure creases are not showing it clearly, since they run horizontally from the radial side of the hand toward the ulnar side or cross the palm in a longitudinal way.

Under the fingers of Saturn and Apollo are the deep longitudinal areas. They are not shaped like mounts or elevations, but regardless, these areas which include the mount of Apollo and the line of Apollo are some of the main focusing points with Palm Therapy especially during the third stage. This is the center for energy flow which awakens the desire for achievement, the urge to "make It"—an extremely important element of success. To some degree it is within this finger, mount and line, that most of the success and achievements characteristics are focused. It is interesting to note that also all three nerves which supply the hand, the radial, median and ulnar nerves, supply together the finger of Apollo (see Appendix A: Anatomy of the Hand). A stimulation of this area helps to trigger success in various aspects of life.

This mount can be stimulated either clockwise or counterclockwise, depending on the type of activity we want to stimulate. For success in material or cognitive aspects of life, it should be a clockwise (*yang* energy) stimulation. For emotional fulfillment, talents development or spiritual growth a counterclockwise (*yin* energy) stimulation is required. The triggering of the Apollo mount brings the need to develop ourselves, to learn, study and grow. It stimulates both hemispheres of the brain and their functions, cognitive, analytical, logical thinking with verbal and mathematical skills or the other side, the imagination, talents, love and joy of art and beauty.

From this type of activity it seems that stimulating the Apollo mount activates the mount of Mercury (learning or training needs) but also by stimulating the Mercury mount, we create the desire for success and fulfillment, so there is some exchange in between these two mounts. Upper Uranus mount brings the devotion and the addictive momentum, so that the person can continue with the task until one achieves one's goals.

When we are not sure as to what direction to stimulate success, then the stimulation of the Apollo Line, on the Mars and Apollo mounts, will be the better choice.

Remember that although success in some areas may be one of our ultimate goals, it should be stimulated on a well-balanced hand. Therefore, we need initially to balance the whole hand in the first stage of Palm Therapy, induce the Release in the second stage, and then activate the energy of success in the third stage of Palm Therapy.

THE MOUNT OF MERCURY

The mount of Mercury (Fig. 28) is located under the little finger. It is the last of the four upper mounts and has a specific aspect of life—learning and adaptation.

Traditionally, the mount of Mercury is considered to be the representative of dealing with other people on a professional level, either as a business man, attorney, physician or healthcare provider. It represents learning and adaptation, speed of thinking, verbal skills and sports abilities. It is considered to represent some negative characteristics as well such as the cheater, the dishonest character. The characteristics were defined according to the mount of Mercury and supported by its finger.

My observation of this mount shows that when we stimulate the mount of Mercury with *yang* energy (clockwise move-

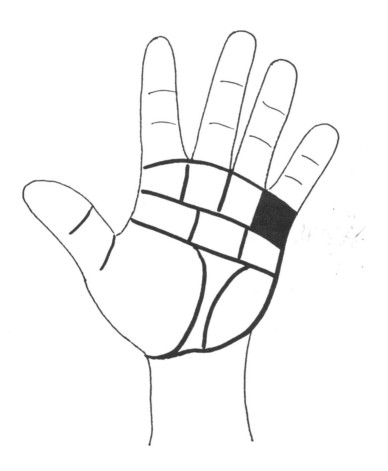

Fig. 28 The Mount of Mercury.

ments), the person feels the need for improvement. It may be improvement of any kind, either to fulfill the expectations created by the Apollo mount or to overcome the inferiority feelings of not achieving or not doing good enough, followed with the need for self-improvement by learning, training or practicing. These findings support the characteristics that are related to the mount of Mercury. They denote the importance of learning and adaptation in all aspects of life.

The need for learning and adaptation to new skills, language, behavior, code of ethics as well as the do's and don'ts of society are crucial tools for every newborn. This process continues throughout life whether we are aware of it or not. The mount of Mercury and other sections of the hand represent this aspect of life to a greater or lesser degree.

We continue to learn, to absorb new information or new skills, even if we don't consider some specific information or knowledge as part of learning. For example, listening to the news, watching TV, reading a simple romance book, encountering various new situations or interacting with others. Our brain, body and mind store information. We may dismiss part of it later on or immediately after, but still it has to pass some mental process including storage in the short- or long-term memory bank.

Those of you who may worry about your learning capability, just don't. We all have this ability and it is much stronger than you ever thought it to be. Your main problem may be the correct use of your memory bank or learning capabilities.

This capacity for learning can be further stimulated so that you can adapt yourself to new skills, a profession, a language or other activities faster, better and more deeply.

The learning and adaptation process starts very early, at some time during the pre-birth stage. Actually, I believe that this process starts as soon as awareness is achieved by the fetus, then immediately after birth the process continues with accelerating speed. In 2-3 years the newborn has to accomplish many new skills, learn a language, new dimensions, new technology, code of behavior, moral issues, how to avoid dangers, love new persons and all the things we take for granted as part of our daily life. We had to learn them at some time back in our childhood.

Somehow, most people attribute their learning skills ability to the experiences they have had in traditional educational methods, which is usually done at officially designated institutions (schools, colleges, universities). Positive achievements usually lead to more self-esteem and eagerness to continue, while negative experiences may prevent one from continuing his/her "official education".

The various aspects of education can be reinforced by stimulating the mount of Mercury. These include improvement of skills of any kind, learning and studying on any level, practicing and exercising any sport, and the ability to better communicate with others.

As I mentioned earlier, there is an interaction between the various mounts. The mount of Apollo is stimulated to activate Success Energy. The expectations to become successful on any level places a demand for improvement which, in turn, activates the mount of Mercury towards learning and acquiring new skills. The process of improving learning abilities can be done, also, more directly by the stimulation of the mount of Mercury which in turn awakens the mount of Apollo for success. This process occurs because all of the mounts are connected with each other in terms of influence and support.

When dealing with young children, ages newborn to 10 years old, it is important to stimulate this mount with *yang* energy (a clockwise stimulation) in order to help them have a good start in learning capacity and better achievements. Of course, other factors should be considered first, such as love, proper diet, elimination (as much as possible) of toxins, allergens, stress, fears or too much responsibility. In addition to these considerations, the stimulation of the Mercury mount can help the child to enjoy the primal instincts—curiosity, learning, studying or adaptation.

THE THREE MOUNTS OF MARS

The three mounts of Mars stretch from the radial to the ulnar side of the palm throughout the center of the palm. The middle of this region is also called the plane of Mars, since it is not really a fleshy elevation but a depression of the center of the palm.

The mounts of Mars represent the power and the courage to get what we want and desire from ourselves, nature and others. It also indicates our ability to fight actively or passively, to resist pressure and overcome obstacles.

The three mounts of Mars from the radial to the ulnar side of the palm also represent the emotional growth and development of the individual.

THE MOUNT OF LOWER MARS

The mount of lower Mars (Fig. 29) is the place of reaction toward the world and other people in an aggressive way. This mount is located under the Jupiter mount and actually supports it. One

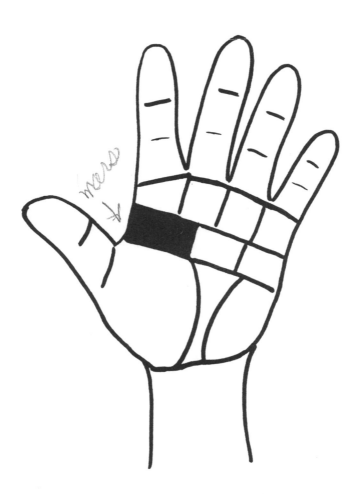

Fig. 29 *The Mount of Lower Mars.*

needs some aggression to become a leader, the boss, the president or the manager. The more aggression (not violence) the person has, the more that person needs an outlet to his/her aggressive energy and to what will support his/her needs to be involved and interact with others from a position of power and influence.

If this mount becomes too developed then it may indicate a violent personality. The mount of Jupiter, then, can be in either extreme; too highly intense with *yang* ability (when well-developed), or too intense with *yin* energy. In this case we will notice that the need for love and appreciation (which are the properties of Jupiter) become secondary and the aggression takes place in its ultimate form—violence.

By considering the qualities of Mars an integral part of the Jupiter mount, it explains the behavior pattern of people more clearly. You also need to remember that the mount of lower Mars is the actual continuation of the Earth mount; the newborn is egocentric in nature. He/she feels and believes that the whole world is oriented to his or her needs and wishes. Some of these are provided, to a certain degree, during our prenatal stage. It seems that part of the basic demands and needs, regardless of other ones which we acquire over the years, stays with us from the time of birth and before to our last day. With time, we learn to move ahead.

I found that the three mounts of Mars actually represent this tendency and it goes along with age. Now, we can see the pattern of the interaction of each mount with the others. Pressing a longitudinal line on the region of Mars at the locations that represent one's age (see Fig. 147a *Age Scale* in Chapter 16) can lead to an immediate relief of emotional pain. If, however, the person does not grow emotionally along with his/her chronological age, then the representative age, even in late life, will still be in the mount of lower Mars. By checking where on the area of three mounts of Mars the person gets calmed or relaxed after a stimulation, we can estimate his or her emotional age.

Aggressiveness, which represents the early childhood, also may represent the more primitive aspects of life. With evolution this mount is weakened and gets smaller in size and intensity. Hopefully, so will the aggressiveness of humanity. Historically we can see that violence such as torture and cruelty is less dominant than it was many thousands of years ago. Although I don't have any documented palms from the past, this is my hypothesis based on logical analysis.

THE MOUNT OF MIDDLE MARS

From the lower Mars we move to the mount of middle Mars (Fig. 30) which is located at the center of the palm. This mount, or actually the plane of Mars, is in constant interaction with the surrounding mounts. It is influenced from the high flow of energy of the bordering mounts. It gets high energy flow which forms what we know as the secondary *chakra* of the heart located in the center of the palm. This area radiates back to Saturn and Apollo mounts and to the line of Apollo, supporting them with the inner aggressiveness energy which enables the person to demand the achievements of success in life. It is the support needed to evaluate one's life and to bring peace of mind. It enriches the characteristics of the Apollo mount and the ability to enjoy the beauty of life, to wish for a better life and to fulfill one's dreams, needs and expectations.

Although there is a linear growth in mastering life from a newborn baby to old age, the peak performance and desires for

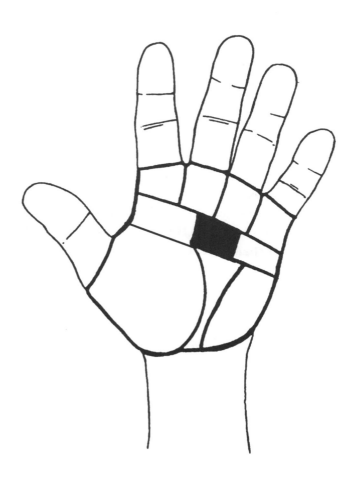

Fig. 30 *The Mount of Middle Mars.*

achievements usually appear at the ages of young adult and adult life. These aspects are presented in the middle Mars, mainly in the region located right under the mounts of Saturn and Apollo.

Middle Mars is also the root of self-discovery which goes into the more elevated aspects of life. As we grow, we go from selfishness and aggression to self-discovery, powerful persistence, patience and inner wisdom (as a continuation from the mount of lower Mars on to middle Mars and to upper Mars). We start to realize that large parts of the expectations we have had are needed to be searched within ourselves. Therefore, we turn inside to find the answers. In this way, the energy of aggressiveness takes another direction inward, leading to self-discovery, patience and inner wisdom. This is reflected in most of us as we grow. It is a gradual change from birth to old age which is manifested in the three mounts of Mars.

When middle Mars is active it is indicated by a darker/reddish color of that region and somewhat more fleshy appearance than expected in this area. It denotes that the person has the ability to grow in the spiritual world as well as in the emotional and cognitive aspects of life. The person, then, can also build a positive approach to his/her own life, but when this mount (actually plane) is too weak, which is indicated by pale color of the area, then the person is more likely to enter into disappointments, depressions, and lack of self-worth and self-esteem.

In terms of Palm Therapy's stimulation on the mounts of Mars, there is not really a fixed place but a journey with our age. Whether it is the emotional or chronological age depends on the individual. In most cases we can notice that these two aspects are represented in two different locations on these mounts, indicating that we usually don't grow up emotionally in accordance with our chronological age.

THE MOUNT OF UPPER MARS

From the child within, from the here and now, anticipation, aggressiveness, disregarding others (in many cases), desires and self-discovery the journey of life continues through the lower and middle mounts of Mars towards the mount of upper Mars.

The mount of upper Mars (Fig. 31) is located under the mount of Mercury. When well-developed, this mount has the qualities of inner strength, coolness in times of emergency and the ability to respond properly and with wisdom in any given situation. It is no wonder that traditionally this mount was considered to be the representative of the inner worrier.

We can see it as the continuation from lower and middle Mars. The emotional progression or growth is needed to pass from aggression, represented in lower Mars, into the hopes, wishes and desire for fulfillment towards balancing as we get older. It lets other qualities that are reflected in the mount of upper Mars to become more active and important; the power to resist, the patience to understand life from the others' points of view, the acceptance of difficulties, the ability to react with wisdom and courage to any given situation with diplomatic skills, calmness and with the inner peace desired. These qualities, although they may be achieved early in life, are more likely to be the qualities of a mature individual over the age of 40-45 years old.

From the ulnar side, the mount of upper Mars with its patience and courage, resistance and wisdom which come with age, the energy continues to flow constantly. It splits into two main directions of energy flow. One flows from the ulnar border through the back of the hands towards the mount of Earth and then continues back to the Mars mounts. The other part, which becomes now a subcurrent, flows backward into the center to

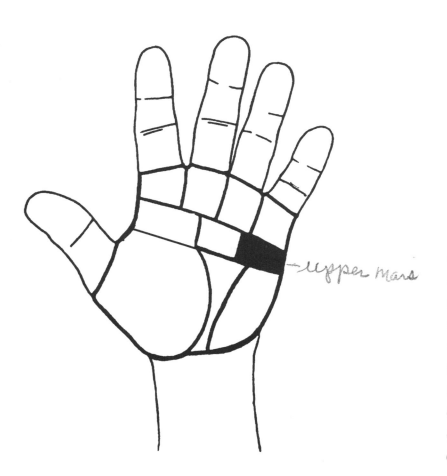

Fig. 31 *The Mount of Upper Mars.*

the mount of middle Mars, forming an energy power that radiates out to all the neighboring mounts.

Being nourished from both sides with the persistence of lower Mars and from the wisdom, patience and courage of upper Mars, the center of the palm becomes a perfect trunk to the energy needed for Apollo to activate success. The mount (or plain) of Neptune also adds its power with a longitudinal stream of energy flow towards this center.

There are many psychological theories that deal with the concept of fulfillment and success. Today, I am more convinced that obstacles can be removed in various ways including through Palm Therapy. We can and should build a better successful life full of love and devotion to ourselves, our families and the whole human race. We should look at all human beings, regardless of any differences, as our brothers and sisters. We need to understand that this is actually our pattern of evolution and a collective success for humanity. This is the best way to live our lives and let the next generations enjoy them too.

Using the energy path which is represented in the center of the palm and along the Apollo finger and its metacarpal can be a strong influence toward this direction. The whole concept and the goal of Palm Therapy, the way I see it, is as a simple tool for humanity to achieve success on the various levels of life including enlightment and a higher awareness which in turn will help in the process of our evolution.

THE MOUNT OF VENUS

The mount of Venus (Fig. 32) is the large mount located at the radial side of the palm forming the ball which is the base of the thumb. This mount is the representative of the vital forces in one's life, or the *chi*.

It is within this mount, which is the largest one in the hand, that our quality of life, our vitality, health, sex life, emotional empathy and the ability to accept ourselves and others into our lives are reflected. The importance of the mount of Venus is far above any of the other ones in regard to these aspects. The mount of Venus also represents the first *chakra* which is one of the main energy centers of the body. This mount is related to reproduction and the ability to love ourselves and others.

Being the largest mount on the palm, it is the source of vital life energy radiation. It radiates its characteristics to other mounts: upward towards the mounts of lower Mars and Jupiter, also toward the ulnar region of the palm to the mounts of Neptune and Luna.

Venus mount is the root for the mounts of lower Mars and Jupiter. The three of them get their influence from the mount of Earth and longitudinal energy flow. Together they form three important aspects:

Physical- Venus
Practical- Lower Mars
Mental/Emotional-Jupiter.

A well-developed mount of Venus means a positive, healthier and happier life. Of course, other factors count as well, but the Venus mount is one of the most important to observe first in the hand.

To determine the quality of this mount it is necessary to check its color, viscosity and its size. Too red or too pale are extreme *yang* or *yin* types. A well-balanced mount has a pink

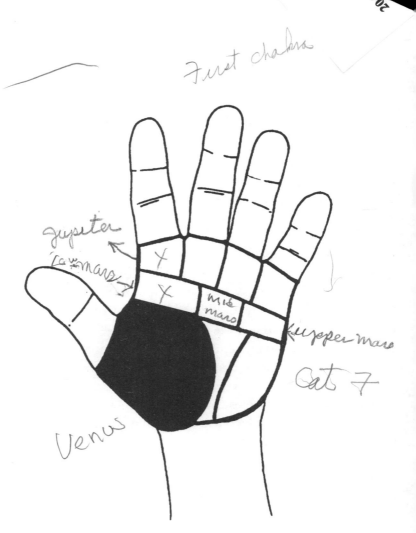

First chakra

Jupiter

(a-mars)

Venus

X

X

mid mars

lupper mars

Cat 7

Fig. 32 The Mount of Venus.

color while a red color may be an indication of hot temper with high blood pressure. A very pale or transparent-like skin (the one which you can see the veins through) is extremely *yin* type. This may indicate low blood pressure or anemia and/or very low vitality.

As mentioned above, the size of this mount should also be taken into consideration. A well-developed mount is measured at about half of the width of the palm from the radial toward the ulnar side. When the mount of Venus is less than that size, it is considered as a small mount, lacking the warmth, love and sound health of a strong Venus mount.

Another important aspect of this mount is the life line (radial longitudinal palmar crease) which encircles it. This line should be unbroken and long enough to circle the mount from its origin to the wrist. If this line appears to be broken or incomplete, it is usually an indication of loss or imbalance of the vitality represented in the mount of Venus. This low vitality and imbalance is usually reflected at the emotional or physical level and in some cases it denotes a medical problem as well.

Thanks to Palm Therapy, you may now increase the size of this mount. The muscles called thenar eminence are located at this region and may increase in size and strength by proper exercising of the thumb. By developing the muscles of this mount you actually will increase its vitality and radiation, influencing in this way the whole hand and thus improving your personality and well-being in general.

If you suffer from any pain or discomfort in the hand, you need to consult with your healthcare professional for the proper exercises according to your age, sex, physical conditions and any medical problem you may have.

In addition to the exercises, you can accelerate the intensity of this mount by a light touch massage. Use a clockwise movement (*yang* energy) applied on the center of the mount with the tip of the first three fingers; increase the cycles gradually until you cover the whole area of this mount.

Another way to increase the vitality of this mount is by imprinting a new and a better life line. Watch how this mount gradually becomes stronger which in turn can be reflected in better health and vitality.

You should remember that as in every other aspect of life you cannot rely on a single factor. In order to have better health, vitality, emotional balance and success, you will have to combine a few aspects which are all related and which interact with each other. The more you understand Palm Therapy the more you will understand this concept.

Another aspect which is important in regard to the mount of Venus is the representation of the left hemisphere of the brain and some other parts of the brain which are responsible for the vitality of life.

The left hemisphere of the brain represents the verbal skills, language, analytical thinking, mathematical skills, a step by step analyzation of the way of functioning and, to a smaller degree, the skills that are attributed to the right hemisphere such as intuitive thinking, talents, musical skills, non-verbal skills, visualization and catching the main point in any issue quickly and by insight.

It is interesting to note that the various mounts which share their bases with the fingers on our hands (the mounts of Jupiter, Saturn, Apollo and Mercury) also share the same characteristics represented by the fingers they are related to. In this manner the mount of Venus is the base for the thumb which, besides willpower, mainly represents logic, analytical thinking and the decision-making ability to continue with goals which are mainly the activity of the left hemisphere of the brain (more about the thumb in Chapter 9).

Now, for the mount of Venus, at a first glance it seems to represent more of the characteristics of the right hemisphere of the brain with its empathy, love, sex, vitality, etc. But actually in the same way that the other mounts share the similar qualities with their relative fingers, the mount of Venus, as the base of the thumb, shares similar characteristics with those of the thumb. Although the characteristics of love, emotional affection, vitality, sex, and energy of life are different from the ones represented by the thumb's (logic analytical thinking and willpower), they are actually the foundation of these more advanced characteristics of the human mind represented by the thumb and in the cortex of both hemispheres.

We can assume that the mount of Venus and the thumb represent the left hemisphere on the right hand, and the characteristics of the left hemisphere which were mentioned above on the left hand as well, but with some activity of the right hemisphere .

We should remember that, ultimately, there are no clear cut characteristics and functions between the right and left hemispheres. The mount of Venus together with the mount of Luna, which is mentioned in the following pages, shows the sharing of functions of both hemispheres in cooperation. Although the main scientifically known activities of each hemisphere are clearly different, some of the activities of the opposite hemisphere are represented in each section as well. Again, manifesting the cooperation between the various parts of the brain.

The mount of Venus also represents the characteristics and functions of the limbic system of the brain which is considered as the seat of the basic emotions and feelings such as anger, fear, depression, aggression, joy and happiness.

Fortunately, our present knowledge of the brain and mind functions is rapidly increasing with the non-invading tools (such as MRI, CT scanning and others). These tools let us watch the brain functions at work. But still in today's knowledge the unknown factors are more than the known ones.

The questions of life itself, what is behind the nervous system of the brain, what is the "I" consciousness, feelings, thoughts, memories, wishes, needs, etc. are not explained so far in a scientific way.

There are many theories and speculations (mine is one of them) but there is no absolute reality yet known to science.

I mentioned this subject in the first and second sections of the book, but it is well-worth bringing it up here when dealing with the activity or the brain.

Is our complex mind with the identity of "I" as a living creature just a collection of nerves, neurotransmitters, hormones and chemicals, or is our soul using the brain as a tool, exactly as we use our cars or other machines ?

Science has found that when there is a damage in a specific part of the brain, the functioning is impaired, therefore the conclusion is that the specific function is actually that part of the brain which has impaired function. This conclusion makes sense, but still it doesn't consider the possibility that there is some intelligent form behind the physiology of the body/brain.

If there is a damage or malfunction of the brain, and the mind does not respond properly, is this damage an evidence of the source of that improper activity? Or, exactly like a car if we have a malfunction in the mechanics of the engine, is that a proof that there is no driver? Can we also conclude that the sole functioning of the car's movement is the tires, and if the tires become flat, then it means that the car cannot move since this is the center of its movement, does it also mean that there is no driver?

The same is happening in the brain and various body activities. We are in the initial steps of discovering the site of the various brain functions and the mechanism of the various mounts, but if there is a higher intelligence that uses the brain (and the body) as a vehicle for its life purpose, there is no way to reach it or measure it through present scientific tools. (See Hand/Mind/Soul Connection, in Chapter 1.

Various religious and esoteric teachings of all ages acknowledged the existence of the soul, near-death experiences, out-of-body experiences, reincarnation phenomena, and regression through hypnosis or trance. These evidences support the idea for the existence of the soul. We can assume that the activities of the brain as part of the physical body and our mind as part of the energy level of our existence are coordinated and managed by the soul. I also believe, as I stated earlier, that eventually science will discover its existence, once the tools to detect the soul will be developed. More about this issue you can read in my coming books: *The Ultimate Prophecy (Book One and Book Two)*.

Personally, since I had a near-death experience at the age of nearly fourteen and since then have had many out-of-body experiences, I am convinced about the existence of the soul as an independent but attached intelligence to the physical body. When death occurs the soul leaves the body as a natural process of cosmic evolution.

Since life energies, or *chi* in Chinese terminology, are also represented in the hand and, more specifically, on the palm in the mounts of Venus, Neptune, and Luna, then some characteristics of the soul should be represented there as well. It is mainly manifested in the radiation of energy through the center of the palm.

THE MOUNT OF NEPTUNE

The mount of Neptune (Fig. 33) is located in between two large mounts: the mount of Venus and the mount of Luna.

This mount is relatively new in the terminology of palmistry and not very well accepted by some palmists. Others view this mount as the one which exists in some people, but not in everyone.

As you can see, the mount of Neptune shares its borders with a few mounts. Its distal border is the mount of middle Mars. Its radial border is the mount of Venus; its ulnar border is the mount of Luna, and its proximal border is the base of the palm (wrist).

If the mount of Venus is very wide, (over half of the width of the palm), then there is little space for Neptune, but still it has enough room in the bottom proximal part of the palm near the wrist.

On the ulnar side Neptune shares its border with the mount of Luna which is another large and powerful mount not very well appreciated. As in the mount of Venus, the wider the mount of Luna is, the less space for Neptune is allowed, but nevertheless Neptune, or the plane of Neptune, exists in between these two large mounts in spite of their sizes and activities.

Neptune is the root of the healing powers within the person. It is nourished from the radiation of Venus mount with its vitality, its love for life and towards others. It also receives energy flow from the radiation of Luna mount with its deepest parts of the subconscious mind, the imagination and the energy of inner esoteric life which is passed from generation to generation in a mysterious way not very well understood by many, but nevertheless, it is represented in the mount of Luna. (This will be discussed in our coming book on palmistry.)

With this influence, Neptune becomes a seat for the inner powers, well-balanced with the physical and spiritual powers creating the practical esoteric energy which is the source for the healing force within ourselves. We all possess some degree of this cosmic universal power to heal ourselves and others and, with proper training we can become effective healers. (If these energies are well-used, then it is for the benefit of that person and humanity in general. If it is not used appropriately in a way of helping oneself or others, it becomes a negative one which is absolutely not recommended. This energy, when used negatively, tends in a karmic way to return against its user.)

How to use this mount's energy for healing, for a stronger immune system, emotional balance, for the reinforcement of middle Mars and Apollo mounts is a whole different story. This is one of the many secrets which some healing occult groups worldwide passed from generation to generation including the masters of the chi-gong (or qigong), the Chinese masters of the chi, and the sages of India. It is involved in activation of the chakras, flow of energy within the whole body, opening the kundalini path along the spine, and increasing the flow of energy into Neptune mount. Some rituals that are intended to focus the subconscious mind toward intensifying this energy are performed as well. (In my workshops I focus only on the positive energy output which includes the healing or the increasing of the healing powers within ourselves with the use of positive Neptune energy. I believe that any negative use of this energy is wrong.)

The mount of Neptune as the source of the healing and balancing energy can be stimulated and reinforced in various ways, mainly through special exercises, meditations and focusing of the mind towards intensifying the energy of this mount.

From the Palm Therapy point of view, in order to increase

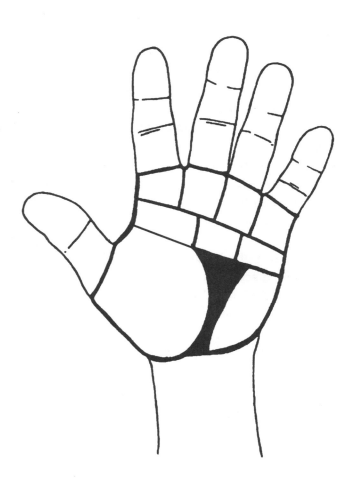

Fig. 33 *The Mount of Neptune.*

the intensity of Neptune mount, you must increase the intensity of Venus and Luna (Moon) mounts first, and be balanced mentally (see Section Four: "The Application of Palm Therapy"). Then apply a light massage with counterclockwise movements on the center of Neptune mount every day on both palms. Do it for 4-6 months (depending on other factors of your condition). It may take a longer or a shorter period of time to develop the radiation of healing powers. Remember, in order to increase the Neptune healing energy you should also balance your diet with minimum or no animal protein (consult a nutritionist) and help your energies with proper meditation and focusing on the radiation of the healing energy from within. Meditate twice a day for fifteen minutes. Then focus on the radiation of healing energy while mentally visualizing yourself healing someone.

IMPORTANT: If you notice with these exercises any negative or adverse reaction, discontinue the exercises immediately, and consult with a qualified Palm Therapist, certified by the IPTA There may be a few reasons for it to happen :

1. Poor and negative state of mind.

2. The wish to acquire power over others.

3. Poor state of health or low energy or intensity of Venus mount.

4. Others are using you without your knowledge, or using their own Neptune energy in a negative way. It may happen in some cults, other groups or near a person seeking others' energies subconsciously.

5. The use of some drugs such as alcohol while increasing the energy of this mount.

6. Imbalance between Luna mount (high energy) and Venus mount (low energy)

7. Other reasons might exist but they are not within the scope of this chapter.

Neptune mount has the power or energy to balance and heal ourselves. It is the practical healing activity within one's body. Therefore, in any chronic disease, reinforcement of the base of the hand, which includes Venus, Neptune and Luna mounts, is of extreme importance. If using Palm Therapy's stimulation, the movement should be clockwise (*yang* energy) on each of the three mounts, although the center of self-healing is in Neptune which is *yin* energy. Start with *yang* energy, then continue with counterclockwise stimulation (*yin* energy) on Luna and Neptune mounts.

Entering the world of Neptune energy and its characteristics is fascinating because of the many esoteric manifestations associated with this mount. Each can be developed and awakened through this area and other parts of the hand with the help of Palm Therapy.

Although in this mount I described the healing energy as esoteric, I am convinced that these energies have a perfect scientific explanation. These energies have some physical characteristics which so far have not been understood or discovered by researchers and therefore we refer to them as esoteric or occult. But once they will be discovered, they will be categorized as another source of energy. Whether you understand this phenomenon or not, this healing energy has been well documented during thousands of years all over the world proving, in a way, its real existence and manifestation.

THE MOUNT OF LUNA

The mount of Luna/Moon (Fig. 34) is located at the ulnar proximal region of the palm.

Luna is one of the most powerful influences in our hands. It is the seat for the self-healing and as such it is one of the main healing energy sources for the Neptune mount. It is also the seat of general physical conditions in the positive or negative aspects of it, wellness or sickness.

Luna is the center of radiation for the subconscious mind which is the representative site of the inner knowledge, needs and feelings. Luna is also the center for imagination, intuition, clairvoyance—the center for passive esoteric powers and talents. This mount serves as the source energy for the mounts of upper Mars and Mercury.

The mount of Luna affects the mount of Apollo with the intuitive insight for a deeper meaning of life, nature, beauty, art and feelings. (Note that upper Mars radiates also upward to Mercury and Apollo.)

By observing the characteristics of the mount of Luna, it becomes apparent that this mount represents mainly the right hemisphere of the brain—the non-verbal skills, imagination and creativity.

With its characteristics and manifestations, the mount of Luna represents the immune-system, the self-healing of body and mind, the connection between body and soul and other aspects which are more esoteric in nature.

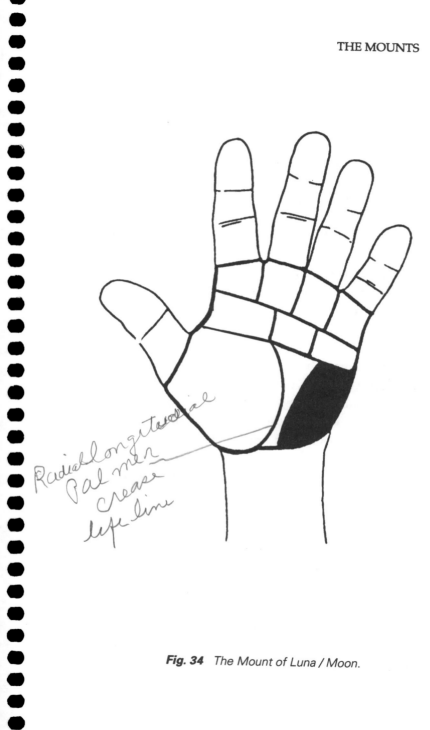

Radial longitudinal
Palmer
crease
life line

Fig. 34 *The Mount of Luna / Moon.*

You may ask, if the mount of Luna is represented on both palms, how then can we relate mainly to one hemisphere and its skills? Do both palms have the same Luna mount interpretation? (The same questions apply to Venus which represents mainly the left side of the brain.)

To answer such questions let's explore for a while the mechanism of the two hemispheres of the brain, their physiological connection to the hands and their activities. We already mentioned the hemispheres of the brain when we dealt with the mount of Venus, but let's further discuss this topic.

The brain is divided into two parts called right hemisphere and left hemisphere. Although they look anatomically similar, they act and store different information, skills and functions as follows:

> **The left hemisphere of the brain** is connected via the nervous system to the right hand. The left hemisphere is responsible for the logical part of life as has been documented in various studies throughout the years. This part of the brain is the center for analytical thinking, logical problem solving, the language center, speech and verbal skills, mathematical skills, order and step-by-step thinking.
>
> **The right hemisphere of the brain** is connected via the nervous system to the left hand. The main responsibilities of the right hemisphere are the non-verbal skills, the imagination in its various aspects and the intuitive thinking. This part of the brain solves problems through insights and intuition. It is open to enjoy music and art. It is the part that recognizes shapes. It loves beauty and enables the individual to grasp the message or the main point in a story, book or real life.

We can see that most of the characteristics of Luna are similar to those representedted by the right hemisphere. And the major characteristics of Venus (and the thumb with its willpower and logic) are similar to those represented by the left hemisphere of the brain.

In traditional palmistry, the upper portion of the palm and that of the fingers represent the mental activity. Nevertheless, we should remember that the whole palm represents the brain/mind and its various activities.

Another point to remember: As mentioned in regard to the mount of Venus, the representation of the various functions of the mind into the right and left sides of the brain are not clear-cut. In each of the hemispheres there are some mental activities originally represented in the opposite hemisphere. For example, verbal skills, grammar and a logical way of talking are the functions of the left hemisphere, but to a lesser degree these skills can be seen in the right hemisphere. Intuitive skills are usually represented as functions of the right hemisphere, but to a lesser degree are also represented in the activities of the left hemisphere.

It is my personal opinion that each hemisphere not only operates within what was originally found to be its mental activities but that also each operates like an imaginary onion with layers of different activities in it as follows:

The left hemisphere with its analytical skills is the main outside layer of activity. Below that, there is smaller portion of activity of the opposite hemisphere. Yet, under that layer there is another layer of analytical skills but with much lesser activity. Under that, there is another layer of intuitive activity and so on. There are many reasons for this hypothesis which explains the logic for the brain/mind to operate this way. For us, the Palm Therapists, it will explain the interconnection and interrelations between the mounts on both hands.. In this case it is the relationship and energy transition from the mount of Venus to the mount of Luna via the mount of Neptune and of course at the same time upwards through the three mounts of Mars and to the mounts of Jupiter, Saturn, Apollo and Mercury.

Therefore, on the mount of Venus, in both hands, there are some representations of Luna which exist on the thumb as well. In the mount of Luna there are some representations of the mount of Venus which now will explain the healing powers of Luna and the representation of the immune system on this mount. The presence of allergies and various diseases will appear on Luna as well, representing, in a way, the emotional aspects of the Venus mount.

The mount of Luna is of utmost importance to work on, because many problems and diseases may be relieved with the help of specific stimulation on this mount along with the mount of Pluto in combination with the mount of Venus. Mental blockages and traumas may be alleviated, too, with counterclockwise stimulation of the Luna mount on both hands.

INTRODUCTION TO THE NEW MOUNTS ON THE ULNAR BORDER OF THE PALM: THE INEVITABLE ADDICTIVE/ATTACHMENT PATTERNS IN OUR LIVES.

The outermost ulnar border of the hand represents the influences and needs we have in our lives. Some of these needs originate as early as the prenatal period of the fetus in the womb. By becoming dependent, or used to them on an increased or regular basis, we develop attachment or addictive patterns that are an inevitable part of life and which have to do with our survival as the human race.

Addictions and attachments are the tools we use as human beings to regulate and stabilize our lives. These tools are our adaptation to our needs at the various levels. As long as they are regulated and steady they may be positive (as long as they are not poisonous by nature or destructive by their patterns). Only when they become overly increased demands, changing the balance of one's life, do they become negative addictive patterns.

The idea that addictions are a normal, natural part of our existence is difficult to accept at first. But if we observe our life patterns very carefully, we can recognize these patterns in ourselves and others.

These patterns or needs can be classified into three worlds or the three levels of existence and are represented by three mounts which are located on the outermost ulnar side of the hand, one under the other, starting from the basal crease/line of the little finger and ending in the wrist bracelet/s, I named them:

The mount of upper Uranus
The mount of lower Uranus
The mount of Pluto

Transverse lines on these mounts are the representatives of the various addictive/attachment patterns we may acquire throughout life (Fig. 35).

We all develop some addictive or attachment patterns to a certain degree on all of the various levels of existence. Let's review some of them:

Emotional/Spiritual: represented in the mount of upper Uranus, it includes love, devotion to others such as for the spouse, boy/girlfriend, higher spiritual entity, God, the creator, etc.

Cognitive/Behavioral: represented in the mount of lower Uranus includes devotion or addiction to work, study, religious activity, sport activity, watching TV, reading newspapers and other routines that are followed on a regular basis.

Physical/Chemical (Substance): represented in the mount of Pluto includes attachment or addiction to a substance such as alcohol, nicotine, coffee, various foods and drinks, drugs, medication, etc. Their use in excess may cause either allergies, chemical sensitivity, immune diseases or auto-immune diseases and psychosomatic disorders. It may also be related to any other disease or emotional disorder.

These three levels of attachments, if carefully checked, seem to have many characteristics of an addiction as defined by the medical profession: physical, or psychological (or both) dependence on a substance, or an activity, with a tendency to use it in increasing amounts in order to continue and receive the initial results. Withdrawal may cause physical or mental pain or stress.

Usually, there is a tendency towards one of these levels of attachments or addictions. It is reflected on the palm by the mount which is dominant in color, relative size and its transverse lines. The other two, then, become less active.

Since attachment or addictive patterns are part of our lives, we can not eliminate them without harming the individual. They form the very basic needs of survival for everyone of us. Only if and when they become excessively out of balance are they then negative addictive patterns, or addictions, as we call them today. In this case we need to replace them with positive ones.

The quality of our addictions or attachment patterns, whether the positive or the negative ones, will determine the need to either improve or change these patterns. From the Palm Therapist's point of view, direct the addictive patterns from Pluto into lower Uranus or upper Uranus mounts.

Fig. 35 Transverse lines on the ulnar side of the hand; the representatives of addictive/attachment patterns in our lives.

Understanding this concept makes it clear for us to realize that the solution to drugs, alcohol or gambling addictions, for example, is not by deciding to avoid them, but by exchanging one addiction that is destructive to our lives with a more positive one.

The Alcoholics Anonymous (AA) in their *Twelve Steps* gives a solution to alcohol addiction by replacing this addictive pattern with positive ones of higher nature.

When evaluating the addictive/attachment patterns in our lives we have to view the whole hand from the self-centered focus to the love, devotion, adaptation and attachment towards our surroundings. In terms of Palm Therapy the evolution of the person is from the mount of Earth, or earlier, towards the mounts of upper Uranus, lower Uranus and Pluto, which represent attachments, love, devotion (upper Uranus) adaptation to regular life patterns (lower Uranus) and physical/chemical attachments or addictions to a substance (Pluto).

The border line between Mercury, upper Mars and Luna mounts on one side and upper Uranus, lower Uranus and Pluto mounts on the other side is unclear. We need to draw an imaginary line along the ulnar border while observing from the side. Then, draw another imaginary line while looking at the palm's ulnar border while the palm of the hand is straight in front of us. The middle line between these two imaginary lines will be the border between the two groups of mounts, i.e., the border between Mercury and upper Uranus, as well as the border between lower Uranus and upper Mars, and between the mount of Luna and the mount of Pluto.

Now that you have gotten a broad view of the three mounts in the outermost ulnar side of the hand, let's discuss each one of them more deeply.

THE MOUNT OF UPPER URANUS

The mount of upper Uranus (Fig. 36) is located on the ulnar border of the palm. The basal crease/line of the Mercury finger is its upper border; the end of the heart line is its lower border. We can say, therefore, that the mount of upper Uranus borders the mount of Mercury and the mount of lower Uranus. Its outermost limit extends up to the end of the dermatoglyphics.

The mount of Uranus represents emotional attachments to others. We call these kinds of attachments, love, friendship or an emotional bond. Actually, if we look at a true loving relationship it has most of the characteristics of an addiction. Initially, it makes us feel great and in a state of euphoria. In a real love the rest of the world seems secondary. We can do almost anything for our loved one/s. As time goes on, we need more stimulation to keep the same initial feelings as at the beginning. A withdrawal period from addiction is very painful. The same as it is from love. The grieving or the emotional pain following a separation from a loved one or from a major attachment figure can be one of the worst emotions that one may ever experience.

All the elements of addiction and emotional attachment are represented in the upper Uranus mount. By itself the upper Uranus mount can be well-developed and prominent from the side of the hand. If the side of the hand is wide (thick hand) the emotional attachment classified as marriage emotional attachment lines are actually starting closer to the back of the hand and continue as transverse lines towards the mount of Mercury.

The location just above the heart line represents attachment in young age and the transverse line/s closer to the basal crease/line of the little finger represents an attachment/s in old age up to about 90-100 years of age.

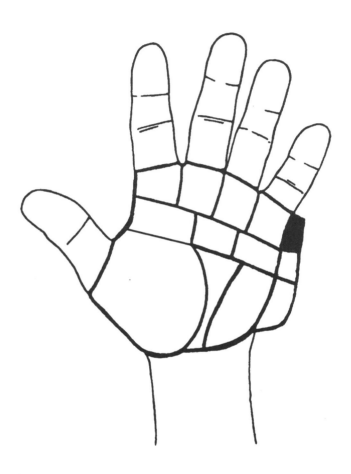

Fig. 36 *The Mount of Upper Uranus.*

The mount of upper Uranus, when well-developed, shows that the person's tendency towards an emotional attachment or addiction leading to marriage and full connections or bond on a stable basis is strong. It is mainly associated with the spouse, boy/girlfriend, but it can also represent the person's spiritual attachment and love for a spiritual power/esoteric belief.

The ability to become devoted to a higher power/God is seen in this mount. The devotion takes the form of a spiritual belief as part of a partnership. From the point of view of the hand this type of devotion to spiritual values is also an addictive pattern. Therefore, an addiction or attachment in this broad concept is much more than a negative aspect. It may be the best one ever experienced without any need for replacement or change. We can consider it as a positive addiction. It may be the perfect solution to some who look for the meaning of life. Love and devotion may be the highest feelings that the human race can ever achieve. It may be love and devotion to our spouse, children, partners, friends, humanity or a more spiritual love, such as love and devotion to God, the Creator, to an organized religion, to a cult or to a group of any type.

How can we, then, distinguish between representation marks of love for the spouse and love for God or love for an established religion/group ?

The transverse lines on this mount usually represent the spouse or loved ones, while the tiny longitudinal lines seen when we stretch the finger of Mercury towards the finger of Apollo, are the representatives of spiritual love and devotion without any giving or actual participation in rituals. But if any giving pattern such as donation or work is involved in the spiritual attachment, it will also appear as transverse lines on this mount. The stronger the lines, the stronger the quality of these emotional or spiritual connections is.

After a long study of this issue, it seems to me that all addictions or attachments on the three levels of existence are natural and part of our healthy life. Yes, these include physical addictions, too. We must understand this issue more deeply. It is within our nature, as human beings, to be attached or addicted; the question is to what? Is it to a regular steady long-term relationship which has a balancing effect and actually helps us maintain a healthy life, or is it to a casual, short relationship that may cause more problems than stability, leading to debilitation of the emotional balance of the individual?

Marriage/attachment lines on the mount of upper Uranus extending towards the mount of Mercury represent the quality of the marriage/emotional attachments. Each of these lines represents a single emotional attachment. The location of the line indicates the period of this relationship. A strong, clearly marked line that ends on the mount of Mercury in a horizontal straight line denotes a strong emotional attachment. If the observed line is weak and turns downward towards the heart line, it describes a poor or negative relationship. The use of biorhythm (see Chapter 19) as a measurement of compatibility between two persons can add another dimension to the evaluation of the quality of that relationship.

The mount of upper Uranus is usually thicker and well-developed in the elementary and the square hand types while the smallest mount will usually appear on a thin hand such as the psychic hand or the conic hand. The qualities of devotion to others and of caring for others in the relationship are a way to secure the emotional addiction one wishes to possess.

Based on my observation, individuals with the elementary hands tend to have a more stable marriage or relationship than others, while many of the possessors of the psychic hands tend to have a shorter relationship than others. Of course, additional qualities must be considered as well, but these examples illustrate the point of a developed or underdeveloped mount of upper Uranus.

The ending of the heart line is at the lower border of the upper Uranus mount. It will determine the length of this mount in comparison to the lower Uranus mount. It is important to understand that the wider the space between the basal crease of the Mercury finger and the heart line, the stronger the influence of the upper Uranus mount—stronger spiritual/emotional attachments to others or to higher powers.

Uranus is considered in astrology a planet of esoteric and occult influence. On the hands it is similar. The mystical influence in this part of the hand is mainly in the area of love and devotion to the elevated feelings either emotional or spiritual while the lower Uranus mount, which appears just under this mount, represents routines, practical rituals and activities, but not the mystical skills or talents as they are represented in the mounts of Neptune and Luna.

Upper Uranus type of addiction, the highest form of addiction is a positive one, whose characteristics of love and devotion may be the tools for evolution toward a better type of humanity. Should we reinforce and increase this mount? It is a philosophical question with more than one answer, one that each individual must answer for him/herself.

REMEMBER unless you become a professional Palm Therapist and you know what you are doing, NEVER stimulate the mount of upper Uranus because there are many implications and systems within this mount that may change or influence the style of one's behavioral patterns.

THE MOUNT OF LOWER URANUS

The mount of lower Uranus (Fig. 37) is located immediately under the mount of upper Uranus and the heart line. We can say that the continuation of the heart line or the mount of upper Uranus is the upper border of this mount, and the imaginary continuation of the head line (in a straight line) or the mount of Pluto is its lower border. The mount of upper Mars is its inner border and the end of the dermatoglyphics on the outer side of the palm is the outermost border.

This mount represents cognitive and behavior addictive or attachment patterns of the individual's to an idea, a belief system or a religious activity, certain behavior patterns, rituals, work, studying, sports, social activity, watching TV, video games, and to other routines which are performed on a regular basis.

The cognitive and behavior addictive patterns, or devotion, which are represented in this mount still can be to a spiritual or religious group, but these kinds of attachments are on a different level. The mount of upper Uranus is characterized by love and devotion to a person, to a group or to a spiritual belief, and the wish to give help and to be part of that activity, person or power. In the mount of lower Uranus, the addictive pattern has a different meaning. In this mount the addictive pattern is to what the group or activity can give to us. The type of comfort, peace of mind, pleasure, entertainment, protection, safety or security can be achieved from the addictive pattern of activity, or in other words it is the addiction to physical or mental activity that can bring us some type of reward.

The dependency we feel towards our parents in earlier stages of life is also represented in the mount of lower Uranus. The more we are attached to our parents/guardians, the clearer the transverse line/s at that area (closer to the imaginary con-

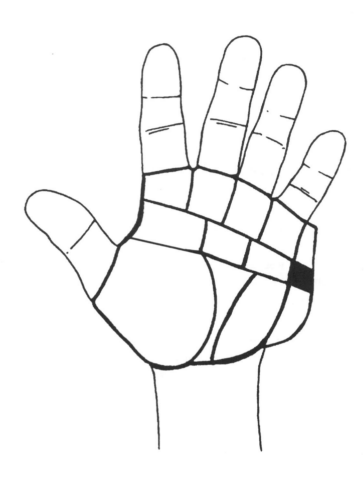

Fig.37 *The Mount of Lower Uranus.*

tinuation of the head line). From the Palm Therapist's point of view, these attachments (positive in nature) are also a kind of positive addiction with all the characteristics of a need for the presence of the supporter and emotional pain if disconnected from them. In a way, we can describe most of human needs and behavior patterns as addictive/attachment patterns in one or more forms.

Lower Uranus may represent positive or negative addictions. These depend on the quantity or level of activity. Any type of activity that becomes so dominant to a degree that it prevents a person from keeping a balanced life becomes a negative addiction. So, actually negative addiction is more of a quantity than the actual thinking or behavior pattern. Any activity, behavior or belief system may become negative if we overuse/do it.

We must remember that we all possess some positive and negative addictions on the three levels. These addictive patterns are more positive or better than the ones represented by the Pluto mount because the addictions or attachments represented by lower Uranus give the person self-gratification, security, satisfaction or entertainment in the positive aspects. When these addictive patterns become negative, it is represented by a more active mount of lower Uranus with transverse lines (not connected and not a part of the head line).

With a careful look at these lines, we can observe the direction of the ends of these transverse lines; whether they curve downward towards the wrist or upwards in the direction of the fingers.

If their ends curve in the wrist direction, the individual is going towards a subsidence or an ending of the addictive/attachment pattern represented by that line. If the end of the line is straight, or in the direction of the fingers, then the addictive/attachment pattern is going to be even stronger.

Transverse lines at the upper part of lower Uranus represent a more cognitive nature of addictive/attachment patterns such as to work and to studying. A transverse line in the lower part of lower Uranus represents more imagination and the entertainment of self-gratification. The addictive/attachment patterns in this part, for example, can be for gambling or watching TV.

Accordingly, we can help ourselves or others in regulating work addictive patterns ("workaholics") or to stabilize an ability to maintain a steady job or business. Also, it may be a good place to help a student towards focusing and devoting him/herself to more studying, or to be more focused in sports, etc.

As you can see, there are many positive aspects of addictive/attachment patterns which we may want to stimulate or reinforce for various purposes in life.

As mentioned in regard to upper Uranus REMEMBER unless you become a professional Palm Therapist and you know what you are doing, NEVER stimulate the mount of lower Uranus because there are many implications and systems within this mount that may change or influence the style of one's behavior patterns.

THE MOUNT OF PLUTO

The mount of Pluto (Fig. 38) is located on the ulnar side of the palm between the mount of lower Uranus and the wrist's bracelet/s. Its inner border is the mount of Luna, and its outermost border is the end of the dermatoglyphics on the ulnar side of the palm.

The mount of Pluto represents physical and chemical addiction, attachments, and interaction with a substance such as alcohol, nicotine, foods, drinks, drugs and medication.This may cause either allergies, chemical sensitivity, immune-diseases and auto-immune diseases. It may be related to any other disease or emotional disorder. It depends on various factors, but as a rule, the stronger the addictive patterns represented by this mount are, the more chances that it will cause some type of negative symptoms or disease. The signs of an addiction or a chemical sensitivity/allergy are marked with transverse lines, dots, islands or reddish areas on some parts of the Pluto mount. These signs may extend toward the mount of Luna as well.

An addiction to a chemical substance, such as drug, has to have a characteristic of use with increasing amounts in order to satisfy or get the same effects as when it was initially consumed. A withdrawal may cause a physical, a psychological, or a mental discomfort/pain while craving that particular substance.

In my opinion, an addiction also may be any dependency and craving for a particular substance which, when using it, leads to satisfaction without the necessity of increasing its consumption, but when avoiding that substance a distress period may be experienced. (So far, this pattern is not considered an addiction by Western scientific medicine.)

We all have addictions or attachment patterns to certain substances as represented in the third level of existence by the mount of Pluto (physical/chemical addictive patterns). They can also be positive such as a craving for regular well-balanced and healthy meals; if we avoid them we may feel some degree of craving for those meals.

Then there are other types of addictions in this third level. They are negative in nature because they represent craving for a strong substance which negatively affects the body and mind (including alcohol and various drugs).

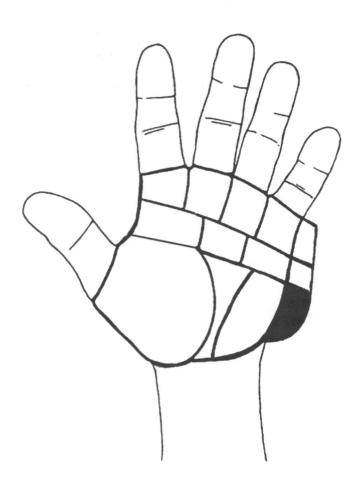

Fig. 38 *The Mount of Pluto.*

People can exchange addictive/attachment patterns of this low level with the cognitive/behavioral, or emotional/spiritual ones. When dealing with the patterns represented by the mount of Pluto it is also important to address the chemical substitute. For example, if there is an addiction to sugar, exchange it for pure honey (don't give an infant pure honey) unless you suffer from diabetes, tooth problems, a metabolic disorder or any other condition which doesn't allow you to use honey. Consult with your healthcare provider for quantities. Any type of chemical addiction may lead to or cause a physical disorder or a disease. It also may be manifested as some type of negative immune reaction which either initiates or aggravates a disease. By pressing longitudinal lines on these addiction lines on the mount of Pluto (and Luna), you may prevent or reduce many physical symptoms of allergies, diseases or disorders.

To the certified Palm Therapist
REMEMBER again, unless you are a licensed healthcare provider
DO NOT ATTEMPT to cure or treat any disease or disorder. Always work in cooperation with a healthcare provider.

It is interesting to note that the thicker the mount of Pluto is, the more positive addictions we can expect. If any disease or reaction connected to negative addiction occurs, it will be more of a *yang* type, such as high blood pressure, heart problems, pains in various parts of the body and headaches. The thinner the mount of Pluto is, the more a *yin* type of problem we can expect such as low blood pressure, fatigue, anemia as well as depression, phobias and some other mental disorders which are related to physical/chemical factors.

Regardless of the type of hand we possess, we all may have negative addictions unless we balance our energies. Palm

Therapy's stimulation may help and change these negative addictions into positive ones.

Those who suffer from negative addictions may switch rapidly into positive ones as soon as they understand the natural process of addictive patterns and how to replace negative with positive ones. Therefore, in these cases explanation about ways to adapt higher, positive addictive patterns and joining specific support groups should be done together with Palm Therapy.

ADDICTIVE PATTERNS ARE AN INEVITABLE PART OF OUR LIVES—SUMMARY

We can explain the life process via the addictive and attachment patterns of any kind or level as a positive tool to survive physically and emotionally, one which helps us regulate and stabilize our lives. By getting used to the surroundings, emotions, social convictions/norms, behavior and consumable items, we don't have to thoroughly analyze these aspects over and over again. By being positively addicted to certain routines at the various level of existence (emotional/spiritual, cognitive/behavioral, physical/chemical), we can regulate our lives in a positive way. Only when these kinds of addictive/attachment patterns become excessive do they turn to negative ones and affect our lives. Then they should be regulated, balanced or exchanged with other attachments or addictive patterns which are better in nature.

Understanding of this concept may be the root for a new therapy approach to any disease or disorder. More research and documentation is needed in order to perfect this approach and to use it as a basis for a therapy system.

As for the Palm Therapists, we must remember that the power of addiction and attachment patterns is a constant energy—equal to the life energy itself. Therefore, we cannot avoid addictions; we can only substitute one addiction for another. If we handle a negative addiction pattern through Palm Therapy or any other method, and don't purposely replace that specific negative addiction with a more positive one, then the individual will change it by him/herself automatically by finding other types of addiction/s which may be positive or negative in nature. (For example, many individuals who decided to stop smoking cigarettes found themselves consuming larger amounts of food or sweets instead.) Fighting negative addictions by forbidding their use (such as the use of drugs or alcohol) without giving a substitute is really ignoring the fact that addiction is a natural process.

In the addictive process, the more we are insecure or afraid in life, the more we become attached/addicted to what we are familiar with and used to. Therefore, it is very hard to stop or overcome a negative addiction. Sometimes, due to unfulfilled needs we try to compensate ourselves by increasing what we believe to be an answer to that unfulfilled need. For example, an unfulfilled need on the emotional level (love) may be compensated with an addictive pattern of a different level such as using drugs or alcohol. An individual who does not have enough financial stability in accordance to his expectation (unfulfilled need) may try to compensate for this need either by becoming a "workaholic" (addiction to work) or an excessive gambler (a destructive addictive pattern). In some other way the "not enough" feeling as a result of unfulfilled need may affect also wealthy individuals and force them to steal and accumulate more and more wealth in order to compensate for their need.

The best way to reduce a negative, destructive addiction is by replacing it with a positive addiction of a higher level, represented by the upper or lower Uranus mounts. As I mentioned earlier, Alcoholic Anonymous is doing it very successfully by replacing a lower addiction of negative patterns into more cognitive, behavioral, emotional and spiritual love and devotion which are positive addictive patterns.

Other groups which take the AA concepts of altering addictions of a negative nature to more positive ones are growing in numbers all over the United States and the world. The best results for those who are members of the AA groups are when they become sponsors to other alcoholics. It is with this purpose of love and devotion to others that the alcoholics overcome their distructive patterns; exchanging their negative addictions from the Pluto mount to positive addictions of the upper Uranus mount.

Although they don't look at this phenomenon as the replacement of lower negative addiction from Pluto into the more developed positive addictions of Uranus mounts, nevertheless they still follow the same pattern.

Understanding this concept can help millions to exchange negative addictions into more positive ones.

Again, we need to remember that addiction is a natural phenomenon. It cannot, therefore, be avoided or prevented. It can only be reduced, changed or replaced with a more positive one. The way to overcome these negative addictions are many; from the various support groups which actually provide a different style of positive addictive patterns (social or spiritual ones) to psychotherapy. Merely explaining to individuals who have negative addictive patterns that what they do is wrong, without providing substitutes of higher nature of addictive/attachment patterns, is unlikely to change their condition.

Groups based on AA (Alcoholics Anonymous) have developed in various areas of life. Part of them address addictions to a substance (e.g., Cocaine Anonymous). Others address behavior addictive patterns (e.g., Gambling Anonymous). Some developed ways to deal with specific mental disorders.

Marilyn Gellis, Ph.D., psychotherapist, followed the principles of helping people through support groups and the replacing of negative addictive behavior patterns with higher beliefs and positive addictive patterns. She founded an organization called:

The Institute for Phobic Awareness
Phobics Anonymous World Service Headquarters (PA)

This organization helps people overcome various kinds of phobias. It is very effective and addresses the emotional needs of the group among the other concepts. Her principles of dealing with phobias, which are actually negative addictive patterns, were summarized in her books: *The Twelve Steps of Phobics Anonymous* (together with Rosemary Muat, M.A.) and *From Anxiety Addict to Serenity Seeker.*

Palm Therapy can be incorporated with other systems in helping individuals who suffer from negative addictive patterns to a substance such as food, alcohol and drugs. Longitudinal lines on any transverse line on the mount of Pluto should be imprinted to help the individual free him/herself from the attachment to a certain substance and from the symptoms which are involved with that negative addictive pattern. This stimulation will make it easy for the person to switch from negative addictive patterns to more positive ones. It is recommended that together with Palm Therapy the individual will be under medical supervision and/or attend a support group which deals with his/her specific addictive problem.

The transverse lines on the mount of Pluto are the only ones on the ulnar border of the hand that can be crossed safely with longitudinal ones.

DO NOT CROSS THE TRANSVERSE LINES ON UPPER AND LOWER URANUS MOUNTS UNLESS YOU ARE A CERTIFIED PALM THERAPIST AND YOU KNOW WHAT YOU ARE DOING. There are many implications and systems within these mounts which may change or influence the style of relationships, one's spiritual/religious belief system, or major behavior patterns.

If you are a client, I strongly recommend, that before you attempt to get a Palm Therapy session, you should look for the certificate of a professional Palm Therapist issued by the INTERNATIONAL PALM THERAPY ASSOCIATION (IPTA). It is the only organization that certifies Palm Therapists. The certificate is given after proper training and wide understanding of scientific palmistry and Palm Therapy with constant updated information. It certifies an acceptance of a moral code of ethics, part of which deals with the aspect of never changing emotional/spiritual attachments or cognitive/behavior patterns without the full understanding and acceptance by the client/individual.

HOW TO STIMULATE OR RESHAPE A MOUNT

Section Four deals with the application of Palm Therapy including suggestions on how to stimulate the mounts. Since this chapter is dedicated to the mounts, let's review some of the basic ways of activating them and the mounts' characteristics:

1. Exercising: The palm is the fleshy area of the hand which also consists of muscles, tendons and fascia. By

exercising a specific finger we increase the strength of the muscles on the palm related to that finger, hence, increasing the size of its related mount. This method will affect the hand type as well, and it does give some results if we exercise the same finger regularly.

The easiest example of how to develop the size of a mount is the development of the Venus mount: Circling the thumb, pressing the first phalanx of the thumb against a hard surface, or flexing the thumb inward can do the job. (Consult with your healthcare professional before any physical exercises, including those of your fingers.)

2. Metamorphosis: Stimulation of the mounts with a very light-touch massage applied in a circular way on a specific mount. This light-touch massage is similar to the way of the *metamorphic technique*. This technique was discovered by the naturopath Robert St. John in 1960. It involves a very light touch massage on the feet, on the head and hand along the places representing the spine. This can release the past traumas from the gestation period (nine months as a fetus). The lower spine representation area shows the connection to the mother or the mother within that person—*yin* energy, and the upper spine representation area shows the father or the father within that person—*yang* energy. The area of the middle spine represents the gestation period of nine months, in which according to this method, most of the life patterns and mentality is based.

Palm Therapy on the mounts is done by gently stimulating a chosen area on the hand in a circular way with the tip of the first three fingers (thumb, Jupiter, Saturn).

Similar to the metamorphic technique, this light-touch massage on the mounts initially releases the various blockages, created at the first stages of life, then evoking and stimulating the healing and creative forces within the mounts. By applying this light stimulation on a certain mount you can heal/balance or stimulate the specific anticipated characteristics represented by that mount. In some cases when you need to create a *yin* energy effect, you need to stimulate the mount with a counterclockwise movement, but when you need to create a *yang* energy effect you can stimulate the mount with clockwise circulation.

To release negative memories from the past you may use a counterclockwise stimulation which also creates a more *yin* energy. Then you can use a clockwise stimulation to create a *yang* energy of the mounts—activating, reinforcing and intensifying its characteristics.

Yang energy stimulation can also be used for the activation of material success and cognitive achievements. A counterclockwise stimulation is recommended when *yin* characteristics are required. These include awakening of talents, emotional fulfillment and spiritual growth. For example, if you want to develop leadership abilities you will stimulate the main mount that represents this ability, the mount of Jupiter, with a clockwise stimulation; for meditation and self-awareness, you will stimulate the mount of Saturn and other areas of the palm with a counterclockwise stimulation; for sexual life and vitality the mount of Venus with a clockwise stimulation; for learning abilities the mount of Mercury with a clockwise stimulation and so on.

Can we go wrong with the light stimulation on the mounts? No. No harm can be caused by that, even if you give a person a different mode of stimulation such as counterclockwise instead of clockwise. We should remember that there is no damage to the tissue, only a light massage on a part of the palm. Your common sense, as well as your experience, should tell you that you have touched and stimulated parts of your hands or palms for as long as you have lived and nothing has happened. So you may ask then, how is it that a light massage can open and release blockages and negativeness of one's personality?

I believe that in our brain there is a center which is unknown as yet to science. This center works with the energy part of our existence and is probably located within the limbic system. I call it "the healing center". It cannot be in the cortex (the new brain) since this healing center is universal to all living things. This healing center is the part which probably sends the primary order to repair or to heal any physical or emotional pain and disorder. Once we let the healing center know that it can start the healing process it will, until healing on the emotional or physical level will be achieved. The mind has its own powers for self-healing if we give it the chance to do so. The light stimulation of a specific mount can activate the healing center, leading to optimum intensity of that mount and what it represents. The mind, in general, and the healing center, in particular, are wise and capable of self-healing. We should trust nature and our inner wisdom that we can heal ourselves and improve our lives.

This does not mean that from now on you will count only on your healing center and not consult with professionals in the fields of medicine, psychology or psychiatry or those of alternative medicine. On the contrary, you should contact them if you think you are having symptoms of a disorder because many times you need further information and feedback in order to heal or improve your life.

Palm Therapy on the mounts is effective. Its influence on specific parts of the personality represented by the mounts becomes clear as you proceed with it. More information on how to apply Palm Therapy through the mounts, you will find in Sections Four and Five. Meanwhile, let's further explore the secrets of the hand.

In the next chapter you will learn about the fingers and the characteristics they represent.

Do your utmost
to achieve your goals.
Continue until you reach them. Forgive
yourself for any failure along the way.
It is natural for all
human beings.

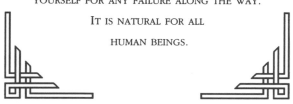

CHAPTER

The Fingers

The fingers (Fig. 39) represent an important part of hand reading. Similar to the mounts in palmistry, they are named after planets and Greek goddesses (an exception to that is the thumb). Their names from the radial to the ulnar side are: Thumb, Jupiter, Saturn, Apollo and Mercury.

We can examine the fingers in a few ways:

-**The length of the fingers**.: whether they are balanced, short or long. This is measured in relation of the middle finger to the length of the palm, also by measuring the length of the fingers and comparing them to each other.

-**The size of each finger's phalanx:** comparing each phalanx to another.

-**The thickness of the fingers**: as seen from the back of the hand and from the side of the hand.

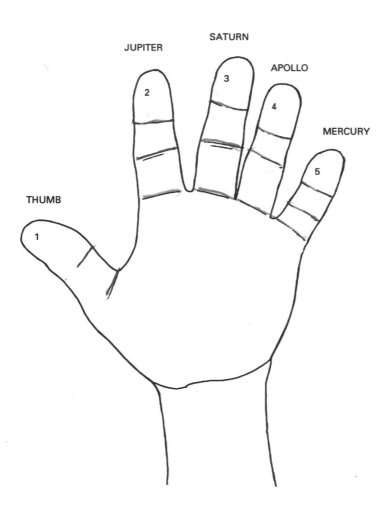

Fig. 39 *The Fingers.*

-The basic types of fingers: smooth, knotty, or irregulars as observed from the back of the hand.

-The basic types of fingertips: conic, square, round, spatulate as observed from the back of the hand, and conic, square, round or bulge as observed from the side.

-The flexibility of each finger: stiff, moderate flexibility or extreme flexibility.

In this chapter we will examine every one of these aspects briefly including the characteristics represented by each finger.

MEASURING THE PALM AND THE FINGERS

When checking the various fingers, we need to compare their size in relation to the length of the palm and in relation to each other.

You have learned to measure the hand at the beginning of Chapter 7: "The Seven Hand Types". For your convenience the procedure for measuring the length of the palm is repeated, here briefly (Fig. 40).

To measure the length of the palm, you need to draw an imaginary line from the radial border of the palm (the side of the thumb) to the ulnar border of the palm (the side of the little finger) starting at the base of the Jupiter finger towards the base of the Mercury finger. Then measure from a midpoint on the wrist's distal bracelet (the one which is closer towards the fingers) to a midpoint in that imaginary line.

When you want to measure the fingers, you measure the longest one which is usually Saturn and you compare its length to the length of the palm.

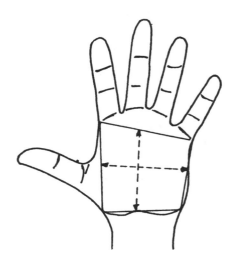

Fig. 40 *Measuring the Palm for finding fingers to palm ratio.*

The Balanced Fingers Hand

In the balanced fingers hand, the length of the Saturn finger is as long as the length of the palm. This is the ideal ratio since it represents the balance between the theory and the practicality of a person. Persons who have this ratio usually have the ability to plan and to achieve their plans. Many leaders possess this type of ratio. They can plan and manifest their planning. The qualities of achieving or doing is stronger in a *yang* type of hand than it is in a *yin* type of hand.

The Short Fingers Hand

In a short fingers hand (Fig. 41) the finger of Saturn is shorter than the length of the palm. It denotes that the person is a practical one and prefers the doing rather than the talking. He/she is

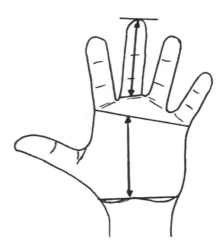

Fig. 41   *The Short Fingers Hand.*

also an achiever. Most of the things that we have in our world are thanks to the short fingers people.

Another aspect of the short fingers people is the emotional one. They have a short temper and may be impulsive in their reactions. They may have less ability to concentrate on theoretical things, but on the other hand, they can be quick and practical in their actions. The shorter the fingers the more technical characteristics versus theoretical ones these persons possess.

The Long Fingers Hand

In the long fingers hand (Fig. 42), the length of the longest finger which is usually Saturn is longer than the length of the palm. This represents the people who mainly live in their imagination. Among them are the artists and the philosophers. They love

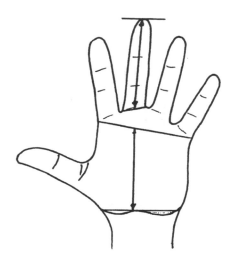

Fig. 42   *The Long Fingers Hand.*

details and have a humanistic approach to life. They may be spir-
itually developed as well. Unfortunately, although these individuals can be very strong in their ideas, they hardly ever become
leaders. Nevertheless, they can be talented and successful in
many fields, especially music, if other qualities as seen in their
hands support this.

We can look at the fingers' length from the various aspects
of the *yin* and *yang, too.* The shorter fingers represent *yang* qualities and the longer fingers the *yin* qualities. Of course, the balanced ones possess the qualities of both.

It is important for us to recognize children with these
types of fingers especially at school when they are very young;
the ones who are short-tempered, quick, and practical (short
fingers hand) or the ones who are patient, love details, slow in
thinking, and full of imagination (very long fingers hand). In

understanding their basic characteristics we need to be patient and direct them to a more balanced way to deal with their sur- roundings and the events in their lives.

COMPARING THE FINGERS

When measuring the fingers, each one of them is measured by comparison to its neighboring fingers (Fig. 43). We also need to compare it to a balanced hand with the balanced fingers in which:

-The thumb and the Mercury finger are equal in length.

-The Mercury finger reaches the base of the upper pha- lanx of the Apollo finger.

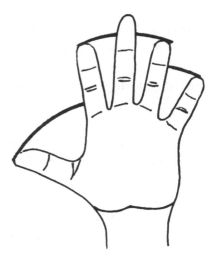

Fig. 43 *Comparing the fingers.*

-The thumb reaches the middle of the third phalanx of Jupiter.

-The finger of Jupiter equals the length of the Apollo finger and also reaches the middle of the first phalanx of Saturn. (If one of the two is longer then its characteristics become dominant.)

-The Saturn finger is the longest in the hand and, also, equal to the length of the palm.

COMPARING THE PHALANGES

We need to measure the different sizes of the finger's phalanges and compare the phalanges to each other in order to see which one is dominant.

Each finger represents a specific quality of the personality and each phalanx represents, in general, a different level of that quality:

I. The uppermost phalanx represents the spiritual and theoretical level of the mind.

II. The middle phalanx represents the practical, behavioral level of the characteristic represented by the finger.

III. The base phalanx represents the physical/body level of the characteristic represented by the finger.

Increasing the quality of a certain phalanx is done by

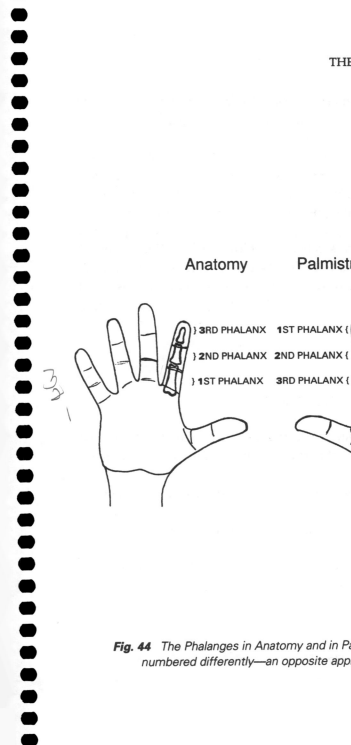

Fig. 44 *The Phalanges in Anatomy and in Palmistry are numbered differently—an opposite approach.*

imprinting longitudinal lines on that phalanx or crossing some transverse lines on the phalanx with longitudinal ones.

When we compare sizes of the various phalanges, it has to be clear that the phalanges flexion lines do not really represent the size or the exact location of the bony part of the phalanges. However, in palmistry, the distance between two digital creases (flexion lines of the finger) is called a phalanx or a phalange.

In anatomy the base phalanx is called the first phalanx and the tip phalanx is called the third phalanx. While in palmistry the tip phalanx is considered to be the first one and the base phalanx is the third one. These differences are illustrated in Fig. 44. In this book we will refer to the phalanges as in palmistry.

THE BASIC TYPES OF FINGERS

We can roughly divide the general shapes of all fingers into three types which can be observed when checking the back of the hand:

-Smooth fingers: either conic or rectangular in shape.

-Knotty fingers: fully knotty or partially knotty.

-Irregular: some bulges at any phalanx as observed from the back or side of the hand.

Smooth Fingers
The smooth fingers (Fig. 45) are smooth from their bases to their tips. Their interphalangeal joints are not prominent along their

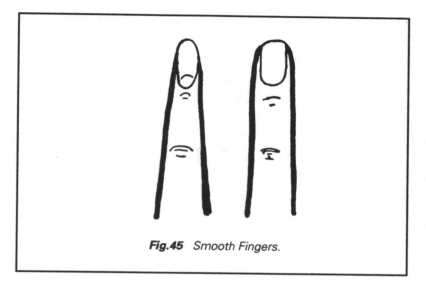

Fig.45 *Smooth Fingers.*

sides. These fingers represent quick, intuitive, non-analytical thinking.

Smooth fingers may be rectangular in shape i.e., the width of each finger is equal from their base to its tip. This can be seen from either the side or the back of the hand.

Another shape for the smooth finger is the conus-shaped finger. This finger is wider at its base and gradually forms a conus towards its tip. It can also be seen from either the side or the back of the hand.

The more pointed the fingertip is, the more of a quick thinker, intuitive and open to influences and ideas the person is.

Knotty Fingers

These fingers have bulges (Fig. 46) at their interphalangeal joints. These fingers are the main representatives of the philosophical hand. In contrast to the smooth fingers, the knotty fingers show a restriction in the flow of thoughts and ideas. They indicate a

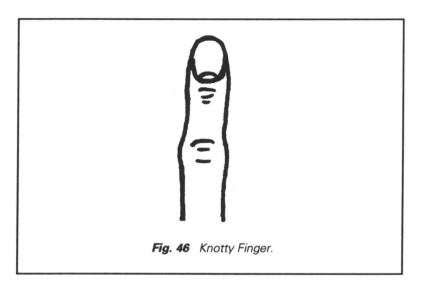

Fig. 46 Knotty Finger.

more methodical, analytical, philosophical thinking in their approach to life. The possessors of these fingers tend to think in depth about information given to them. They don't hurry to make conclusions, to answer or act before they have considered all facts or possibilities.

Sometimes these fingers are not completely knotty, but partially knotty, which means that there may be only one bulge joint on a finger while the other interphalangeal joints (either upper or lower joint) may be smooth. In this case the characteristics of the knotty fingers can be attributed to the two phalanges which border with that bulge.

Irregular Fingers

As mentioned above, irregular fingers (Fig. 47) may have some bulges at any phalanx as observed from the back or side of the hand or have other irregularities. It can be due to genetic factors, due to diseases, accidents or other reasons. Since an external

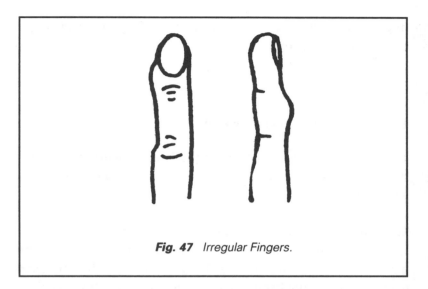

Fig. 47 *Irregular Fingers.*

change leads to a change in thoughts, behavior and personality in general, the fingers should be observed carefully and have to be compared with other components of the hand. You may find some contradictions if the irregularities in the shape of fingers has happened recently. If the irregularity has been in existence for a long period of time, the new changes in personality have been established and the other components of the hand will probably support such modifications which will also be represented, in the lines and the mounts.

The location of the irregularity will usually weaken the characteristics represented by that finger or that phalanx.

The Thickness of the Fingers

The thickness of the fingers is another aspect to look for when examining any finger type. The thicker the finger is, the more *yang* quality its basic characteristic possesses. The thinner the finger, the more *yin* characteristics it possesses. The thickness of the finger can be checked as seen from the back of the hand and as seen from the side of the hand.

THE BASIC TYPES OF FINGERTIPS

There are many shapes of fingertips. The following are some of the main classifications. They should be observed from the back and the sides of the hand

The fingertips as observed from the back of the hand:

The fingertips should be observed from the back of the hand for their characteristics. They should also be observed from the side of the hand to check the strength of these characteristics. There are four basic shapes of fingertips.

-Conic
-Square
-Round
-Spatulate

Conic Tip (Fig. 48)

The finger forms a tapered conus at its tip. This shape indicates a more intuitive, quick-thinking, artistic characteristic. The possessors of this fingertip love beauty and pleasure in life.

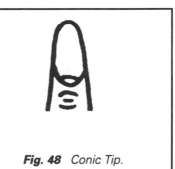

Fig. 48 Conic Tip.

Square Tip (Fig. 49)
The shape of this fingertip looks almost straight. It represents love for routine and a methodical, systematic way of living. The more square the tip is, the more it indicates a tendency of checking or of holding the flow of energy in such a way that the logical mind assesses it.

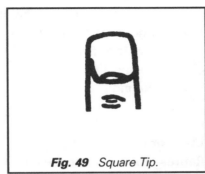

Fig. 49 Square Tip.

Round Tip (Fig. 50)
The characteristics of the round tip finger are somewhat between the conic and the square tips. They are intuitive, yet, with a logical mind. Although this finger represents a less practical characteristic than that of the square one, it indicates a better ability for accumulating wealth and properties.

Fig. 50 Round Tip.

Spatulate Tip (Fig. 51)
The spatulate fingertip is wider than the width of the finger. This tip indicates practicality, high energy and creativity. The wider the fingertip is, the more *yang* qualities the finger has.

Fig. 51 Spatulate Tip.

The fingertips as observed from the side:

The fingertips should be observed from the side as well. You may notice three main shapes:

-Conic or flat tip
-Bulge
-Round

Conic or a Flat Tip (Fig. 52)
Represents the influences of *yin* qualities on the finger.

Fig. 52 *Conic or Flat Tip.*

Bulge Tip (Fig. 53)
Represents the influence of *yang* qualities on the finger.

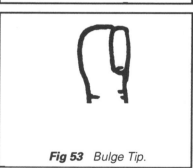

Fig 53 *Bulge Tip.*

Round Tip (Fig. 54)
Represents the influence of a balanced quality in terms of *yin* and *yang*.

Fig. 54 *Round Tip.*

THE FLEXIBILITY OF THE FINGERS

The flexibility of the hand or of the fingers is an important variable in hand reading. As a rule the more flexible the fingers are, the more open-minded the person is to new ideas, changes and adaptation to new life patterns.

The flexibility can be checked in various places of the hand. Bending each finger carefully towards its back can give us a good indication for the range of flexibility of that finger. This may change from finger to finger and from phalanx to phalanx of the same finger.

When the flexibility is too extreme (fingers or distal phalanges easily bent backward), it denotes generosity, lack of self-decisions, extreme changes in moods, a person who is easily influenced by others, and one who is involved in a more *yin* type of activity.

When the fingers are stiff they denote an insecure personality, one which resists new changes or ideas. It may also indicate stubbornness, determination, persistence and a more *yang* type of activity.

A moderate flexibility indicates an open-minded personality, generosity, acceptance of changes, adaptation to new life patterns and a well-balanced quality of that finger.

* * *

Now, let's learn about the characteristics of each finger. We will start with the thumb and end with the little finger.

Please note, in traditional palmistry the fingers are numbered from one to four starting at the pointer and ending with the little finger while the thumb is not numbered. This was established because the thumb was, and still is, considered as a very special component of the hand which cannot be compared to the other fingers. But for simplicity, the fingers in these sections are numbered from one to five (from the thumb to the little finger).

THE THUMB

The thumb, traditionally, plays an important role in the diagnosis of the hand. It can be short or long, of a low setting or high setting, narrow or wide in the first and second phalanges and with various degrees of flexibility.

When you observe hands, you will notice that the thumb is opposing the four fingers and is actually the strongest finger in the hand.

The mount of Venus forms its base and it is the main power behind this finger. As described before, the mount of Venus represents the vital energy, love, and the sex energy one possesses, in addition to the left hemisphere of the brain and the limbic system.

The length of the thumb is determined when the fingers are straight and the thumb is straightly closed to the fingers. While looking at the palm we examine the tip of the thumb against the third phalanx of Jupiter. A normal well-balanced thumb is one which reaches the middle of the third phalanx of Jupiter (Fig. 55). If it reaches longer than the halfway of the third phalanx of Jupiter (Fig. 56), we consider it as a long thumb which, in general, indicates a strong willpower and a better ability to achieve goals in life. It also suggests a good, logical, analytical mind.

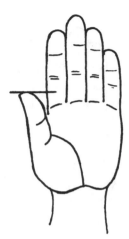

Fig. 55 *A balanced thumb.*

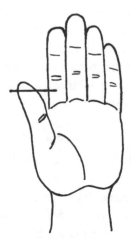

Fig. 56 *A long thumb.*

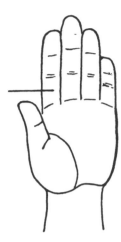

Fig. 57 A short thumb.

A short thumb is one which does not reach the middle of the third phalanx of the Jupiter finger (Fig. 57). This kind of thumb is one of the first evidences of mental weakness which includes poor willpower, poor logic and poor analytical ability. On the other hand, it indicates an intuitive mind and a tendency toward an imaginative, non-analytical approach especially if supported by a well-developed mount of Luna.

One of the main characteristics of the ape's hand is a short thumb with a high setting (Fig. 58) which means that the origin of the second phalanx of the thumb is higher and closer to the base of the fingers than to the wrist. The higher the setting, the less sophisticated the person is and vice versa. The base of a low-setting thumb (Fig. 59) is closer to the wrist than to the fingers. The way to measure high and low setting is by drawing an imaginary line from the base of the Jupiter finger to

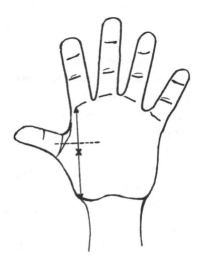

Fig. 58   *A short thumb with a high setting.*

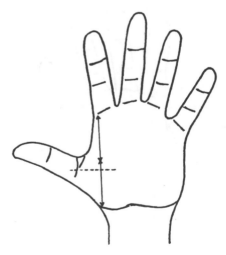

Fig. 59   *Finding the base of the thumb setting.*

the base of the wrist. The midpoint on this imaginary line represents a normal setting of the thumb

We need to remember that the thumb is only one aspect
of the hand; the total components of the hand will give us the
best indication of one's personality. Palmistry is never based
on one or two features, but on the studying of the entire hand.

The thumb and other supporting components in the hand
may indicate to what degree a person can build his life according to his goals. The willpower is represented in the first phalanx of the thumb, and the logical mind is represented in the
second phalanx of the thumb. Since most of our plans, activities and goals require determination and a logical mind, it is
most important to evaluate the thumb in that respect.

How do we determine, in the thumb, if the person has a

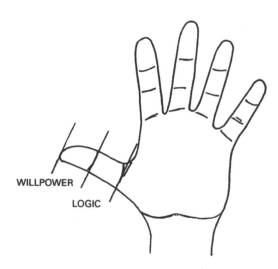

Fig. 60 *A balanced willpower to logic ratio is represented by the equal
length of the first and the second phalanges of the thumb.*

good, logical mind? You need to compare the first and the second phalanges of the thumb. The longer phalanx is the dominant one. A balanced willpower to logic ratio is represented by equal lengths of the first and second phalanges of the thumb (Fig. 60). But, remember, we can check this characteristic after we decide if the thumb is long or short, as well as the type of setting i.e., high or low.

In general, we can assume that a wide and long thumb represents a *yang* type of personality and a narrow and short thumb indicates more *yin* type qualities.

If the second phalanx is short (in a short thumb), then instead of having a logical approach, the person is more emotional with a more primitive approach to life or with primary instincts and wishes as described by S. Freud.

A stimulation with longitudinal lines on the first phalanx of the thumb is applied to increase willpower and determination, while a stimulation with longitudinal lines on the second phalanx of the thumb is applied to increase logical powers. A clockwise stimulation on these phalanges can bring similar affect.

THE FINGER OF JUPITER

Jupiter is the second finger after the thumb (Fig. 61), or the first one of the four fingers, as numbered in traditional palmistry. This finger is known as the index finger. It represents the person's reaction to the outside world. Jupiter finger has the clue towards many of the illnesses that come as a reaction to outside stimulation. This finger also manifests the control of the person towards others and some aspects of self-control. The length of the finger shows the level of dominancy of its characteristics.

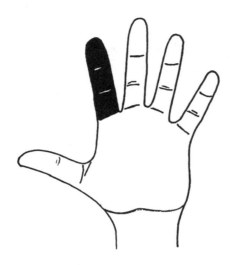

Fig. 61 *The finger of Jupiter.*

The measurement of the Jupiter finger is done by comparing it to the fourth finger, known as the finger of Apollo.

Measure from the tip of the finger to the base of the third phalanx to decide which finger is longer. The ideal length for the Jupiter finger will be the one which is identical to that of the Apollo finger and reaches the middle of Saturn's first phalanx (Fig. 62). In this case, the person has both the ability of leadership and the enjoyment from an equal relationship. A balanced finger indicates a minimum tendency towards either psychosomatic disorders or high-stress related problems.

A long finger of Jupiter (Fig. 63) represents a stronger control over others as a dominant characteristic. You may notice that those who are entering into leadership or running for the management of any institution, corporation, or state, as well as those who usually are in control, have a long Jupiter finger. A

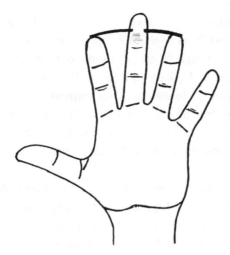

Fig. 62   *The ideal length of the Jupiter Finger is one which is identical to that of the Apollo Finger and reaches the middle of Saturn's first phalanx.*

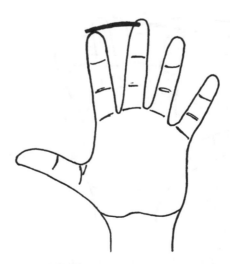

Fig. 63   *A long finger of Jupiter.*

long finger of Jupiter is also associated with a tendency to develop stress related disorders. The main problems would be of the *yang* type such as high blood pressure, ulcers, digestive problems, skin disorders, heart problems and others.

A short finger of Jupiter represents (Fig. 64) those who are controlled by others. I found out that individuals who, by accident, had lost the first phalanx of Jupiter lost most of their wish to command, rule or influence others. In this case a change in one's character occurs along with the artificial shortening or loss of that finger.

I, personally, was witness to the cases of two people who lost their first phalanx of Jupiter. Both changed a career into a less competitive one. More information of cases similar to the above should be obtained for a statistical proof. (If you have

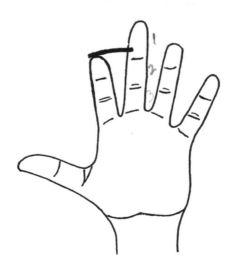

Fig. 64   *A short finger of Jupiter.*

such data please write to us and we may include the appropriate data in future writings).

When the finger of Jupiter is short, or shorter than average, it denotes that the person lacks in *yang* energies, hence, lacks control towards others. In this case most of the problems will be of psychosomatic aspects such as asthma, bronchitis, chronic pain, tiredness, hypotension and lack of energy, which attributes to *yin* energy. If the third phalanx is wider at the base it has the tendency for laziness and obesity.

You can manipulate this finger by increasing its vitality with a longitudinal line. But we must remember, nothing has been done just by dealing with one aspect. It is always the combination of all the elements that contributes to a success in dealing with any problem or disease.

Now, let's observe the finger's phalanges: The finger of Jupiter, like the other fingers but the thumb, is divided into three phalanges, each one of which represents another characteristic of this finger.

The First Phalanx of Jupiter Finger

The first phalanx is also known as the nail phalanx. It is measured from the top end of the finger to the first dominant horizontal line of the finger which is the digital flexion line. A good size will be equal to the second and the third part of the finger.

This phalanx represents the mental aspects of the person's attitude towards others, the intellect, the wisdom or the cognitive part of the brain in respect to others and to the outside world. The longer this phalanx is, the stronger the self-confidence is, sometimes to such a degree as being arrogant and very inconsiderate of others. If this phalanx is shorter than the others phalanges of that finger, it indicates a low ability to manage the outside world and others.

The Second Phalanx of Jupiter Finger

The second phalanx is actually the practical part of this finger. Whatever the person wants to achieve in this world, this part, if well-developed, will increase his/her chances to take advantage of it. In other words, from the Palm Therapy's aspect, this part— if we increase its quality— will increase the success momentum of the person. This can be done by marking longitudinal lines on it or by applying a clockwise stimulation. Another way to do it is by lowering the horizontal line between the second and base phalanx or by marking a new transverse line above the first flexion line of the first phalanx.

The Third Phalanx of Jupiter Finger

This phalanx is controversial among the various professionals in the fields of palmistry. The reason is philosophical in nature. The third phalanx is the base for the culinary, sex and other types of joy and entertainment which come from the outside. (For example, masturbation is indicated in the third phalanx of Saturn and not of Jupiter. The reason is that Saturn deals with the self, while Jupiter deals with the outside world in its various aspects.)

How far should we enjoy life? How far should we expose ourselves to the indulgence and the satisfaction which the outside world can offer us?

Some believe that the more is the better, assuming that the purpose of life is pleasure. In this case the bigger this phalanx is, the better its quality domain. Others believe that endurance and self-control are the best qualities. Hence, the smaller and thinner this phalanx is, the better it serves these believers.

These questions become more important when using Palm Therapy because, by applying Palm Therapy, you actually have a control over these aspects. You may improve or reduce the quality and the influence of this phalanx

My opinion is that you may do these changes only on yourself as desired while in relaxed state of mind, but never impose your view/beliefs on others.

To the certified Palm Therapist

You should not make any changes without consulting with your client and checking his/her ideas, beliefs and wishes. Remember that consulting and pointing out the various options is a part of the Palm Therapist's code of ethics. This is required from every Palm Therapist, even if, according to his/her belief system, some qualities are better than those which the client believes.

THE FINGER OF SATURN

The finger of Saturn (Fig. 65) represents the person's attitude towards him/herself. In this finger the energies of life are directed towards the various emotional or cognitive functions, but not social, as in the finger of Jupiter. From the standpoint of Palm Therapy many chronic diseases are associated with this finger.

The finger of Saturn is, also, the finger of the religious, metaphysical and philosophical outlook of life. A well-balanced finger has to be slightly higher than both Jupiter and Apollo. If it is equal to one of these fingers (a short Saturn finger) it would be a good idea to check these fingers as well. It may be an indication of an hereditary mental imbalance unless the neighboring fingers are very long, too.

As a general rule, the shorter the finger of Saturn, the

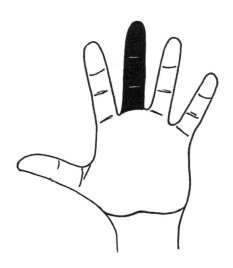

Fig. 65 *The Saturn Finger.*

lower the self-esteem of the possessor. If it is extremely short it is very likely that the person will develop a psychotic approach to life. Always take into account the other components of the hand before coming to such a conclusion.

The First Phalanx of Saturn Finger

The first phalanx of Saturn represents the philosophical approach to life, the ESP, religion and belief system but also sadness, grief, depression, sorrow and various emotional pains.

The Second Phalanx of Saturn Finger

From the Palm Therapy point of view, the second phalanx of Saturn represents the basic satisfaction from oneself but also chronic conditions that may have originated from psychosomatic diseases that are environmental in origin. An example for this is a case of the child who develops chronic asthma due to living in a non-functional family lacking love or affection. The middle phalanx represents the sorrow the child feels about himself, not the relationships with his parents. Although this is very important it would be represented in the parents' affection lines on the mount of Venus and in other places such as the finger of Mercury, the head line and heart line. (The aspect of parent-child relationship will be covered in more detail in our coming book on palmistry.)

The second phalanx also represents the practical part and the way in which we evaluate ourselves. People who don't take care of themselves practically will have horizontal lines on this phalanx. The neglected part of the body is detected through the location of the horizontal lines. A line on the upper part of this phalanx will represent the mind and the head, while a line on the lower part will represent the legs and the feet. Longitudinal lines on the second phalanx represent the overcoming of this type of difficulty and the improvement of the quality of this phalanx while deeper horizontal lines reduce the quality of this part.

The Third Phalanx of Saturn Finger

The third phalanx of Saturn represents the physical fitness and health of the person as well as psychosomatic disorders. Allergies can be detected in this phalanx in combination with other signs on the mount of Luna and that of Pluto. Many times it denotes various physical ailments which have no other clues. In the base phalanx, as in the other phalanges of Saturn, horizontal lines will represent difficulties or psychosomatic disorders on a physical level. Also, if you want to see the origin of the problem, this finger will be the best source of information; according to the horizontal lines, the strongest (darkest) one represents the most active problem. Since you now know that lines do change, develop or diminish, you might encounter lines that are new (in case of a newly developed problem) or diminished ones when some steps are taken to correct a situation. You may help yourself by creating longitudinal lines over the horizontal ones. (Cross the lines with longitudinal ones in at least three places on those horizontal lines.)

THE FINGER OF APOLLO

The finger of Apollo (Fig. 66) is very valuable in Palm Therapy. It is the seat of talents, imagination, artistic activity, creativity and

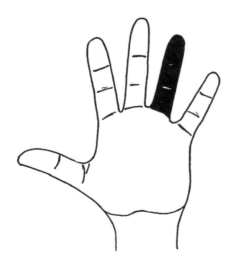

Fig. 66 *The Finger of Apollo.*

success in whatever aspect of life one chooses. This finger together with the mount of Apollo and the line of Apollo is the main place of focus during the third stage of Palm Therapy.

The finger of Apollo, as a whole, represents by some authorities the heart. From my point of view, this finger represents the emotional part of the self. Attracting joy and happiness can be activated by the stimulation of this finger. Interestingly enough, Chinese medicine considers the heart as the seat of joy and happiness.

The finger of Apollo is balanced when its length is equal to that of the Jupiter finger and reaches the middle of the first phalanx of the Saturn finger. This indicates a loving personality with love for beauty, harmony, art and a desire for fame, money and fulfillment.

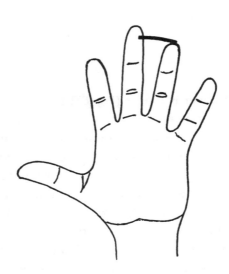

Fig. 67 *A long finger of Apollo.*

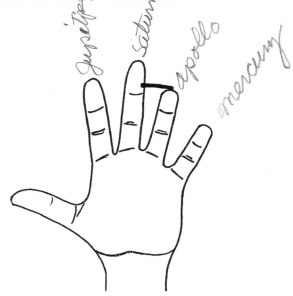

Fig. 68 *A short finger of Apollo.*

If the Apollo finger is longer (Fig. 67) than that of Jupiter, or as long as Saturn, it also indicates an artistic, aesthetic approach to life, living in a world of imagination. These people do not care to control others. In most cases one's view of life will be "I'll do my job and you do yours." These people can be introverts too (with the condition that in addition to a long Apollo finger, the head line and life line commence together).

If the Apollo finger is shorter than that of Jupiter (Fig. 68), there is little room for one's imagination. These subjects usually act without much thought. They are seeking success and are into controlling others. Usually it is manifested in their lives and careers.

The First Phalanx of Apollo Finger

If the first phalanx of Apollo is dominant it represents the highest form of fulfillment, as well as the spiritual, emotional or charismatic energy required for success. The larger or longer this phalanx is, the more achievements in life that person possesses (if other parts of the hand support this). The first phalanx of Apollo also represents the altruistic joy of fulfillment (without physical enjoyment).

The Second Phalanx of Apollo Finger

The second phalanx of Apollo represents the practical approach towards fulfillment in whatever area of life. Traditionally, it was attributed to practicality in art/talents, but it is also to the practical achievement in any area of interest including business, study, sports, hobbies or lifestyles.

The Third Phalanx of Apollo Finger

The third phalanx of Apollo represents the enjoyment from art or from life with materialistic desires, such as beauty, comfortable living, etc. It is the base for joy and satisfaction from the outside world, such as enjoying a good movie, music or vacations. This kind of satisfaction is versus the one represented by the third phalanx of Jupiter that also reflects enjoyment from an outer source, but in a more physical level such as from food and sex.

THE FINGER OF MERCURY

The finger of Mercury (Fig. 69), the last and the smallest one , represents in palmistry the thyroid functions as related to quick-

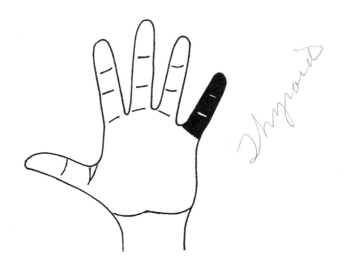

Fig. 69 *The finger of Mercury.*

ness or slowness of the physical and mental capacities.

The finger of Mercury is considered to be well-balanced when its fingertip ends at the first digital flexion line of the Apollo finger, between the distal and middle phalanges (Fig. 70).

A balanced finger in a long fingers hand will demonstrate more quickness of the mind, and a well-balanced finger in a short fingers hand will demonstrate quickness of physical activity (both have to be supported by complementary signs).

If the finger of Mercury is shorter than the base of the first phalanx of Apollo (Fig. 71), it indicates an ability to be good at expressing oneself in front of one person or a small group, but lacking the talent or ability of lecturing to the public. It also denotes that the possessor of this type of finger prefers the "doing" over the "talking."

Those who possess a long Mercury finger (Fig. 72) have more verbal capabilities and may be good as lecturers, teachers or at any instructional job.

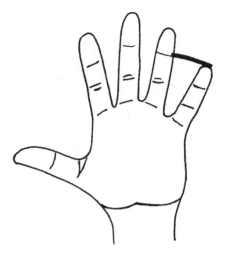

Fig. 70 *A well-balanced length of Mercury finger.*

Fig. 71 *A short finger of Mercury.*

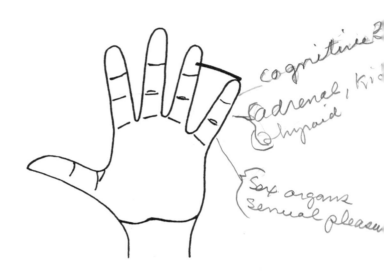

cognitive?
adrenal, kid
thyroid

Sex organs
Sensual pleasu

Fig. 72 *A long finger of Mercury.*

The physical health is also reflected by this finger. The first phalanx of Mercury is associated with the cognitive brain; the second with the adrenal, kidneys and the thyroid; the third phalanx is associated with the sex organs of the male and female and with sensual pleasure of both genders.

Since this finger is the base for quickness and health, longitudinal lines are very important. The health line which appears in some of the palms is associated with this finger.

The direction or the inclination of the finger provides some information as to how its possessors approach others. If the little finger is inclined towards that of Apollo, especially when the hand is at rest, palm down and somewhat loose, these people usually refuse to disclose themselves to others. This may be due to low self-esteem or emotional trauma at a young age. Traditionally, this sign is considered as an indicator of people who don't tell the truth. I realized that once we improve their self-esteem or remove the initial traumas from their lives, these individuals become more open and direct with others. People who possess this inclined finger are also considered as having good talent for business (if the other components in the hand support this, too).

If the finger is extended outward, away from the other fingers, it shows some difficulties in relationships. These people prefer being isolated from society. The condition also can be solved by improving their self-esteem.

The First Phalanx of Mercury Finger

If the first phalanx of the Mercury finger is dominant, it represents good verbal skills and easy communication with others. If the whole finger is long, it denotes an ability for public speaking. It also indicates good learning skills and a special interest in scientific researches and factual information.

The Second Phalanx of Mercury Finger

If the second phalanx of the Mercury finger is dominant, it represents a more realistic, practical approach towards business, science or medicine and thus is manifested in one's career.

The Third Phalanx of Mercury Finger

If the third phalanx of Mercury is dominant it denotes sensuality and physical activity which is manifested in sports, work and sexual life.

CAN WE CHANGE THE QUALITY OF THE FINGERS?

As mentioned in regard to the general shape of the hand, our fingers undergo natural changes throughout a lifetime. Special exercises can induce some changes as well. It may take many months, but it is possible. A change in the thickness of the fingers can lead to a corresponding change in the personality.

When evaluating the characteristics of the fingers and the various phalanges, we must pay attention to the transverse lines (other than the flexion digital lines). These lower the quality of the phalanges while longitudinal lines increase the potential represented by the phalanges.

Through Palm Therapy's stimulation, you can accelerate or decrease specific characteristics that are represented by the various fingers or their phalanges. Longitudinal lines or a clockwise stimulation can be applied for awakening certain qualities, while the marking of transverse lines or a counterclockwise stimulation will either balance or decrease the intensity of the characteristics represented by the finger/phalanx.

CHAPTER **10**

The Major Lines

The study of the lines on the palms is very important for Palm Therapy. Before you can correct any line, you must understand the normal pattern and representation of each line, as well as the effect of the minor lines on the hand (Chapter 11). Also, you need to pay attention to special marks and signs (Chapter 12) which may appear on the hand. Remember, all the markings on your hands may naturally change in shape and direction during your life.

The focus of energy keeps shifting gradually as life proceeds from the prenatal period to birth, to young child, young adult, adult and gradually to old age. So does the focus and the influence of the main lines on the palm shift gradually from their origin near the mount of Earth towards their destinations either towards the ulnar side of the palm (the heart and the head lines) or in a curve towards the wrist (the life line).

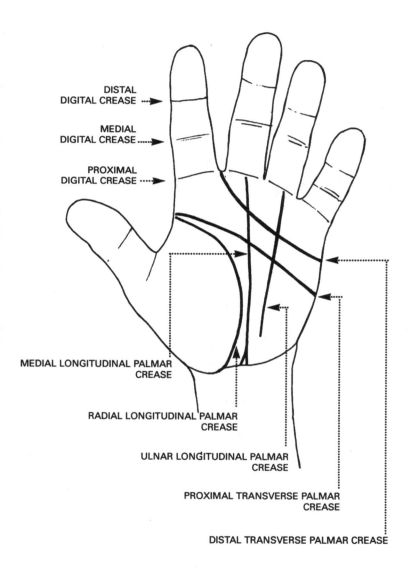

DISTAL
DIGITAL CREASE ····▶

MEDIAL
DIGITAL CREASE ······▶

PROXIMAL
DIGITAL CREASE ····▶

MEDIAL LONGITUDINAL PALMAR
CREASE

RADIAL LONGITUDINAL PALMAR
CREASE

ULNAR LONGITUDINAL PALMAR
CREASE

PROXIMAL TRANSVERSE PALMAR
CREASE

DISTAL TRANSVERSE PALMAR CREASE

Fig. 73 *The major lines and their anatomical terminology.*

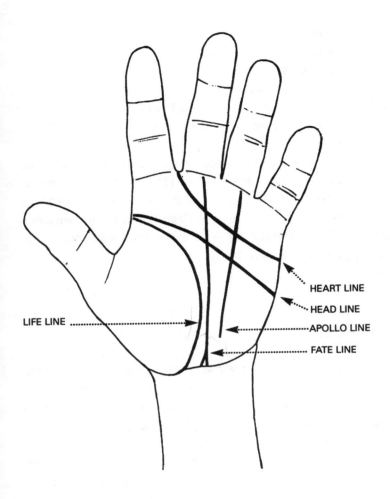

HEART LINE

HEAD LINE

LIFE LINE

APOLLO LINE

FATE LINE

Fig. 74 *The major lines and their terminology in palmistry.*

The major lines include:

The Heart Line
The Head Line (Brain Line)
The Life Line
The Fate Line (Line of Saturn)
The Apollo Line (Sun/Success line)
The Mercury Line (The Line of Health)

An illustration of the various major lines and their terminology in anatomy are presented in Fig. 73 (but the Mercury line). Pay attention to the location of the terms: distal, proximal, radial and ulnar. (You may refer to Page 129 or to the "Anatomy of the Hand" in Appendix A.) The major lines and their terminology in palmistry appear in Fig. 74.

THE HEART LINE

The heart line (Fig. 75) is important from the standpoint of Palm Therapy. It is a transverse line that lies under the mounts of the fingers, usually commencing at the mount of Jupiter or between this mount and the mount of Saturn. In anatomy this line is known as the distal transverse palmar crease.

In traditional palmistry the heart line indicates the condition of the heart. Some palmists went so far as to indicate the possibility of heart attack at a certain time in a person's life, as well as the related emotional aspects such as love relationships and expectation from others on the emotional level. A perfect heart line is smooth and deep, starts with a curve and continues horizontally straight toward the ulnar border of the palm. A per-

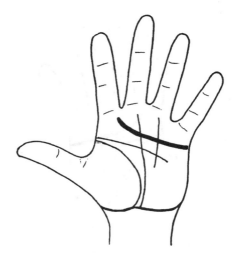

Fig. 75 *The Heart Line.*

fect heart line demonstrates a healthy, balanced mental approach.

When there are some emotional difficulties during one's life, it will be represented on the heart line. The hypothesis is that any emotional difficulties force the person to stop the natural energy flow which runs on that line, so he/she can focus on the problem or the emotional pain. The more severe the stressor is for that person, the more the person has to stop the energy flow. According to the severity of the case, the disturbance of energy flow on the heart line will be represented in an upgrading scale from a dot (Fig. 76), an island (Fig. 77), a chain (Fig. 78), and in severe cases, a breakage/s (Fig. 79) on the line.

Unless the person takes some form of a therapy, this disturbance will create problems in the future of that individual which will be manifested as accumulated stress, mental disorders and a variety of physical diseases.

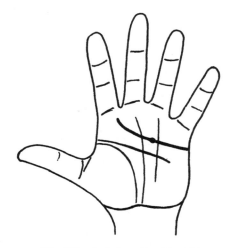

Fig. 76   *A dot on the Heat Line.*

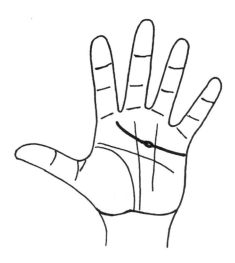

Fig. 77   *An island on the Heart Line.*

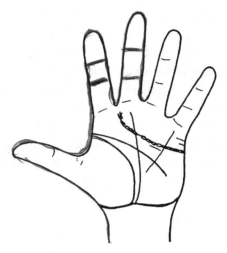

Fig. 78   *A chain on the Heart Line.*

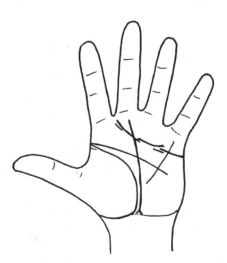

Fig. 79   *A breakage on the Heart Line.*

If such marks are clearly seen on the heart line, Palm Therapy can be applied simply by working and smoothing such marks. If emotional problems exist, and no evidence is seen on the heart line, the use of a magnifying glass, or even a microscope, will be efficient in the effort to locate the source of that emotional problem and to handle it as well.

As a rule, the larger the breakage on the heart line is, the higher the stressor is. This manifests the endurance and ability to survive under a traumatic situation, reacting like a sensitive fuse which disconnects the energy flow or the electricity of that specific event.

Palm Therapy improves and balances the energy flow of the lines. If the energy flow of the heart line cannot move smoothly through its channel (line) it may lead to further emotional reactions ranging from a light depression to other disorders, from fears to severe panic attacks, or from being slightly annoyed to strong anger, frustration, hate, or violence. Many emotional disorders can be expected when there is a breakage or other interruption to the heart line.

Some people possess a very short heart line (Fig. 80), which commences from the mount of Saturn or the mount of Apollo. These people are usually of short temper and have difficulties dealing with emotions, therefore, they are hard to live with. Imprinting a longer heart line can improve their nature. Before we do so, we need to verify what emotional approach one would rather possess. In reality these individuals don't cooperate in the first session and are not able to understand the meaning of it. The denial of their emotional state is preventing them from accepting help and from treating themselves. For such a type of personality, I usually extend the heart line with a slight curve towards the finger of Jupiter by imprinting and marking this extension on the original line. In many cases, these individuals can feel the difference after the first session and become more

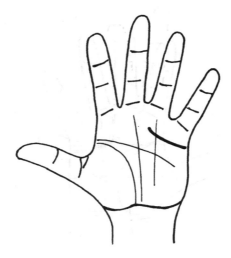

Fig. 80   *A very short Heart Line.*

cooperative in discussing their feelings regarding the direction of
the emotional qualities which they wish to achieve.

To the certified Palm Therapist:
For an individual with physical or emotional problems of any kind, Palm
Therapy serves as an additional tool, combined with a proper treatment
by a healthcare professional.

The location of the heart line is also important for hand
analysis. An ideal location of the heart line is when the distance
between the base of the finger of Apollo and the heart line
(Fig.81) is equal to one-third of the length of the palm (from
the base of Apollo finger to the wrist's distal bracelets), dividing
the palm into three sections which represent the three worlds:
spiritual/emotional, practical/behavioral and physical/chemi-
cal.

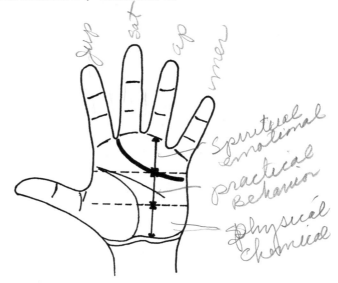

Fig. 81 *An ideal location of the Heart Line.*

The distance of the first part (i.e., from the basal flexion line of the Apollo finger to the heart line) represents the spiritual/emotional world. The longer the distance between the base of the fingers to the heart line, the stronger the emotional/spiritual basic capacity of the person is.

The distance between the heart line and the head line is measured at the closest part between them (it is parallel to the fingers of Apollo and Saturn). A normal distance (Fig. 82) is about one half of the width of the first phalanx of the Saturn finger (measured at the base of the nail). This distance denotes a balance between the ability to accept new ideas in general, and the ability to accept new ideas only through the control of the belief system one possesses. A wide distance between the heart line and the head line (Fig. 83) is one that is more than the width of one half of the first phalanx of the Saturn finger. This distance demonstrates the ability to be open-minded and to accept new

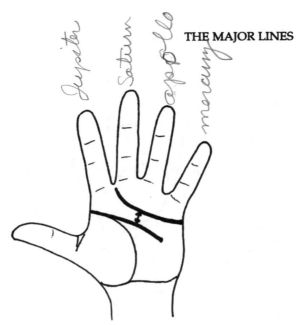

Fig. 82 *A normal distance between the Heart Line and the Head Line.*

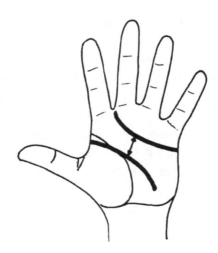

Fig. 83 *A wide distance between the Heart Line and the Head Line.*

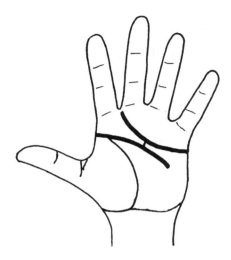

Fig. 84 *A short distance between the Heart Line and the Head Line.*

ideas without restricting it with previous belief system guide-lines.

A short distance between the heart line and the head line (Fig. 84) is one which is shorter than the width of one-half of the first phalanx of the Saturn finger. A short distance denotes fixed ideas and the ability to accept mainly information which is large-ly based on an established belief system. (Previously in tradi-tional palmistry, the width between the heart line and the head line was believed to demonstrate kindness versus selfishness which a person possesses. The wider the distance was, the more good-hearted the person was considered to be, the narrower the distance was, the more selfish character the individual was con-sidered to have.) After observing hands of many individuals I did-n't find evidence for that assumption.

A downward heart line (Fig. 85) is a line which originates

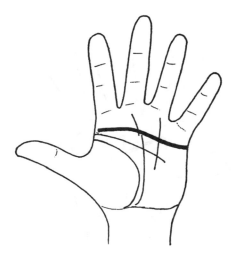

Fig. 85 *A downward Heart Line.*

closer to the head line. It denotes a control of the emotions by the cognitive mind and shows that the person's attachment to others is on a logical basis rather than on an emotional one.

THE HEAD LINE

In traditional palmistry, the transverse line which starts in the radial side of the palm and runs almost parallel to the line of heart is called the head line or the brain line (Fig. 86). This line represents the brain physiology and logical mind activity. In anatomy this line is known as the proximal transverse palmar crease.

The two hemispheres of the brain were mentioned in Chapter 8. Now, let's describe some of the brain and the mind

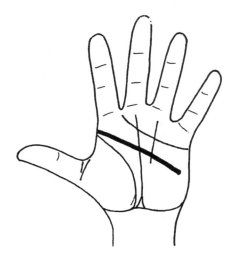

Fig. 86 *The Head Line.*

characteristics which are represented by the head line.

Taber's Cyclopedic Medical Dictionary defines the brain as a large, soft mass of nerve tissue contained within the cranium. It is the cranial portion of the central nervous system. The brain is the primary center for regulating and coordinating body activities. Sensory impulses are received through certain nerves (afferent). These register as sensations which are the basis for perception. The brain is known as the seat of consciousness, memory, thought, reason, emotion and judgment. Motor impulses are discharged through another group of nerves (efferent) to muscles and glands initiating such activities. Through reflex centers automatic control of body activities is maintained. The most important reflex centers are the cardiac (of the heart), vasomotor (of blood vessels) and respiratory centers which regulate circulation and respiration.

The mind is defined as the integration of the brain's functions, resulting in the ability to perceive the surroundings, to have emotions, imagination, memory, will and to process information in an intelligent manner.

The largest part of the brain is the cerebrum. It is divided into right and left cerebral hemispheres. The two sides of the cerebrum send impulses to, and receive impulses from, the opposite sides of the body.

The right hemisphere, which is known to represent imagination, fantasy, the ability to visualize and use intuition, love, art, physical activity and more, is connected to the left hand. While the left hemisphere, which is related to logic thinking, complex mathematics, writing abilities and science, is connected to the right hand.

This is the case when the dominant hand is the right hand. If the left hand is the dominant one, we assume that the hemisphere functions are reversed, too.

The head line represents both the cognitive and the imaginative thinking of the mind. According to the various components of the hand as well as to the head line, we can draw information regarding the mind activity and tendencies of an individual. A long and straight head line (Fig. 87) represents a more mathematical or logical thinking. While a head line which inclines all the way in a curve towards the mount of Luna denotes of more imagination than logic. If this curve is way down toward the wrist (Fig. 88), and this condition appears in both hands, the owner of this hand may live in his/her own world of imagination to a degree that may indicate mental disorder or insanity. A head line which ends in a an upward curve towards the heart line (Fig. 89) shows restricted cognitive patterns of the mind, or an extreme tendency for idealization.

The origin of the head line is separated from that of the life line. If the head line commences together with the life line (Fig. 90), it

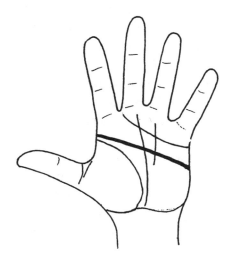

Fig. 87 *A long and straight Head Line.*

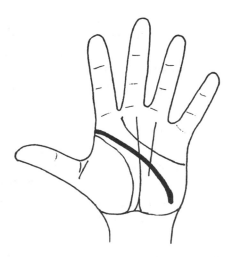

Fig. 88 *A Head Line which is curved towards the Mount of Luna.*

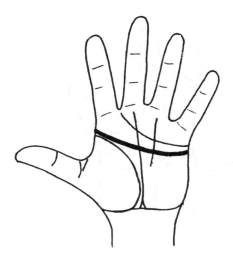

Fig. 89 *A Head Line which is curved towards the Heart Line.*

demonstrates an introvert personality. If the head line is attached and runs together with the life line as one line and then at a certain point splits (Fig. 91), it may signify an introvert personality and a stressful childhood. Sometimes the head line commences from the curved border which is formed by the life line (Fig. 92). In such cases, it shows an inferiority complex starting in childhood. While in other cases the head line may be absent at the normal beginning of it, in the radial border of the palm, but commences at some later point, towards the middle of the palm (Fig. 93). This demonstrates a high stress as a young child, usually in individuals who tend to forget their very early childhood years.

A chained head line (Fig. 94) shows an impaired thinking and some emotional restrictions which the person is trying to control logically.

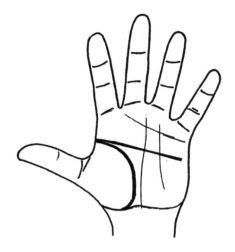

Fig. 90 *The Head Line which commences together with the Life Line.*

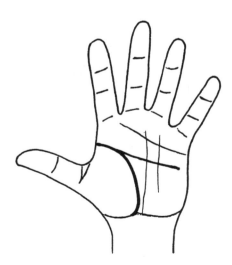

Fig. 91 *The Head Line which is attached and runs together with the Life Line as one Line, then splits at a certain point.*

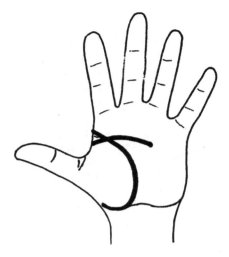

Fig. 92 *A Head Line which commences from within the curved border formed by the Life Line.*

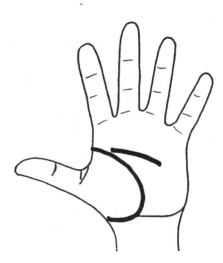

Fig. 93 *A Head Line which does not commence at the radial border but at some later point towards the middle of the palm.*

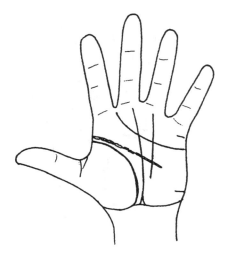

Fig. 94 *A chained Head Line.*

A broken head line (Fig. 95) usually presents when the cognitive hardship is too extreme so that the only solution is running away. It mostly happens after a traumatic event that was very hard to handle.

The next two shapes of the head line may be misleading, and always should be supported with additional data from the other components of the hand, as it is always recommended.

A short head line (Fig. 96) usually shows a practical and quick approach to life without investing time to learn or think much.

The other possible shape for the head line is the simian line (Fig. 97). If the head line and the heart line are formed as a single transverse line, it may be an early sign of Down's syndrome, but it may merely demonstrate a control of emotions or restricted behavior patterns.

From the standpoint of Palm Therapy, the way to improve

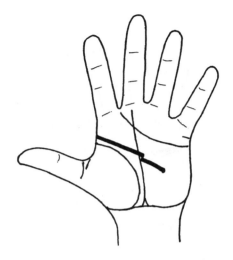

Fig. 95 *A broken Head Line.*

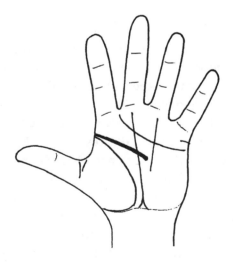

Fig. 96 *A short Head Line.*

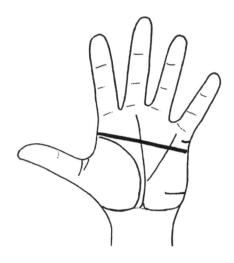

Fig. 97 *The Simian Line.*

the condition is to imprint a better head line which is slightly curved towards the mount of Luna. This should be done often until the new line starts to shape and take its place, thus improving the mental ability and well-being.

A quality head line is deep, clear and at least reaching the finger of Apollo. This usually indicates a good IQ and proper brain functions. (One of the first things which I concentrated on, back in 1985, when I started to check the effectiveness of Palm Therapy, was working on the head line to improve my own IQ.)

Stimulating this line improves the IQ, as well as concentration, memory and other talents we possess.

Since these can be improved by stimulating the head line, it becomes a great tool for students of any age. This line can be stimulated providing they don't suffer from any emotional disorder which might be provoked when activating this line. It is not dangerous, but may be unpleasant. If that occurs, use your thumb nail and press an age line (a longitudinal line which crosses the head and the heart lines parallel to the fate line, in the locations representing the current age on these lines (see the *age scale* Fig. 147a, Chapter 16). Press for a few minutes in each hand or until relief is achieved.

For the reinforcement of one's learning abilities, the Mercury finger and mount should also be taken into consideration.

Nevertheless, I don't recommended the activation of the head line in the first stage of Palm Therapy because this line represents past memories. Its stimulation can initiate the release process. Since most of us did suffer at some stages of our lives, the memories from childhood, or earlier, can be vivid and express themselves in dreams or by changes of mood. Therefore, it is not recommended to start with the head line (prior to the Balancing Stage).

Those people on whom I worked on their head lines prior to the Balancing Stage reported, after a few minutes of stimulation, anger, stress and the wish to terminate the session. Usually, unless you prepare the clients with enough reinforcement or balancing at the first stage, they may never come back for another session and so lose the opportunity to get rid of emotional problems that interfere with their happiness, relationships and fulfillment.

As mentioned above, although the head line is one of the perfect tools to improve memory, concentration and the IQ, it is not the place to start. It should usually be activated in the second and the third stages of Palm Therapy. (The heart line in most cases will be the first line with which to start, then the life line, the fate line, and the Apollo line. Palm Therapy for the three stages is reviewed in Section 4.)

The first part of the head line, which is between the thumb and the Jupiter finger, represents the childhood. This part should be observed very carefully because if there is any trauma, fear, or mental problem rooted in the early childhood we should locate it there.

During the Release Stage, the second stage of Palm Therapy, by stimulating and smoothing that part, a healing effect to the memory storage from negative feelings and traumas is taking place and may improve life.

The head line is just one part of what should be observed in a person's hand in order to determine the IQ and mind abilities. Other factors are the thumb, the general shape of the hand, the distal phalanx of each finger, the finger of Mercury and its mount.

As a rule, to examine the quality of the mind, the general shape of the hand should be classified first, then check the fingers and specific phalanges, usually the tip phalanx of each, and then the head line. The use of a magnifying glass will be helpful for detecting the small lines crossing the head line as well as islands or dots on the line. The color and resistance of the line should be checked next.

The head line plays a very important role in Palm Therapy, but we must deal with it very carefully and only after the person can undertake the emotional pain from past memories.

In cases when people went through a major trauma, like those who experienced the concentration camps and, as a result of it, are on the borderline of sanity, or are so depressed that they threaten very often to commit suicide, Palm Therapy can serve as an effective tool. The work is done by imprinting one or more small vertical lines to cross the head line at the places that represent the current age of the individual and the period of the trauma.

To the certified Palm Therapist:

Remember, in those cases mentioned above, this work can be only secondary and in addition to the treatment of a licensed psychotherapist. By all means, never claim or suggest that you can solve mental problems by Palm Therapy alone. Always work with the cooperation of a practitioner and consult with him/her for the benefit of the client. If such client is not under medical care, refer him/her to such a professional.

THE LIFE LINE

The life line (Fig. 98) is one of the most important lines of the hand. This line encircles the mount of Venus starting on the radial border of the palm, from the middle point (more or less) between the thumb and the Jupiter finger, and goes all the way towards the wrist. This line is clearly marked in most hands and is known in anatomy as the radial longitudinal palmar crease.

As mentioned earlier about the head line, sometimes the life line is attached to the head line at the beginning of the line. This usually demonstrates an introvert personality. If the life line commences separately from the head line it indicates an extrovert personality. The space between the two starting points of these lines indicates how dominant this extrovert tendency is.

Another possibility is when the life line and the head line are attached and run together as one line and at a certain point split to form the head line and the life line. In this case it will demonstrate an introvert personality starting in childhood and a stressful period which continued for as long as the lines run together.

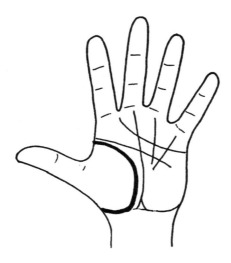

Fig. 98 *The Life Line.*

Up to now you have learned about the characteristics of the life line in regard to psychological conditions (i.e., introvert when attached in a way to the head line). But actually the main characteristic of the life line deals with the various aspects of health and vitality.

In ancient palmistry a long life line was believed to represent the longevity of a person, while a short life line or the point of break or absence of the life line was considered the date of death of the individual. This assumption is totally wrong and misleading. There is no direct connection between the length of the life line and the actual longevity.

The life line shows the vitality and the energy a person possesses. A short life line (Fig. 99) shows a normal start in life in terms of vitality and health. An absence of parts of the life line, or the presence of a dot, breakage or an island on the line, represents a loss of vitality and energy at the age related to the loca-

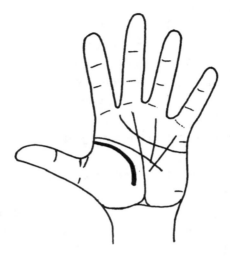

Fig. 99 *The short Life Line.*

tion of that sign which may lead to chronic conditions.

The life line, therefore, is an important tool for drawing information regarding the health and the general level of vitality of the person. You can improve the line and mark it all the way toward the wrist, encircling the mount of Venus. By correcting this line you actually improve the vitality as well as the healing forces within you.

We must remember that, in many cases, this line should be reinforced regardless of the problem or disease that one has whether it is a physical disorder or an emotional/mental one. Reinforcing the life line is actually reinforcing the *chi* energy, or the primary energy of life, which is described in Chinese medicine.

Another aspect of the life line is that it forms a border line for a very special mount—the mount of Venus. It may encircle this mount closer to the radial border, making this mount narrow (Fig. 100) or encircle it to form a wide mount of Venus (Fig. 101). The larger the mount of Venus is, the more vitality a person possesses. By marking a wider borderline with the life line (including activation of specific muscles in the hand) you increase the size of this mount. But don't over extend the life line towards the ulnar side in a way that will affect the mounts of Neptune or Luna. These mounts are important for our balance. The life line will lose its characteristics if you do so and become ineffective.

Islands, dots, cutting lines and breakages on the life line should be considered as negative and, therefore, should be corrected by smoothing the line. As I stated before, it is absurd to foresee a trouble or a disaster a person may encounter at any specific time during his/her life as seen on the line and not to do anything about it. In the past, the palmist used to predict a disaster or a problem that might occur at a specific time in one's life. Now that we understand the mechanism of the hand from the standpoint of Palm Therapy, it is our obligation and duty to correct these negative events immediately upon seeing them on the hands. I believe that my strongest contribution to life is this active prevention approach, which means don't be a passive viewer anymore, correct and improve the quality of your life! Prevent negative events before they happen! Do it in an active way with the use of Palm Therapy or other tools and therapies.

Some of you may question this approach and wonder if it is right to prevent or avoid specific events in a person's life, thus changing one's karma/fate. The answer is positive. It is more than correct. It is our obligation. It would be the same as asking if it is right for a doctor to prescribe a remedy to fight a disease and by doing so to actually change the karma or the course of the disease; also if it is right for a doctor who recommends a periodical test to make sure that everything is OK. When he sees

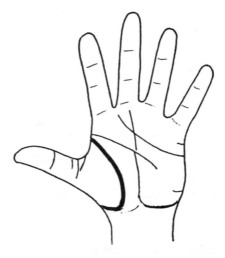

Fig. 100 *A Life Line which encircles the Mount of Venus closer to the radial border of the palm decreases the size of this mount.*

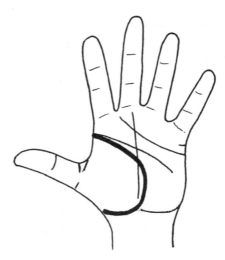

Fig. 101 *A Life Line which widely encircles the Mount of Venus increases the size of this mount.*

something wrong it is his/her responsibility to help to prevent it as soon as he/she can, before further complications appear. The physician's approach should be applied to Palm Therapy. This means that you may prevent a problem, disease or even a disaster by working out problems with a simple, easy technique— Palm Therapy. Again, as previously stated, this work must be in addition to the diagnosis and treatment by a licensed healthcare professional.

You can increase the energy of life simply by pressing and working on the life line (especially towards the wrist). Working on the line of life usually means concentrating the stimulation on the place representing the actual age of the person also smoothing any island or connecting any breakages. But, as a general practice, it is a good idea to mark the whole line from the beginning to its end (on the wrist) in both hands.

Usually, when there are specific problems we need to remember that the left hand represents the left part of the body, but the right hemisphere of the brain. The left hemisphere will be represented by the right hand which also represents the right side of the body. But since in most problems and diseases both parts of the body are included, it is wise to to stimulate the line on both hands.

THE FATE LINE

The line of fate (Fig. 102) is the medial longitudinal palmar crease (anatomy) which runs from the mount of Neptune toward the finger of Saturn.

This line is also known as the line of Saturn or the line of destiny. It is one of the main longitudinal lines which, in traditional palmistry, is attributable to the fate of a person, his/her career, direction, goals and tendency to a secure or an insecure life. It, also, represents any change in life modalities such as changing homes or locations during childhood or later in life.

When this line commences at the mount of Neptune it shows that the person had balanced supervision as a child and enjoyed freedom as well.

People who possess a fate line which starts within the mount of Venus (Fig. 103), were overprotected as a children. The more to the radial side the origin of this line is, the more a rigid and overprotective experience was involved. The location where the fate line crosses the life line, leaving the mount of Venus, represents the phase when they got free from the over-protective guardians or became independent.

If the fate line starts at the mount of Luna (Fig. 104), it denotes a lot of freedom during childhood and it shows a much more independent person. The negative part of it is that it may

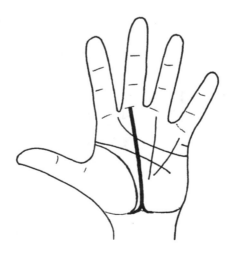

Fig. 102 *The Fate Line/The Line of Saturn.*

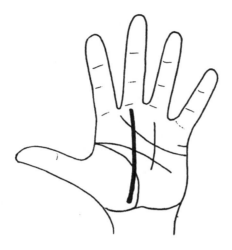

Fig. 103   *The Fate Line commences within the Mount of Venus.*

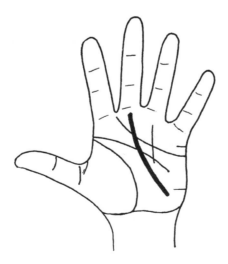

Fig. 104   *The Fate Line commences within the Mount of Luna.*

sometimes create a cold personality which is less affectionate towards others. These people tend to be good in business or, feeling the lack of supervision, they may subconsciously want to correct their past by becoming teachers of any kind. When the Jupiter finger is short, the tendency will be towards practical issues. If the Mercury finger is long the tendency will be towards teaching theoretical studies. In some cases both conditions apply.

In some cases, the fate line twists towards either the finger of Jupiter or that of Apollo. When it ends near the Jupiter finger (Fig.105), it demonstrates that these subjects' directions in life are more toward self-control. They also tend to be self-centered and they are self-motivated in their main work and activities in life.

If the fate line is naturally twisted towards the finger of Apollo (Fig. 106), their career is involved with the public. These individuals are more inclined towards an open social life. It also shows that the motivation for the main work and activities of these persons is connected to an external stimulation. If the fate line goes towards the base of Apollo, it also tells us that these subjects, in their careers, aim to build security for themselves and their family. They may also prepare themselves for a more active social life at a mature age.

In most cases, the line of fate is found broken into many segments (Fig. 107). The locations of these segments indicate many changes in one's life, as well as the period when these events occurred.

Sometimes the line of fate starts much higher, distally, from the wrist towards the middle of the palm (Fig. 108). If the fate line is partly absent, or can hardly be seen on the hand, then it demonstrates that the person's purpose or direction in life is unclear, without any goals or stability. The more stable one's life is, the clearer the fate line appears on the hand.

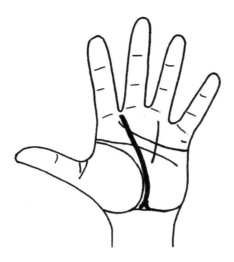

Fig. 105 *The Fate Line which ends near Jupiter Finger.*

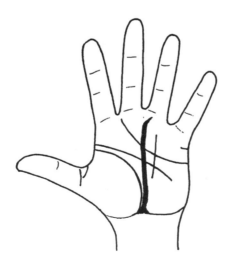

Fig. 106 *The Fate Line is twisted towards the Apollo Finger.*

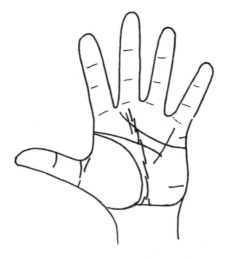

Fig. 107 *A broken Fate Line.*

When the fate line can't be seen, it shows that the person is thinking in various ways and is likely to have instability in life. For Palm Therapy, if you create a new line which is well-balanced from the middle of the wrist toward the base of the Saturn finger, you may create a more stable frame of life for yourself. If you are a certified Palm Therapist, you always need to verify with your clients their needs and expectations before you attempt any change.

Generally, you should not interfere with the fate line by creating new lines. Although, if you want to initiate calmness, imprinting this line can help to reinforce and balance a more secured state of mind.

It is important to remember that by pressing a parallel line/s (the age line) to the fate line equivalent to the places where this line crosses the heart line and the head line, you can create a relaxation state. The fate line and its parallel lines may play an important role in stabilizing a person's life.

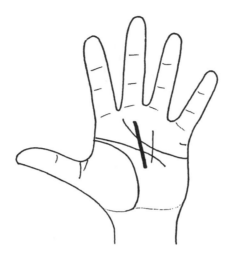

Fig. 108   *A Fate Line which commences distally from the wrist.*

You can choose to work either on the left or the right hand. But, first, you need to analyze the need for stability. If the need is practical in nature, you work on the right hand (if you are a right-handed person); if it is emotional in nature, work on your left hand (if you are a right-handed person).

To the certified Palm Therapist:

The issue of interfering with one's destiny/karma has moral and spiritual implications. While it is a must to interfere with karma in order to help one to overcome health problems for restoring good health and a more balanced energy, it is not for the Palm Therapist to decide on the kind of life path for their clients. In general, the fate line is the stabilizer of the life path. Since we might change one's destiny by working on this line, you should be very careful to reinforce mainly the existing line or to go according to the client's expectations. Never create a new fate line without the understanding of the client and his/her permission. More about destiny from the spiritual point of view, see my books *The Ultimate Prophecy (Book One and Book Two)*.

THE LINE OF APOLLO

The line of Apollo (Fig. 109) is known also as the line of success, the line of Sun or the ulnar longitudinal palmar crease (anatomy). This longitudinal line starts at the mount of Luna and continues all the way towards the finger of Apollo. The line of Apollo actually a luxury to have. In most individuals you may see only parts of it, usually between the line of heart and the finger of Apollo. In some individuals there is a double line (Fig. 110) which denotes success in two different areas of activity.

In traditional palmistry the line of Apollo represents success, love, and talents of any kind such as talents for drawing, painting, acting, crafting, music, writing and any other type of art.

Palm Therapy attributes to this line, also, peace and harmony. The line of Apollo is an excellent line to work on for relaxation. Stimulation of this line helps in situations of stress,

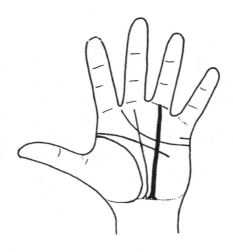

Fig. 109 The Apollo Line.

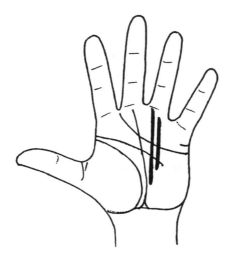

Fig. 110 *A double Apollo Line.*

depression and mood swings. It also brings a sense of security and well-being to the individual. Therefore, it becomes one of the most important tools for emotional balancing which is essential for achieving success of any kind.

The line of Apollo represents the fulfillment and achievement factor in human beings. Therefore, stimulation of this line is highly recommended for the activation of Success Energy.

Success is a very subjective issue. Each one of us has different expectations and needs, therefore, the line of Apollo represents the owner's view of success which can be in any aspect of life. My finding in Palm Therapy regarding this issue is that, through working on the line of Apollo, it actually stimulates success and achievements in any direction people wish to advance themselves.

When this line commences in a curve from the mount of Luna (Fig. 111) it shows the type of success which comes from

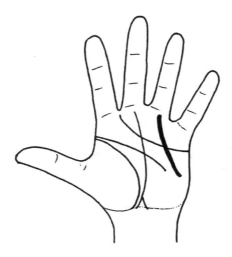

Fig. 111 *Apollo Line which commences in a curve from the Mount of Luna.*

interaction with other persons, such as success in business, success as a teacher or recognition and fame as in the case of movie stars.

When the line of Apollo clings too closely to that of the fate line (Fig.112) it denotes that the main success comes from within—from their mental activities and talents. These persons are more devoted to their own development, creation, inventions, crafts, writing, or scientific researches. Unfortunately, these people are not always recognized by others.

If the line of Apollo starts above the line of heart (Fig. 113) it denotes success after age 40. In order to be recognized by others, the upper part of Apollo line should end toward the Mercury mount and finger.

Various factors are involved with the achievement of true success. They are well-known to many individuals who fulfilled their dreams. We all possess some of them naturally. But for

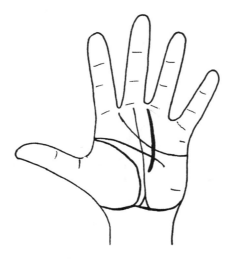

Fig. 112 *Apollo Line which clings too closely to the Fate Line.*

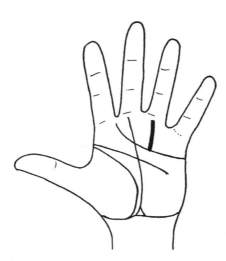

Fig. 113 *Apollo Line which starts above the Heart Line.*

many reasons they are sometimes hidden or sabotaged somewhere in our complex personality. Each one of those aspects is vital for success. They may all be stimulated by Palm Therapy.

Let's review, now, what usually it takes to become successful, achieve your goals and fulfill your dreams.

The main factors for success :

1. Decision
Make a commitment to succeed.

2. Look inside yourself.
Find your own special talent, skill, or knowledge. Each one of us has a quality at which he/she is good and which can be developed further to be used for your success. It can be anything. It is not necessarily related to your level of education, although any learning can further develop what you already possess. Through Palm Therapy, you may sharpen your special talent/s which can be further stimulated with education and training.

3. Planning
Any successful venture starts with a proper plan.
Know what you want to achieve. Remember that success is not limited only to financial aspects. It is a broad term for any positive way in life that you want to have, be, or experience. It may include a loving relationship, knowledge, wealth, special skills and talents. So take the time. Sit down and list all the goals you want to accomplish. When you are done, plan how to achieve them. By doing so, you will awaken many of the success elements in your mind to work for you.

4. Visualization

See the target as clearly and in as much detail as you can. We all have daydreams. Direct those daydreams to your goals daily. Dream about your success, enjoy it as if you have already achieved it. Use all of your senses: see, hear, feel, smell, taste. The more vivid you picture your success, the faster you will achieve it! (More about visualization in Appendix B.)

5. Faith

Have faith. Believe with all your heart that you are going to achieve your goals. Do not allow any doubts of failure to cross your mind. If this happens, immediately correct them with a positive visualization of the best outcome for you. Faith is essential for your success. Faith is the vehicle driving your mind toward success.

6. Grateful attitude

Give thanks continually for every good thing that has come and will come to you. This will increase your connection with God/the creator/karma/divine powers and will help you to be even more faithful and to focus on the positive things in your life.

7. Persistence

Be determined. Do your utmost to achieve your goals. Continue until you reach them. Forgive yourself for any failure along the way. It is natural for all human beings. Learn from your mistakes and continue with your goals and plans.

8. Enjoyment and Satisfaction

You deserve to enjoy your life at all times, including while in your persistent pursuit to reach success. Remember, that when you accomplish one goal, you immediately set another —higher in nature than the previous one. This is a natural process. So, don't wait to enjoy your life *only* after you accomplish all of your goals. It may be too late. Look around you. There are at least a few things to be happy about in every single day! By enjoying yourself on a daily basis, you will create a positive energy which will work for you during your journey towards success!

***

Stimulation of the success/Apollo line in the right place, as well as other areas in the palm, which are specific to your own personality, awakens the various factors of success in the subconscious mind to work for you. It pushes you to become successful from within. The urge to fulfill oneself is being triggered rapidly this way. Success follows quickly and naturally. It usually takes the form of positive coincidences which happen frequently, opening the gate to success. You don't have to understand the process in order to achieve yours. Some individuals who experienced Palm Therapy didn't connect their achievements with the stimulation of the various lines including the line of Apollo. In some cases, people would claim that they just felt great, with more energy, and that their success came from their own initiative or from encounters with others. Since an unusual urge towards success arose in them, they decided to put more efforts into achieving it, and were lucky as well. This is what Palm Therapy stimulates!

A large part of the work with Palm Therapy focuses on this line. Whether at the first phase, the Balancing Stage, to initiate relaxation and a balancing effect, or at the second phase, the Release Stage, when needed, and, of course, during the third phase, the Fulfillment Stage, for the stimulation of harmony, fulfillment and Success Energy.

It is so natural to become successful once we reinforce the Success Energy through the line of Apollo. This way most of us all over the world can fulfill dreams and live better with the help of the energy stimulated through this line and other areas in the hand.

THE LINE OF MERCURY

The line of Mercury (Fig. 114) is one of the longitudinal lines on the hand. This line, when it appears, runs usually from the mount of Neptune towards the Mercury finger and ends at the base of this finger.

For many centuries there was a controversy in traditional palmistry regarding the meaning of this line and its relationship to health, learning, body/mind awareness, physical and sport activities.

Is this a negative or a positive line to have? It presents an interesting dilemma in Palm Therapy. Some authorities in palmistry claimed that the appearance of the Mercury line is a sure sign of a disease or of physical or mental problems. Then, when the person regained good health the line supposedly disappeared as well.

If we take this approach then it would be to our benefit to eliminate this line and weaken its affect through Palm Therapy.

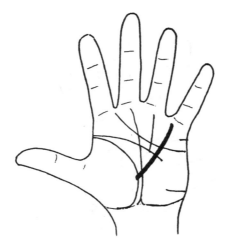

Fig. 114 *The Mercury Line.*

Other researchers in palmistry considered this line as an indication of well-being. Therefore, accordingly, a large, clear line would demonstrate a strong, vibrant health. A line which is broken into many little segments (Fig. 115) may indicate health problems and a low immune system. When there is a significant break in the line of Mercury (Fig. 116) it shows specific chronic diseases that the body is fighting to balance, such as rheumatism, arthritis, diabetes, a heart condition, chronic asthma, etc.

It is more likely to find this line in the hands of mature people (over 30 years), rather than in young children. This, theoretically, supports the claim of no line equals better health.

My findings, after trying to analyze this line, are based on a very practical assumption. If a person feels better after stimulating or creating a new Mercury line, then it supports the claim that a strong Mercury line represents vitality and health.

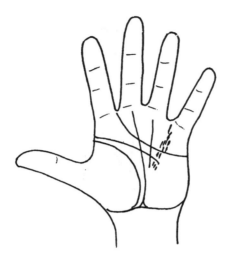

Fig. 115 *Mercury Line which is broken into many segments.*

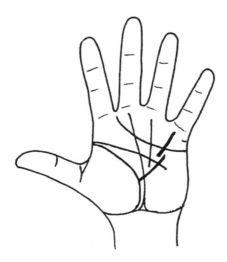

Fig. 116 *A significant breakage on Mercury Line.*

After a lengthy research, I am convinced that this line represents healing factors and it will be a good idea to stimulate this line in order to increase the vitality. If there is any breakage in the line of Mercury, then we have to correct it into a clear, solid line. Remember that vertical lines on the palm are balancing and reinforcing everywhere. Therefore, we should approach this line as a positive one.

A clear, strongly marked Mercury line denotes that the healing forces of the body are activated. Therefore, a stimulation of the line will further activate the healing process which involves the immune system as well.

For many palmists, the fact that there was a need for healing indicated that there was a disease or a problem. Since they only analyze through the hand, this line was attributed to health problems regardless of the healing forces involved. For others who were more into the healing arts, this line represented the healing and the recovery forces within our system.

The effect from the stimulation of this line together with the life line helps to promote healing and the overcoming of many physical and mental ailments in our body and mind.

Success Energy

IS ONE OF THE MOST INTERESTING ASPECTS OF
PALM THERAPY. SUCCESS ENERGY DOES NOT TEACH YOU HOW
TO BE SUCCESSFUL, BUT IT REMOVES THE FEAR OF SUCCESS; IT
BUILDS UP HIGHER EXPECTATIONS AND A BETTER CAPACITY TO
LEARN NEW SKILLS, TO BECOME SUCCESSFUL AND TO
SUBCONSCIOUSLY ACT AND BEHAVE IN A WAY
THAT DRAWS MORE SUCCESS TO YOU.

11

The Minor Lines

The minor lines (Fig. 117) represent some aspects of the personality. The various lines, which we call the minor lines, appear only in part; some people do not have them at all.

From the standpoint of Palm Therapy it is important to reinforce some of these lines and to eliminate others.

The Main Minor Lines are:

A. Ring of Solomon
B. Ring of Saturn
C. Ring of Apollo
D. The Girdle of Venus
E. Secure Lines (Caring and Devotion Lines)
F. Fulfillment Lines (Caring and Devotion Lines)

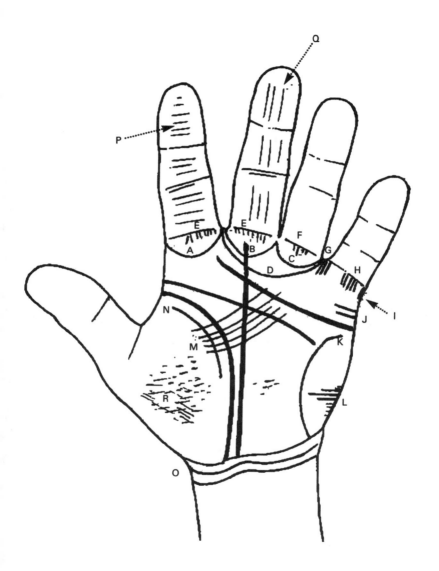

Fig. 117 *The Minor Lines.*

G. Lines of Medicine (Caring and Devotion Lines)
H. Children's Lines (Caring and Devotion Lines)
I. Spiritual Worship Line/s (Caring and Devotion Lines)
J. Marriage (Affection) Lines
K. Line of Intuition
L. Allergy Line/s (Including the Via Lasciva Line)
M. Family Influence Lines
N. Parents' Line
O. Life Bracelets
P. Transverse Lines on the phalanges of the fingers
Q. Longitudinal Lines on the phalanges of the fingers
R. Sensitive Lines

THE RING OF SOLOMON

The ring of Solomon (Fig. 118) is located at the mount of Jupiter.

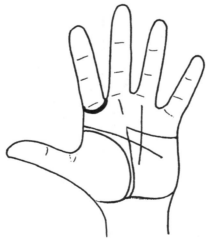

Fig. 118 *The Ring of Solomon.*

This ring is actually a reinforcement to the finger of Jupiter. It indicates satisfaction from sex, food and other excitements. The ring, also, increases the whole finger of Jupiter which, in a way, accelerates the characteristics repressed by this finger including the need and the power to control others.

Some charismatic people possess this ring shape or, actually, a small segment of it. It is very rare to find a complete ring of Solomon.

THE RING OF SATURN

The ring of Saturn (Fig. 119) encircles the mount of Saturn. This sign is rarely found. This ring actually increases the base phalanx of the Saturn finger, causing a more self-approach, self-satisfac-

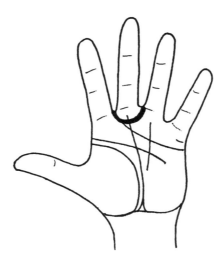

Fig. 119 *The Ring of Saturn.*

tory personality. On the other hand, this ring is not beneficial to the holder since it is cutting the end of the fate line and indicates tendencies towards depression and becoming more introverted.

Through Palm Therapy, the effect of this ring should be reduced by reinforcing and marking a stronger fate line all the way up to the base of the Saturn finger.

THE RING OF APOLLO

The ring of Apollo (Fig. 120) located under the finger of Apollo increases the properties of the third phalanx of the Apollo finger which represents the joy and self-satisfaction from art, beauty and other aesthetical properties. It is a passive reinforcement towards the enjoyment of beauty. Therefore, it is a debili-

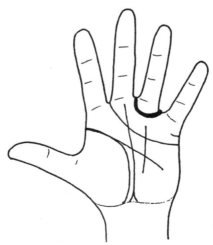

Fig. 120 *The Ring of Apollo.*

tating ring for those who want to be actively successful in life. This should be corrected through Palm Therapy by imprinting a stronger line of Apollo for success. In this way the ring of Apollo loses its influence.

THE GIRDLE OF VENUS

The girdle of Venus (Fig. 121) is located above the heart line. It is semi-circular in shape. It usually starts at the base of the index and the middle fingers and ends between the fingers of Apollo and Mercury. It has various meanings according to different researchers in palmistry.

During my work with Palm Therapy, I found that the girdle of Venus usually appears incomplete or broken. The line repre-

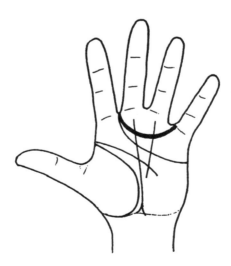

Fig. 121 *The Girdle of Venus.*

sents, in reality, a sister line to the heart line. Often it is a repair line or a protection to the heart line.

When this line exists, it usually demonstrates a tendency towards anxiety, phobias and hysteria. The possessors of the girdle of Venus are highly sensitive and emotional people.

Many times, we can see that this girdle crosses the heart line at the areas below the fingers of Saturn and Jupiter. It is important to correct it by imprinting and reinforcing the line of heart in those areas.

CARING AND DEVOTION LINES (IN GENERAL)

Caring and devotion lines (Fig. 122) are the representatives of the various kinds of emotional developments one goes through dur-

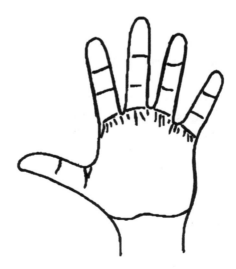

Fig. 122 *Caring and Devotion Lines in general.*

ing a lifetime. These may be manifested on the hands of children and adults, reflecting the level of one's potential emotional development. The various levels of caring and devotion towards oneself, towards others and towards a spiritual power are represented in the various longitudinal, small lines which may appear under the fingers of Jupiter, Saturn, Apollo and Mercury.

The process of emotional development in regard to the ability of caring and being devoted either to ourselves or to others can be divided into five main groups:

1. Caring for the basic security of oneself
   (secure lines)
2. The need to fulfill and enjoy life in a successful way
   (fulfillment lines)
3. Caring for others with or without loving emotions
   (lines of medicine)
4. Caring for others on a loving emotional basis
   (children's lines)
5. Caring and devotion to God, the Creator or other
   spiritual realities (spiritual worship lines)

All emotional levels of caring and devotion may appear on the hand. There is no contradiction if only part, or all aspects are, represented on the hand.

CARING AND DEVOTION LINES: SECURE LINES

The small lines under the fingers of Jupiter and Saturn (Fig. 123) represent the person's way to secure him/herself in life since

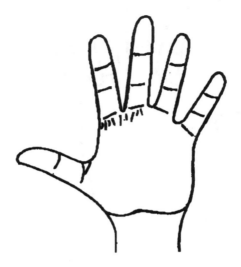

Fig. 123 *Caring and Devotion Lines:*
Secure Lines.

childhood. The more one feels secure the more he/she becomes emotionally developed and vice versa.

CARING AND DEVOTION LINES:
FULFILLMENT LINES

After the basic needs are satisfied and the person feels emotionally secure he/she looks for the self-fulfillment on a higher level. Fulfillment of these needs, which come as a result of success in various areas of life, appear as small, longitudinal lines on the mount of Apollo (Fig. 124).

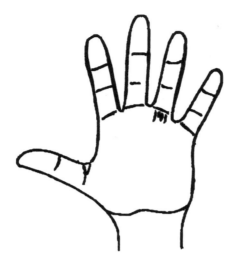

Fig. 124   *Caring and Devotion Lines:*
Fulfillment Lines.

CARING AND DEVOTION LINES:
LINES OF MEDICINE/HEALER'S LINE

As the person becomes more mature in emotional needs, he/she is able to take care of others with or without a loving, emotional connection. This will be shown between the fingers of Apollo and Mercury as small, longitudinal lines (Fig. 125) which, traditionally, are called the lines of medicine or the healer's lines. These lines may also represent a profession which involves taking care of others, such as the various healthcare providers—a physician, a nurse, a psychotherapist, a physical therapist, a massage therapist, etc.

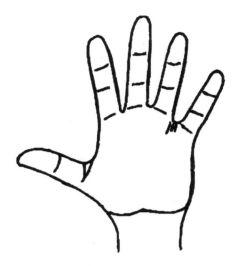

Fig. 125 *Caring and Devotion Lines:*
Lines of Medicine/The Healer's Lines.

CARING AND DEVOTION LINES:
CHILDREN'S LINES

A higher level is the need and ability for one to take care of and be devoted to others including one's own children with feelings of love and responsibility towards them. This is shown in the next group of small, longitudinal lines just under the Mercury finger (Fig. 126). Traditionally, they are known as the children's lines. These lines appear in the hands of most mothers but also in the hands of many devoted caregivers.

During the centuries the children's lines were used for predicting the actual number of children a person may have.

After close observation, I found this not to be the case. I saw many older people with six or more lines who never had children or had a fewer number of children than those lines indi-

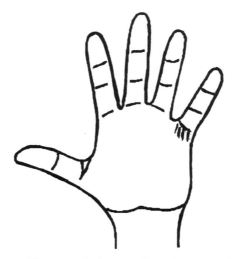

Fig. 126   *Caring and Devotion Lines: The Children's Lines.*

cated. In the psychic type of hand with the many tiny lines of hysteria, the number of children's lines is numerous, regardless of the actual facts. Therefore, I concluded that these lines represent the potential for emotional caring and responsibility for others.

Caring for our pets will appear as a longitudinal line/s between the children's lines and lines of medicine. It is hard to differentiate between them and the children's lines.

CARING AND DEVOTION LINES: SPIRITUAL WORSHIP LINES

The last group of the caring and devotions lines represent devotion on the highest level. It is the care and devotion to the ultimate authority/ies in one's life which is usually the spiritual one/s. It can be a devotion or worship to God, the Creator or any other spiritual entity. This is manifested in small, longitudinal lines on the mount of upper Uranus (Fig. 127). I named them "spiritual worship lines." Ministers, Priests, Rabbis, Imams and others whose lives are involved in connection with higher entities usually possess these lines.

Fig. 127 *Caring and Devotion Lines:*
Spiritual Worship Lines.

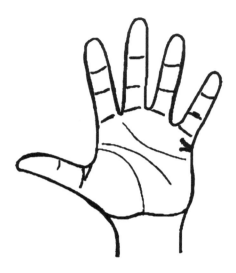

Fig. 128 *The Marriage / Emotional Attachment Lines.*

THE MARRIAGE/EMOTIONAL ATTACHMENT LINES

The marriage/emotional attachment lines, also known as the affection lines (Fig. 128), are transverse lines that commence at the ulnar border of the palm between the base line of Mercury finger and the heart line. They start at the mount of upper Uranus and extend to the mount of Mercury.

The marriage lines are the most impressive lines.These lines do not necessarily represent marriage, but mainly the emotional attachments to other people, usually of the opposite sex. It can also represent a physical or emotional connection or even a platonic love without any physical contact. The direction of the lines indicates the nature of the relationship.

THE LINE OF INTUITION

The line of intuition (Fig. 129) is a line that curves from the mount of Luna towards the finger of Mercury.

In theory, this line represents a strong intuition. From observations, I found that it indicates an active imagination that reinforces the mount of Luna.

In a way, the imagination is the basis for any intuition and metaphysical development, but this line itself does not indicate strong mystic powers.

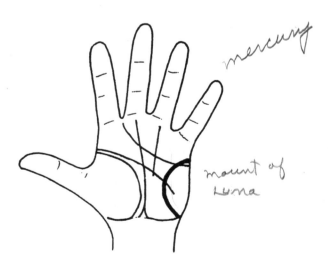

Fig. 129 *The Line of Intuition.*

THE ADDICTION/ALLERGY LINE/S

The addiction/allergy line/s (Fig. 130) is a transverse line/s that may appear on the mounts of Pluto and Luna.

Traditionally, according to some authorities in palmistry, the line/s was also called *via lasciva*. This transverse line represented a variety of aspects from traveling overseas to allergies.

From observation, I concluded that this line or a series of a few parallel transverse lines on the mounts of Pluto and Luna are actually the representations of some physical/chemical addictive patterns which may involve allergies, chemical sensitivity and the body's immune system (refer to my findings about attachment/addictive patterns in our lives as seen on the mounts, Chapter 8). The physical/chemical addictive patterns which are represented in these allergy lines may initiate or maintain a variety of diseases. My experience reveals that by reducing the effect of these lines through Palm Therapy (i.e.,

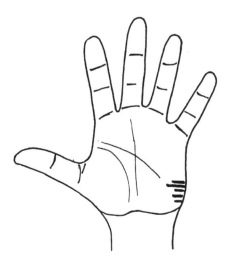

Fig. 130   *The Addiction / Allergy Line/s.*

crossing these lines with longitudinal lines), many symptoms of allergies and chronic diseases are lessened or significantly reduced. These include emotional problems that are related to a use of a substance (see Section Five: "Palm Therapy for Mental Disorders"). Therefore, working on these lines is a must for many physical and emotional disorders. Remember, if you suffer from any symptom do not attempt to treat it only by yourself. Always seek the help of healthcare professional.

THE FAMILY INFLUENCE LINES

Family influence lines (Fig. 131) are lines which run from the mount of Venus towards the fingers of Saturn or Mercury. These lines represent the effect of the various psychosocial stressors a person experienced through his/her family. These lines are

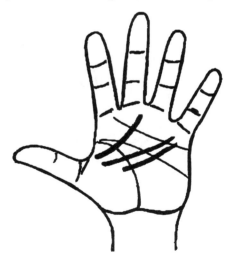

Fig. 131 *Family Influence Lines.*

more likely to be found in the hands of the *yin* type personalities such as in the psychic, the conic and part of the mixed hands.

THE PARENTS' LINE/S

The parents' line/s (Fig. 132) is actually a line that runs parallel to the life line on the mount of Venus. The stronger the line appears, the stronger was the influence of the parents on that individual.

I found that a well-marked parents' line also indicates the degree or length of the period of stress while growing up in the family. This line is more likely to be seen in the hands of those

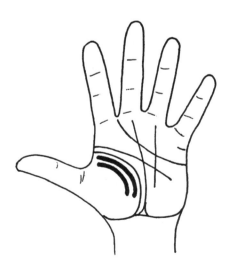

Fig. 132 *The Parents' Lines.*

who had controlling parents, but it is more common in females than in males. Some palmists call this line "sister line" or "double life line." Since this usually represents the parents' figures of an individual, it seems that a parents' line is a more suitable name for it.

THE LIFE BRACELETS

The life bracelets (Fig. 133) are the transverse lines that appear on the wrist. According to some authorities these bracelets have no significant meanings in palmistry. However, by working with Palm Therapy, these lines showed a balancing effect and a reinforcement of vital energy. It looks as if these lines should be

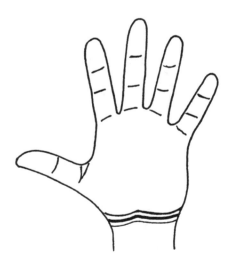

Fig. 133 *Life Bracelets.*

called "balancing lines" or "energy lines." Palm Therapy's stimulation on these lines enhances calmness and helps to balance the sleeping patterns, including those of insomnia.

THE TRANSVERSE LINES ON THE FINGERS' PHALANGES

The little transverse lines (Fig. 134) on the fingers (not the flexure digital lines) represent a deterioration and debilitation of the characteristics represented by a specific finger or a phalanx. ·

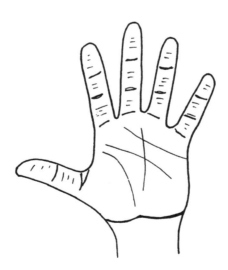

Fig. 134 *Transverse lines on the fingers' phalanges.*

THE LONGITUDINAL LINES ON THE FINGERS' PHALANGES

Longitudinal lines on any phalanx (Fig. 135) of the fingers serves as a reinforcement to the characteristics of that finger or phalanx. You should look for those longitudinal lines which appear on dry hands. (Longitudinal lines are naturally seen after you immerse your hand in water for a while, leading to what we call "prune skin".)

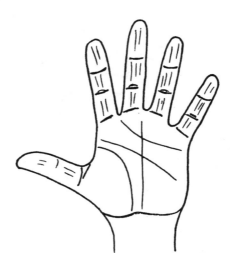

Fig. 135 *Longitudinal lines on the fingers' phalanges.*

THE SENSITIVE (HYSTERIA) LINES

The sensitive lines (Fig. 136) are tiny hairlines which cover the whole palmar side of the hand or a large part of it.

Their location and the direction in which they run have some meaning in terms of reinforcement or debilitation of certain characteristics represented on specific areas of the hand.

These small lines are also called hysteria lines and in many cases they show anxiety, fears and panic.

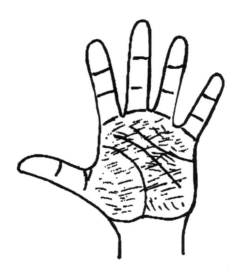

Fig. 136 *The Sensitive Lines.*